THE
MUSCULAR
GOURMET

THE
MUSCULAR
GOURMET

MANDY TANNY

1817
HARPER & ROW, PUBLISHERS, New York
Cambridge, Philadelphia, San Francisco, Washington
London, Mexico City, São Paulo, Singapore, Sydney

Cover photography: Harry Langdon
Cover design: Ed Passarelli

Food styling: Mary Ann Mucica and Iola Vosburg
Makeup: Melody Jaisson
Workout fashions: Danskin and L. A. Gear

FIRST EDITION

Designer: Abigail Sturges
Copy editor: Ann Finlayson
Indexer: Alberta M. Morrison

Library of Congress Cataloging-in-Publication Data

Tanny, Mandy.
  The muscular gourmet.

  Includes index.
  1. Cookery. 2. Bodybuilders—Nutrition.
I. Title.
TX652.T35 1988   641.5′63   86-45700
ISBN 0-06-096096-5 (pbk.)

---

88 89 90 91 92 RRD 10 9 8 7 6 5 4 3 2 1

This book is dedicated to
all my bodybuilding friends
who made The Muscular Gourmet *possible*.

CONTENTS

ACKNOWLEDGMENTS

A special thanks at *Muscle and Fitness* magazine to the art staff and the editorial staff, Renee Mudgett, Chris Glass, and, of course, Joe Weider.

A very special thanks to my father Armand, my aunt Ola, and my son Mario, who stuck by my side every step of the way.

FOREWORD

If you're going to be a winner, you have to eat like one.

I've always believed that success is not a goal in itself, it's how you achieve it. For me, determination, hard work, and a zest for life is the key. I always knew where I wanted to go, and I got there with the attitude of winning. No challenge went unconquered. Each and every competition I've won and film I've made has been one more step on the ladder of success. And I'll tell you with certainty that I couldn't have done it without the help of good nutritious food, the kind I find in this cookbook by Mandy Tanny.

Healthy food gives you the necessary stamina and vitality for taking the road to the top. If the food is deliciously prepared, it gives you a much needed psychological boost as well.

I'm a firm believer in the priority of good wholesome food for building the perfect body, so I don't agree that you have to deprive yourself of one of life's great pleasures to get into shape. All the while I was in competition, I really enjoyed having well balanced meals. I built muscle on them. I functioned better than I did with spartan diets and crazy food fads. Looking forward to good food stabilized my morale and helped lighten the load for a hard job well done.

Now that my schedule is more demanding than ever, I have to pay particular attention to my food intake. The stress of filming fifteen hours or more a day, usually on location, calls for a well-rounded diet with interesting recipes like the ones in this cookbook. Let's face it, everybody loves to eat, and making food work for you as well as making it appealing is what this book shows you how to do. Men and women, from executives to athletes, will benefit from it. Whether you're working long hours, training hard, raising families, or just enjoying life, there's something in this book for everyone.

I have been reading Mandy's food column in *Muscle and Fitness* magazine for years, and it has always delighted me. In the many visits I've made to the Weider Health and Fitness headquarters in Woodland Hills, California, I've continually had the pleasure of renewing my friendship with Mandy with long, fun conversations. They've often included discussions on food and suggestions for recipes I've found satisfying and enjoyable. With that in mind, I'm pleased to present *The Muscular Gourmet,* a culmination of those years of effort and expertise. My only regret is that I didn't have this cookbook when I was bodybuilding.

In parting I would like to conclude that *The Muscular Gourmet* is a forerunner in books of its kind. It offers gourmet recipes backed by a philosophy of good looks and good health through sound nutritional advice and regular workouts. I think Mandy Tanny's clear outlook and long experience in the bodybuilding field takes one of the most innovative and realistic approaches to the winning combination of intelligent eating and training I've seen. Anyone following a fitness life-style who is motivated by success and hungers for the good life should not pass up this book. By using it as a guideline, you'll be one step closer to your goals.

ARNOLD SCHWARZENEGGER

THE
MUSCULAR
GOURMET

1
THE ART OF
THE MUSCULAR GOURMET

The Muscular Gourmet is unique. It's more than a collection of gourmet recipes. It's a life-style cookbook that embraces a philosophy of fun and fitness, natural food values, and the art of good living. Today's move toward muscle calls for eating the right foods and following a regular exercise program. This book will teach you how to live by this plan and get the most out of life without being obsessed by dieting.

In the scheme of fitness, goals become impossible when approached without the right working knowledge of diet and exercise. With an intelligent, logical, and accurate view, *The Muscular Gourmet* will show you why some diets don't work and how others do. You will learn the fail-proof way to attain and maintain optimum health and successful weight control with a balanced diet of superior foods and the correct moderation of calories. You will even discover some surprising facts on protein and muscle building that will assist you in your training program to build the ultimate body. You'll learn supermarket savvy, with a complete and informative guide to pro shopping that will teach you how to select only the healthiest, highest quality foods available for your diet. These important fundamentals will give you basic knowledge on which to build your Muscular Gourmet life-style.

The reward of living a Muscular Gourmet life-style is creating a better body through a more attractive way of life. The very implication of the concepts ''muscular'' and ''gourmet'' suggest having the time, the strength, and the zest for living life to its fullest potential. The art of the Muscular Gourmet is that of mating fine living and fitness with vital nutrition and good cooking.

Knowing how to cook well is an art, and that art takes its highest form when it's combined with knowledge of proper nutrition and food values: use of wholesome unprocessed foods, adding herbs and other natural flavor enhancers, and employing healthy methods of food preparation. This is precisely what the Muscular Gourmet offers you.

You'll find in this cookbook over 300 original, kitchen-tested recipes, designed to help you follow a Muscular Gourmet life-style diet.

Natural

All the recipes call for primary wholesome ingredients. No ready-made, re-fined, or overprocessed foods are used. That includes (with a few isolated exceptions) canned and packaged foods, any foods with chemicals or fillers added, "fake foods" such as imitation dairy products and foods that are OVERCOOKED.

Not overcooked—that's the passport to good health. The value of eating raw foods (or foods as close to their natural state as possible) has been un-fairly ignored and misinterpreted. Quite simply, raw foods contain all the live enzymes, all the fiber, and all the vitamins and nutrients that nature intended them to have. Cooking always destroys or breaks down these elements to some degree. To help you understand, ask yourself this question: If you're going to sustain a live healthy body, are you going to feed it nonvital, nutri-tionally depleted foods? The answer, of course, is no.

Still, if raw or lightly cooked foods are best, then why a book on cooking? Because it's impractical and nearly impossible to enjoy a normal life today without some cooked foods in the diet. The solution is to cook foods with the smallest possible amount of destruction and to include in your diet as much raw food as possible: fresh vegetables, fruits, salads, raw nuts and seeds, unpasteurized dairy products, and even good rare meat (excluding pork).

If you haven't been following this kind of diet, you could probably im-prove your looks and your health noticeably by changing your ways. You've got to keep those live enzymes flowing and the Muscular Gourmet will help you to do this.

High Protein

Don't shortchange yourself. Protein is necessary for cellular growth and res-toration, so put some power into your diet. The Muscular Gourmet recipes stress plenty of first-class protein, an absolute must in stabilizing hunger, building muscle, and getting the most out of your workout program.

Low Calorie

The Muscular Gourmet does not take shortcuts on nutrition and quality for the sake of low calories. But by virtue of using only essential, healthy ingre-dients, it eliminates the excessive use of fats, oils, and refined starches that add unnecessary calories and do little for the flavor and nutritional value of food. You can therefore count on recipes that are low to moderate in calories, yet are nutritionally balanced.

Balance

As you will learn in the next chapter, your daily diet must have balance—a certain proportion of protein, fats, and carbohydrates. This is necessary to moderate hunger, to control body weight, and to maintain good health. These recipes were formulated to keep that balance as close to the recommended proportions as possible.

Easy Preparation

* The information on which the nutritional calculations are based was obtained from the Nutrition Almanac, revised edition (New York: McGraw-Hill, 1979), and manufacturer's labels. All figures were worked out on a calculator, computer, and spread sheet.

This is THE best cookbook for the gourmet who likes to prepare natural, elegant meals without putting a lot of effort into cooking. The "gourmet" lies in the ingredients, such as herbs, savory stocks, and fresh earthy fare, rather than in a lot of cooking and elaborate preparation. It's a gourmet's dream with muscle added.

Breezy but informative introductions launch exciting, easy-to-read recipes, followed by nutritional calculations to help you count calories, protein, fats, and carbohydrates.* Other highlights of this cookbook include interesting side bars, offering helpful Tidbits on food preparation and Fat Busting tips on diet and nutrition. Each chapter also features Celebrated Meals, menus designed to give you ideas for spectacular meal planning and entertaining with Muscular Gourmet recipes.

Now, let the Muscular Gourmet flex for you. Let it be your inspiration and guideline to a better way of life, and results you can live with—for good.

2
MASTERING THE DIET MYSTERY FOR A MUSCULAR GOURMET LIFE-STYLE

When Exercise Is Cheating

Beyond a doubt, exercise is the surest way to a beautiful body and glowing good health. Whether you're training a heavy two hours every day or doing fifteen minutes of aerobics once a week, you will better yourself physically and mentally. Every able body, young and old alike, should incorporate some form of exercise or vigorous activity into his or her life-style on a regular basis.

This does not mean, however, that's it's all right to eat the wrong foods because you have a good exercise routine to keep you in shape. Nor does this mean that you should go out once a week and overexert yourself, trying to burn off calories after a weekend binge. You risk injury that way. If you *have* to exercise to keep from getting fat—or, worse yet, *are* fat even though you *do* exercise—there's something wrong with your diet.

Exercise should never be a crutch for bad eating habits.

Sensible eating is the partner of sensible exercise. A life of diets, feast or famine, and junk foods only leads to a roller coaster ride of weight control and a lifelong battle with fat. Quite simply, diets don't work. Here's why.

Why Diets Don't Work

Your body has an instinct all its own when it comes to dieting—much like a chipmunk hoarding nuts for the winter. When faced with a sudden drop in food intake, your body will start hoarding calories. That includes food that is nutritionally empty but often high in calories. Your body will then store those extra calories as fat, as if preparing for a lean season. The fewer calories you eat, the more your body will hoard and the slower the fat loss, if any, will be. Eventually your body adapts to a lower calorie intake; then the moment you begin to eat normally again, you gain the lost weight right back, and possibly more.

Now here's the rub, particularly for bodybuilders and athletes. Fat is more important to basic survival than muscle, because it takes fewer calories to burn fat than muscle. When you go on a crash diet, your body prepares for a "state of emergency" by burning muscle tissue for fuel, saving that easy-burning, insulating layer of fat for last. So while you may be getting thinner, due to loss of muscle, you're actually adding fat—exchanging it for muscle.

"Skinny fat" might be the best way to describe the look. The weight loss is only temporary as long as you stay on the diet. You may well end up looking both flabby and gaunt, especially as you get older, definitely not the image of vibrant good health. Remember, you want to be strong, not weak; you want to build your body, not break it down.

These hard-hitting facts may seem like an injustice on nature's part, but then nature didn't set standards for strength and beauty—people did. In fact, nature predisposes the body to favor fat to muscle. Fat is an automatic acquisition, necessary for survival. Muscle is earned. The harder we work, the more we get. Conversely, to lose muscle mass, you simply stop working out. To lose fat, you have to work hard at it—and intelligently.

This is why so many diets don't work. Now learn how they do.

The Secret to Successful Weight Control

If you follow a Muscular Gourmet life-style, there will be no need in your life for excesses of anything. Everything will be accomplished with balance and moderation, and tempered with positive energy. Begin with your diet. Forget about calories and vitalize your way of eating. Concentrate on balance and incorporate natural foods more and more into your daily fare.

As we have seen, everyone needs a balanced amount of carbohydrate, protein, and fat in his daily diet. If you cut out any one of them or alter the recommended ratio, you will eventually cause an adverse chain reaction in your body's metabolic and muscle-building functions.

Carbohydrate should make up about 60 to 70 percent of your daily food intake. If you don't eat enough carbohydrates, especially when you are training, the liver will convert protein from your muscle tissue into glucose for energy, and there go your beautiful, hard-won muscles. Specifically, they give you the fuel to function. Try to focus on complex carbohydrates such as fresh fruits, vegetables, grains, and legumes. Stay away from simple sugars and refined carbohydrates that wreak havoc with your blood sugar level.

Fats are necessary in the diet to give the body internal supportive structure and, assist in the chemical reaction of the metabolic and tissue building processes. Fats satisfy the craving for carbohydrates that could cause you to load up and get fat. You should get between 10 and 15 percent of your daily intake of calories from fats, both saturated (meat and dairy products) and unsaturated (nuts, seeds, and vegetable oils). But beware! Too much fat in the diet will be readily stored in places you don't want it.

The Power of Protein

The true power of protein has been overestimated, underestimated, and long misunderstood, but its nutritional value is undisputed. Twenty-two amino acids combine to form all the known proteins. Eight of the amino acids are essential (the body cannot synthesize them) and are found in meat, fish, and fowl, and all twenty-two are necessary for tissue building.

To be sure, the body requires that between 15 and 25 percent of the daily caloric intake be composed of protein. A more exact estimate depends on a variety of conditions. Following are the major factors that will help you determine how much protein you need.

An average 160-pound adult requires a minimum of 60 grams of dietary protein per day. But an athlete or bodybuilder who wants to gain muscle needs up to three times that amount, and even if he just wants to maintain a lean body mass, he needs 20 percent more protein than the average person of the same stature. These calculations are based on an optimal diet, with a protein utilization of at least 65 percent. If the diet is too low in calories, protein will be used as fuel instead of for building muscle.

Too much protein converted to energy can cause kidney and liver disorders and vitamin and mineral deficiencies. Too much protein in the form of calories can be stored as fat. A diet too high in calories or out of balance in the ratio of carbohydrates, fats, and protein, can cause any one of these antimuscle-building functions.

Other factors affect the assimilation of protein in athletes and nonathletes as well. Protein should have a high biological quality—that is, the less processing the better. Food loses as much as 80 percent of its protein value when cooked, leaving only about 20 percent of assimilable protein for tissue building. The nonessential amino acids should be in balance with all of the essential amino acids. An excess or absence of one amino acid can affect the body's need for another amino acid. Additional protein is needed in times of physical injury or emotional stress. Both cause a prolonged loss of nitrogen, which results in lack of muscular growth and tissue repair. In addition, when a person is bedridden or immobile, the body loses some of its ability to assimilate protein efficiently. Cold weather also increases the body's need for protein, as much as tenfold in subzero climates.

Last but not least, consuming either too much or too little dietary protein can lead to foul-ups in weight control. If the caloric value of the diet is too high, the added protein will be stored as fat and cause bloat, especially if it's second-rate protein (overprocessed and fatty meats, protein powders, and protein foods not containing all eight essential amino acids). People following those newfangled theories favoring no fats and very little protein are hungry all the time—notorious for carbohydrate loading and binging, while their weight goes up and down like a yo-yo. It's damaging to the health, not to mention the adverse effects it has on muscle building.

How much or how little protein do you need? Assess your activities and goals, then adjust your diet according to these Muscular Gourmet guidelines. Take a balanced approach, always start out in moderation, and above all, learn to listen to your body's needs.

Fighting Fat with Fiber

One of the major causes of overweight today is the lack of fiber in the diet. The American diet particularly is overabundant in fiberless foods such as fatty meats and full fat dairy products (40 percent of the average American's food intake is fat), and refined starches and sugars.

Body fat comes mainly from the fats that we eat—not from carbohydrates. It takes eight times more energy from the body to burn carbohydrates as it does to burn fat. Hence, dietary fats end up easily as stored body fat. Carbohydrates have to go through more metabolic steps than fats to be stored as fat in the body. This constitutes a greater heat loss that stimulates the burning up of more calories, thus the burning up of more bodyfat.

Fiber is found in complex carbohydrate foods that are natural and unrefined. These fibrous foods such as raw (as opposed to cooked, since the cooking process breaks down the fiber) fruits, vegetables, nuts, seeds, grains, and legumes are slow-burning, efficient sources of fuel, which keep your blood sugar stable and control hunger. And because of their high fiber content, these foods contain more bulk, so you eat less to get full. Finally, as they sweep through your digestive system, they take with them waste calories that linger there and metabolize into fat. Once again, the more raw, natural foods replace refined and fatty foods in your diet, the trimmer and healthier you will be.

The Real Way to Lose Fat

As we discussed, the secret to good health and successful weight control is maintaining balance and moderation. You now have a foundation of knowledge with which to begin a serious diet that will revitalize and energize you and help you keep off excess fat for good.

Before you begin, however, remind yourself that there are no shortcuts to successful weight control, but there is no journey longer than a lifetime of unsuccessful dieting.) If you want to lose weight the real way, start by cutting back only 500 calories a day below the intake considered average for a person of your sex, age, and height. Remember to keep your protein, fats, and carbohydrates in the recommended proportions. Don't omit anything that's good for you; simply eat less. And don't tamper with calories. Your metabolism is in training; don't confuse it.

This cutback will amount to 3,500 calories per week—or the loss of one solid pound of fat. On diet alone, you don't want to lose any more than that, or you can be assured that it is not just fat you're losing but fluids and muscle tissue as well.

Maintain that regimen until you have reached your desired weight. In the beginning you may find your weight loss a bit irregular at times, due to the adjustment in body fluids. Sometimes it will even seem as if nothing is happening, but if you're sticking to your diet, it is. Metabolic changes may be taking place that you don't detect on the scale. As you get closer to your goal, you may even find the pounds coming off faster than you would expect. This is due to the fact that as you lose fat, your metabolism steps up to where it should be. Now it's helping you burn fat instead of dragging you down.

On this way-of-life diet you will not be hungry, you will not be undernourished, and unless you overeat, you will *never* gain the weight back. Maintaining your ideal weight will become automatic. You may only have to adjust your daily food intake a few hundred calories either way. Let your body be the judge. It will tell you what it needs. And if you've treated it right, a healthy, properly functioning body will make the right decisions.

Tailoring Your Diet for the Body You Want

If a sleek physique is the way you want to go, you're on the right track, but it's muscle that puts you on the map. Muscle give the body that developed, defined, and highly coveted look that can only be acquired with exercise training. It's a quality that just doesn't come without some degree of muscular growth, for men or women.

The amount of muscle you pack on for the look you want depends on the type of exercise you do and the intensity of your effort. But you can assist your body in gaining muscularity by tailoring your nutritional requirements. If exercise is the ultimate bodybuilding weapon, then good nutrition is your ammunition.

A body in training will react better and acquire maximum muscle mass when the dietary ratios of protein, fats, and carbohydrates are kept in correct proportion with each meal. Fuel burning and tissue repair are given a better chance. Depleting one nutrient and loading another will ultimately hinder muscle gain. Even if you're a nonexercising person, you will want to sustain your natural musculature by maintaining a relatively similar balance.

It has been established that a person's daily food intake should contain 15 and 25 percent protein, 10 and 15 percent fat, and 60 and 70 percent carbohydrates. Within that scale, adjustments need to be made according to the person's level of activity. Bodybuilders, power lifters, and strength athletes need between 20 and 25 percent protein in their diet every day to build and maintain muscle mass. Those in endurance training, such as swimming, bicycling, running, or aerobics, need around 15 to 20 percent protein, and the nonactive person should have between 10 and 15 percent. The ratio of carbohydrates is lower for strength training, around 60–65 percent, than the need for endurance training, which requires 65–70 percent. The nonathlete requires up to 80 percent carbohydrates in his daily diet. This shift from higher protein to higher carbohydrates is due to the greater need for muscle in strength activities and the higher fuel-burning need for endurance activities. The more strength and development desired, the more protein required. All active people, whether they're training with weights or doing aerobics, need between 10 and 15 percent fat in their daily diet. Nonactive people should have no more than 10 percent.

Using these guidelines now, you can select recipes from this book to tailor your daily dietary needs according to your level of activity. The demand for carbohydrates is higher in the morning than later in the day, to handle the day's fuel requirements. Choose recipes that provide a ratio of carbohydrates closer to 80 percent, or supplement your meals with extra carbohydrates.

But remember, if you are training very hard and require a lot of carbohydrates for fuel, you'll need an ample amount of protein to provide that essential balance. Eggs and dairy products are an excellent source. Moderate your carbohydrates and increase your protein slightly as the day progresses. Muscles at rest require protein for repair and growth. Choose recipes that will fulfill your highest protein need, somewhere between 25 and 30 percent (or even higher if you're on a hard cycle of training to build muscle). If you eat meat, fish, or fowl for your evening meal, combine it with comparable portions of fresh vegetables, potatoes, legumes, or whole grains to meet your carbohydrate requirement.

As long as you're eating a well-balanced diet, the amount of saturated and unsaturated fats your body requires will be found in the right proportions naturally in wholesome, unrefined foods. Try to keep fats at a ratio of 10 to 15 percent of your diet at all meals and closer to 15 percent if you're training hard and consuming additional protein.

Remember that the more perfect assimilation is, the better foods will interact to build muscle tissue. To insure this, don't overload your system at mealtime. Ideally, you should eat frequent, small meals instead of few, large ones throughout the day to keep digestion working at a steady pace. At mealtime, eat protein foods first, to allow your body to assimilate all the protein it can and stabilize hunger before you get to the carbohydrates. And always eat slowly for optimum digestion and protein utilization.

Exercise, the Ultimate Bodybuilding Weapon

As I pointed out earlier, you must not rely on exercise to compensate for an incorrect diet. But if you want to look and feel your absolute best and speed up weight loss, exercise is the final answer.

It doesn't matter if you pedal or pump your way to fitness. It all adds up to better health and vitality and ultimately a better look. There's no denying it. When peole see a firm, shapely body constituted by vibrant muscle, it stirs something primal inside of them, and they react with excitement. They want what they see, and what they see goes beyond diet.

Muscle gives the body tone, shape, and symmetry that bone and fat cannot. It supports the skeletal structure and acts as a protector of the internal organs. When muscle is allowed to atrophy, a person becomes physically and physiologically weak, and fat will accumulate where muscle should be.

This same principle applies to the heart as well. The kind of shape a person is in generally indicates the kind of shape the heart is in. The heart is a muscle also, so the more muscle density a person has, the stronger his heart will be and ultimately the better his overall health.

Exercise keeps excess fat at bay. Some fat is necessary on the body, but too much can be dangerous, especially to the heart. It can make you feel tired and sluggish and can even cause stress and emotional instability, and it can make the body look distorted and out of shape. Here's how exercise keeps excess fat off and that magnificent muscle on.

Exercise itself is a form of stress that causes muscle fibers to build up a "wall of defense." The more you exercise, the denser this wall becomes, hence the bigger your muscles get. You might even consider muscle a "hot" item. Muscle in its resting state burns more calories than fat does. Muscle also contains fat-burning enzymes within its fibers. Therefore, the denser the muscle, the stronger the fat-burning enzymes, and the more energy you will burn just to maintain it. Muscle does not favor fat but keeps it in check.

When you don't exercise, your body's metabolism is working at a low setting. Calorie burning is slow, so fat will readily accumulate. The more fat you have, the slower your metabolism will be and the less fat you will burn. It's a vicious cycle that can only be broken by severe dieting (which is dangerous) or exercise. Exercise raises the body's metabolic setting. Hence, once you begin an exercise program, your body will burn more calories at a faster rate, even at rest. Last, and of course not least, exercise itself burns calories. Without changing your caloric intake, you can lose weight on exercise alone. As we have seen, you can also lose weight (one pound per week) on just a sensible, lower-calorie diet alone. But the two combined are dynamite. With a vigorous exercise program and good diet, you can safely and sensibly double, and even triple, your fat loss in the same amount of time, while changing the shape of your body (and your life) for the better.

Nothing can beat the dynamic duo of a bodybuilding diet with training. You will look better, feel better, and live a better life-style. Let's close this chapter with one thought that says it all. "Living well is the best revenge, but looking great is winning the war."

3
SHOPPING WITH SAVVY

Launch your Muscular Gourmet life-style by learning how to select the best foods available. In this section we show you some new and possibly controversial concepts concerning the *real* meaning of quality. Fitness and awareness go hand in hand, so it's important that you understand what you're going to be cooking with and why.

How to Shop for Quality Foods

High quality does not necessarily mean high cost, and vice versa. In fact the best foods are usually not expensive at all, yet can be considered every bit as "gourmet" as the pricey items in the specialty department of your supermarket. This is not to say that gourmet foods are not worth it (many *are* better than "commercial" foods), but the primary consideration in quality should be given to biological value.

How foods rate on the biological scale is determined by the degree to which they have been processed and with what—preservatives, emulsifiers, stabilizers—or whether they were treated with heat at all. The less processing, of course, the better. Many of the characteristics of gourmet foods—the size and shape of the produce, the cuts or tenderness of meats, the herbs used in condiments, the term "fancy" on bottle or can—only add to appearance and price. What counts is nutritional value and freshness.

With the exception of dried fruits, nuts, legumes, certain grains, raw honey and nut butters, cold processed vegetable oils, and products that are meant to be aged, fermented, or pickled within the container—*anything* that comes in a bottle, can, or package that has a shelf life—has been processed to some degree. "Processed" includes being treated with heat, which partially (or totally) destroys the value of most foods. For instance, some bottled juices are touted as superior because they're unfiltered, yet filtered or not, they still have to be pasteurized (heated) in order to be bottled and stored. Healthwise, they're no better than filtered juices; they may just have a better consistency and taste. Though not quite as flavorful at times, fresh frozen juice concentrates are actually better. Many are made with a special dehydration process that doesn't require high heat and thus are healthier to drink. Better yet, many markets now squeeze their own citrus juices fresh daily, and these juices can usually be found in the produce section of the store.

In shopping for quality, let the biological scale be your guide. The longer the shelf life of foods (including foods that are refrigerated and frozen), the greater their degree of processing and the less nutritional value they have.

Buying Fresh Produce

There should be no contest between fresh and frozen or canned foods. Fresh is best, but even at that be wary in selection. Avoid produce that has bruises, brown spots, or a waxy outer covering. It's a sign that they may be old and inferior. On the other hand, beware of perfect, brightly colored skins. They may have been coated with a food coloring to conceal their lack of quality, or worse yet, preserved by a radiation process. With greens, discard the outer leaves and rinse the remaining leaves before using them. Wash all fruits and vegetables gently with a soft brush to remove any wax and chemical residues. If there's doubt about how the produce was grown or stored, remove the skins. There are other ways to make up for the lost roughage without adding chemicals to your system.

Some health food stores have produce sections that carry "organic" fruits and vegetables. Though not always consistent in their shape, color, size, condition, and availability, they are supposedly grown without the use of pesticides or fertilizers. If the issue of chemicals and pesticides is one that concerns you, organic produce (or even growing your own) may be an answer to the unknown.

Frozen Versus Canned

Should fresh produce be out of the question and the next question is whether to use frozen or canned, the answer is to use frozen. Some frozen vegetables are parboiled, and most are packed with added salt, so you'll need to rinse them and only briefly heat them through to cook them. Watch out for frozen fruits packed in sugar.

For the most part, canned fruits and vegetables are off the list. They've been soaking for a long time in salt, sugar, or additives, but worse, have been thoroughly processed at a high heat (remember, anything that comes in a can cannot be raw). If necessity has you buying canned produce, always get them packed in water or their own juices without anything else added.

When it comes to buying meats and fish, the same "frozen instead of canned" rule applies, providing they have not been breaded or otherwise altered. Most canned meats and fish come packed in a briny solution often laced with preservatives and partially hydrogenated oils, so they'll need to be rinsed and drained before use.

Meats, Poultry, and Fish

When shopping for meats, always select the leaner cuts. This includes organ meats such as heart, liver, kidneys, and yes, brains. Not only are organ meats lean, they have a higher nutritional value than muscle meats and as a rule are less expensive. Stay away from steaks and chops and gourmet cuts with a high fat content characterized by white marbling or a lightish pink color. Domestic poultry should be pink and firm. A yellowish skin indicates that the bird has a lot of fat. Even skinned it may contain a lot of intramuscular fat that is hard to remove. Stewing chickens are much leaner than frying chickens but require a lot of cooking with moist heat to make them tender.

The continual controversy surrounding the hormones and feeding methods in raising commercial livestock is something to consider. If you're apprehensive, look for markets and butcher shops that carry meat and poultry grown naturally without the use of chemicals and hormones, sometimes for average prices.

Fish and shellfish are a pretty good bet, but more and more they too are being grown on aqua farms where methods of fertilizing, feeding, and transporting the fish to market could very well call for some thought. Protect yourself and know your source. If there's doubt, ask a knowledgeable person at a fish or meat market to give you the scoop.

Dairy Products

Now here is something you should know about dairy products and your health. According to government regulations, virtually all dairy products have been pasteurized and homogenized—that is, processed. Pasteurization heats the milk to a very high temperature to kill harmful bacteria and prolong shelf life—that is, in your refrigerator—but it also kills some of the milk's beneficial enzymes and reduces its nutrient content. Most milk sold in stores is also homogenized—a process by which the large fat molecules are broken down into tiny ones, giving the milk a uniform creaminess and better storageability. However, the combination of pasteurization and homogenization gives the fat molecules "artery clogging" properties, much the same way hydrogenated oils do.

Unfortunately, pasteurization and homogenization are necessary in packaging, transporting, and marketing a satisfactory product to a wide range of consumers. It's a dilemma to your good health, but here are some ways to get around it. If you or your children drink milk, drink nonfat milk. Even though it has been pasteurized, the homogenized fat molecules have been removed, but not the remaining nutrients. It's higher in protein than whole milk, with a little over half the calories. Low-fat milk is the next notch down but better than whole milk. Use it for baking or making richer sauces or desserts. Avoid pasteurized whole milk products. Choose nonfat yogurt and low-fat or part-skim soft and hard cheeses. If you're a cheese lover, try to buy aged cheeses. They're relatively high in fat and sodium, but they have a redeeming value—most aged cheeses are made with raw cultured milk and are probably the only raw commercial dairy product you'll get. Read the label to be sure. If it does not say "pasteurized," then it's raw.

In some areas—New York State is an example—it is illegal to sell unpasteurized milk except at the farm where it was produced. Elsewhere it is possible to buy raw "certified" milk products. If you're lucky enough to live in such an area, by all means buy them. Not only are they nutritionally superior, but they have to be produced with an extremely high standard of cleanliness and low bacteria count to bear the label "certified." That way you can be safe and certain that you are getting a high-quality product.

A word about yogurt. Yogurt cannot be raw to be cultured, but the culture itself has live enzymes and healthful benefits. Read the carton to see that it's pure and not cut with gelatin and stabilizers. If it contains fruit, be sure that it doesn't contain sugar also.

In the case of margarine versus butter, butter wins hands down. Even though margarines may be made from 100 percent polyunsaturated oils, they must be partially hydrogenated, a process of high heat and chemical purification that is ironically linked to cellular and arterial damage. In addition to the hydrogenated oils, you get stabilizers, food coloring, preservatives, and other chemicals. Margarine is not a good bet. Caloriewise margarine and butter are equal, but butter is natural, it has more nutritional value and more flavor. Unless you're on a very strict diet, there's nothing wrong with a bit of butter in cooking. As you will find, the Muscular Gourmet uses only small quantities of butter for taste, not texture or richness. With a few exceptions where the recipes specifically call for unsalted butter, the choice is yours. Although salted butter has more flavor, it is recommended that you use sweet or unsalted butter, so that you have full control of your salt intake.

Butter is better than margarine, but if you do use margarine, buy the types made exclusively from polyunsaturated vegetable oils such as corn and safflower. Likewise, if you are using store-bought mayonnaise, buy the type made from safflower oil. Among the best oils to cook with are safflower, sunflower, soy, corn, peanut, sesame, and olive oil. They contain no saturated fats and no cholesterol. A little oil goes a long way, so vegetable oils are also used sparingly in the Muscular Gourmet recipes. And absolutely nothing is deep fried. If your health food store carries them, get "cold pressed" oils. They are better because they have not been refined through heat or chemical methods. Try to save them for noncooking purposes such as homemade salad dressings and mayonnaise. They are a little stronger in flavor, but well worth it nutritionally. Two oils to avoid are coconut and cottonseed as they are high in saturated fats.

Read the Label

Nearly all commercial condiments and sauces are made with such additives as sugar, salt, hydrogenated oils, preservatives, or other chemicals. Look for terms like "lite," "dietetic," "low calorie," "mild," "low sodium," "naturally aged," "naturally fermented," or "natural style;" then *read the label* to see if they contain any of the above additives. A natural brand of catsup will carry the word "imitation" on the label because it's made with honey instead of sugar, whereas a national brand is allowed the term "natural style" on the label, although it contains sugar. So watch out! Canned or bottled "gourmet" items as a rule are purer and made with better quality ingredients than "commercial brands," and may be a smarter buy in the long run.

Sweeteners

For a sweetener, always try to use raw, unfiltered honey. It's rich in nature's nutrients and provides a smooth, low-key flow of energy to the body. Blackstrap molasses and pure maple syrup are good also as they are high in vitamins and minerals. Never buy white sugar. It's a highly processed, nonnutritive chemical that causes the blood sugar to go up and down, due to insulin reactions. Brown sugars are tricky, because unless they are the real thing, they could simply be white sugar with molasses added in varying quantities. Raw sugar is a cut above, but unfortunately it is not actually "raw," only less refined than white sugar; nevertheless, it contains a few residual nutrients. Fruit sugars such as fructose, beet, and date sugars are both good and bad. They burn slower and have a better effect on the blood sugar level, but they are highly refined and contain very few, if any, nutrients. If you must use an artificial sweetener, go with NutraSweet. Its sweetness is derived from a formation of amino acids, and it is the safest of all the artificial sweeteners on the market.

Flavoring Agents

It's always wise to regulate your salt intake, especially if you have problems with fluid retention. But let's face it: Some things just don't taste good flat. With very few exceptions, where salt is called for in an exact amount, most of the Muscular Gourmet recipes only call for salt "to taste." This does not mean to wield the salt shaker with wild abandon. Start out with less, then add a little more until the food suits your taste. You may even want to undersalt it. Food has a tendency to taste saltier as you go because the flavor of sodium lingers.

Commercial table salt is a potent, processed chemical. Avoid it at all costs. Instead, use sea salt, which is derived from a natural source and contains some of the minerals found in the sea, or, vegetable salt, a combination of earth and sea salt, dehydrated vegetables, and a yeast concentrate. Although the two types of salt are interchangeable in most of these recipes, vegetable salt imparts a slightly seasoned flavor, so you may not want to use it in sweet and baked goods. Both of these salts should be available in the health food section of the supermarket.

Freshly ground pepper is a must. The taste of it is exceptionally robust. Keep whole peppercorns in a pepper mill ready to go in your kitchen. Since most of these recipes call for pepper ''to taste,'' all you need to do is give the pepper mill a few grinds as you cook. There's no need to measure. Store unused pepper tightly sealed in a cool place. Commercially ground pepper gets stale and flat especially fast, so don't leave it open.

Whole peppercorns can be bought in the supermarket, but you may find some of the more exotic spices such as cardamom and cumin seeds, saffron threads or whole nutmeg a bit more difficult to find. Many health food stores have a spice section that carries these whole, hard-to-find spices. If not, ask your grocer to order them for you and keep them in stock. Then invest in a little spice mill for grinding them. It isn't often that fresh or exotic spices are called for in these recipes, but when they are, they lend an unbelievable flavor that's well worth the effort of obtaining them.

Herbs are a key ingredient in gourmet cooking and a much more intelligent choice than the abundance of rich creams and butters that characterize so many gourmet recipes and anesthetize the taste buds into overeating. It's not always easy to make a recipe taste good without such dangerous ingredients, but the challenge can be met. It takes awareness, willpower, and the ability to reeducate your taste buds in the true gourmet sense. Let herbs be the star in their combinations and complexities. Growing herbs at home or obtaining them fresh and drying them out yourself is the best way to capture their full flavor and aroma. However, commercially dried herbs that have been stored properly are quite adequate to use. Just remember, if you are substituting dried herbs for fresh in a recipe, use ¼ of the amount called for. This amount may vary slightly, depending on the variety, quality, and shelf life of the herb.

Grain Foods

Breads and pastas are starches, and highly refined ones at that. Be careful of the flours and grains they contain. In checking bread labels and cereal boxes, be alert for enriched or white flours, even unbleached flours, and avoid them. Look for whole wheat flour, whole wheat berries, sprouted wheat, wheat germ, rye, whole barley, oats, stone-ground cornmeal, and bran. Again, watch out for sugar and preservatives. Choose pastas made from whole wheat or some of the newer varieties made from vegetable flours such as spinach, artichoke, or tomato. Never buy white rice, only brown (which has the bran left intact) or wild rice. When buying legumes, get the whole beans and peas, since they are more complete nutritionally. Many whole legumes (and grains) can be sprouted for healthier soups, salads, and baked goods.

Wines and Beers

Here is a note of interest for the occasional wine and beer drinker. Avoid capped wines; most of them have been chemically fermented and often have added sugar. Look for corked wines or wines with a vintage date. Most widely marketed bottled and canned beers are pasteurized, though some regional beers from smaller breweries are not. Keg beer, on the other hand, is normally unpasteurized and has a superb taste, as do aged wines.

Leave hard liquors alone. In rare instances, I have called for small amounts of liquor in recipes as a flavoring agent—an exception. But on the whole, stay away from something that is, in the end, not good for you.

Fitness and good health don't fall in your lap; you have to go out and get them. Likewise, many commercial foods are not naturally healthful, so you must become a discriminating shopper. You may have to explore a bit before you discover where certain ingredients can be obtained. It doesn't matter if it's a computerized supermarket, a gourmet mini-market, the corner butcher shop, or a roadside health food store. Go where you get what you need, but shop with savvy.

Once you elevate your standard of living, smart shopping and eating will become second nature to you. It's fun to know the facts, to leave your old habits behind, and put your new knowledge to work for a happier, healthier life-style that's a cut above the rest.

4
MEAT

GREAT ROASTS

Cooking a good roast is an art, and probably anyone who has ever made the gallant attempt has ruined at least one. So rather than compromise a magnificent meat roast for the sake of trial and error, follow these fail-proof roasting tips.

For starters, cut off excess fat from meat, but leave a thin layer to keep it from drying out during roasting. Give it a quick rinse under tap water and pat it dry with paper towels to clean the outside for seasoning.

Ideal oven temperature for juicy roasting is between 300° and 350°, usually around 325°. For beef and lamb roasts use a meat thermometer inserted into the thickest part of the meat; the internal temperature should read 120° to 130° Fahrenheit for rare, 140° to 150° for medium rare, and 160° for medium. Veal is best done at medium to medium well and registers between 155° and 165°. Pork should always be well done and registers 170° to 175°.

For truly great roasting, a convection or turbo oven is unsurpassed. It circulates the hot air during cooking, so that it seals in the meat juices all around the roast as it cooks off the fat. Meat cooks about 30 percent faster at 25° to 50° lower temperature than in a standard oven, so it saves energy too. The convection oven turns itself off when it's done cooking, and since it's small and cools off fast, you can let the roast sit in the oven without taking it out right away.

For better results, start all meat at refrigerator temperature. Thaw out frozen cuts if possible. However, if you must start with frozen meat, the cooking time will be approximately 10 to 15 minutes per pound longer. Whether the meat is frozen or not, take off 2 minutes per pound for bone-in if the prescribed cooking time is for boneless and add 2 minutes per pound for boneless to the prescribed cooking time for a bone-in roast. And in timing your meal, always remember that it's better to undercook than overcook a roast. If you start late, diners will wait a few minutes more for perfect meat. But if you start too early and the roast is overdone, you have no recourse.

Roasts cook best in a roasting pan with low sides; they cook more evenly

Fat Buster: To deglaze a roasting pan or skillet of browned meat drippings, drain off fat, then pour a small amount of wine, herbed vinegar, apple, or citrus juice into the pan. Stir over a medium heat scraping off any brown bits. Cook until sauce becomes syrupy, then spoon over the meat.

when there is less moisture surrounding them. A shallow pan also makes basting easier. Cook boneless or fatty roasts on a rack in a shallow roasting pan. It keeps them in a dry heat and out of the fat drippings.

Never cover a roast during cooking. It will lock in steam and cause the roast to overcook and lose that "roasted" flavor. For the same reason, do not add liquid to the roasting pan until the meat is done. If a roast seems to be browning too much on the outside, lower the heat a little or set a piece of foil loosely over the meat.

If you wish, you may baste a roast with its own juices several times during cooking. This will help keep it moist and give it more flavor from the seasonings you have used.

It's always best to let a roast stand 15 to 30 minutes before carving. That allows the juices to simmer down and permeate the meat so that they don't spill out when you cut into it. Take into account that meat will continue to cook a little more during this time, but not enough to change its rareness drastically.

Carve meat on a platter, not in the roasting pan, so that escaping juices will not mix in with the roasting pan fats. To separate fat from warm meat juice in the pan, let it cool slightly first; fat rises to the top, and it's then easier to skim off. There's also a nifty little houseware item, a cup for pan drippings with a spout stemming from the bottom, which enables you to pour out just the juice. Make a good lean gravy, or serve the juice as is with the meat. If drippings are scant, due to lack of juice, add a little water or stock to the pan to stretch it.

Reheating rare to medium leftover meat is tricky; often it overcooks. Leftover roast is best eaten deli-style, cold, but if you prefer to warm it up, put it uncovered in a 250° (or less) oven until it is palatably warm. Cut off a slice to see. If you make it too hot all the way through, it will probably be overdone. Never attempt to reheat meat in a microwave oven. You might as well give it to the dog.

Yes, cooking a roast just right *is* an art. Try these recipes, and you'll have to agree that, when it's succulent and cooked to perfection, there's nothing like a great roast. On the following pages, you'll find a lineup of the heavyweights.

Note: The following nutritional calculations are for 4 ounce servings of lean meat plus the recommended individual servings of vegetables, dressing, or whatever else is part of the dish.

PERFECT PRIME RIB

Here's what you've been waiting for—perfect pink prime rib rolled in a home-blended prime rib seasoning that's better than restaurants.

Per serving:
418 calories
16 g protein
39 g fat
0 g carb.

1 tablespoon vegetable salt (low-sodium salt optional)
1 teaspoon each paprika and dehydrated parsley flakes
½ teaspoon onion powder
¼ teaspoon each garlic powder, celery seed, dried oregano, and rosemary
1 bay leaf, finely crumbled
4 whole black peppercorns
1 beef rib roast (about 5 pounds)

Finely grind all seasoning together in a high-speed grinder. Arrange seasoning evenly on a piece of wax paper and roll the roast around thoroughly to coat it (or put seasoning in a shaker and sprinkle it on).

Place roast, fat side up, on a flat rack in a shallow roasting pan. Roast in a 350° oven exactly 20 minutes per pound or for 1 hour and 40 minutes. Skim off the fat, and save the juice to serve with the meat. If you want to serve prime rib "au jus," add clear stock to the meat juice to make enough for all, and season with prime rib seasoning. Serves 8.

ITALIAN ROAST VEAL

Per serving:
285 calories
25 g protein
11 g fat
19 g carb.

1 boneless veal loin roast (about 3 pounds)
3 cloves garlic, peeled and split into quarters
Vegetable salt and freshly ground pepper
1 teaspoon dried basil
½ teaspoon each dried oregano and thyme
1 sprig fresh parsley, chopped
1 pound Italian plum tomatoes, chopped
½ green bell pepper, julienned
1 large white onion, quartered
1 can (8 ounces) tomato puree
1½ cups medium-dry red wine

With a small sharp knife, pierce veal roast all over and insert into it slivers of garlic. Place the veal in a large roasting pan. Salt and pepper it to taste, and sprinkle it with herbs. Arrange vegetables around the veal. Mix tomato puree and wine together, and pour over veal and vegetables, making sure vegetables are moist with sauce.

Place roast in a 350° oven, and bake ½ hour, basting once. Turn roast, and reduce heat to 325°. Cook for 1 hour more, basting several times. Meat thermometer should register 155° when done. Serves 4.

PORK SHOULDER ROAST WITH CHESTNUT STUFFING

Per serving:
331 calories
16 g protein
25 g fat
10 g carb.

Note: Don't be
fearful and overcook
the pork to the point
that it is dry and
leathery. Use a meat
thermometer, and
pay attention to the
recommended
cooking time. It will
be well cooked yet
juicy.

1 tablespoon butter
¼ cup shallots, finely chopped
½ cup celery, finely chopped
1 cup fresh mushrooms, sliced
¼ cup dry sherry
¼ teaspoon each dried marjoram, sage, savory, and thyme
Vegetable salt and freshly ground pepper
1 boneless pork shoulder roast (about 5 pounds)
¾ pound chestnuts, cooked and peeled; or 1 can (15½-ounces), drained
Ground sage

In a medium, nonstick skillet, melt butter, and lightly sauté shallots, celery, and mushrooms. Add sherry for liquid. Mix in herbs and salt and pepper to taste, then set aside. If roast is tied, cut the strings, and unroll the meat. Make necessary cuts to lay it out flat. Spoon sautéed mixture across the center, then arrange a row of chestnuts over that.

Carefully roll up the roast, and secure it with string. Dust it all over with ground sage, and salt and pepper to taste if desired. Place it on a rack in a shallow roasting pan. Roast it in a 325° oven for approximately 30–35 minutes per pound until a meat thermometer reaches 170°. Serves 8.

TRADITIONAL LEG OF LAMB

Per serving:
211 calories
17 g protein
15 g fat
0 g carb.

1 leg of lamb (about 5 pounds)
4 cloves garlic, peeled and split into quarters
3–4 sprigs fresh rosemary
1 tablespoon olive oil
Vegetable salt and freshly ground pepper

With a sharp narrow knife, make a slit in the lamb about 1–1½ inches deep into the meat. Press in a sliver of garlic and several needles of rosemary. Repeat this all around the lamb until the garlic is used. Brush the leg all over with olive oil, and salt and pepper it to taste.

Place lamb, meaty side up, on a rack in a shallow roasting pan. Lay the whole sprigs of rosemary across the rop of the lamb. Roast in a 325° oven at 20–22 minutes per pound, about 1 hour and 45 minutes for medium rare. Serves 8.

ROAST LOIN OF VEAL IN A PECAN MUSTARD CRUST

Per serving:
281 calories
23 g protein
21 g fat
2 g carb.

1 veal loin roast (about 4 pounds)
Vegetable salt and freshly ground pepper
2 tablespoons butter
2 tablespoons Dijon mustard
1 tablespoon plain nonfat yogurt
½ cup pecans, finely crushed

Sprinkle veal with salt and pepper to taste. Melt butter in a small saucepan, and blend in mustard and yogurt. Brush sauce all over the meaty sides of the roast. Spread pecans out on a piece of wax paper. Roll coated areas of the roast in the pecans. Sprinkle any remaining pecans over the top. Place roast, meat side up, in the bottom of a shallow roasting pan. Roast in a 325° oven at 25–30 minutes per pound, or until a meat thermometer registers 160°. Serves 6.

CROWN ROAST OF LAMB

Per serving:
307 calories
14 g protein
28 g fat
0 g carb.

1 rack of lamb (8 ribs)
2 tablespoons Dijon mustard
1 clove fresh garlic, pressed
Freshly ground pepper

Crack the connecting ribs along the meaty end of the roast. Blend mustard and garlic together, and lightly brush over the meat. Add pepper to taste. Bend the end ribs together, meat side in, and secure it with a string or skewers. Place it, ribs up, on a flat rack in a shallow roasting pan. Cover the tip of each rib with foil to keep it from burning. You may stuff crown with a ball of foil to help roast retain its shape.

Roast it in a preheated 325° oven approximately 9 to 10 minutes per pound for rare. When done, move it to a serving platter, and remove foil. Serve filled with Saffron Rice (page 193). Serves 4, two chops per person.

MARINATED BEEF TENDERLOIN ROAST

Per serving:
307 calories
22 g protein
23 g fat
1 g carb.

¼ cup olive oil
¼ cup dry red wine
3 cloves fresh garlic, pressed
½ teaspoon each dried basil, marjoram, and parsley
¼ teaspoon dried oregano
4 whole cloves
Vegetable salt and freshly ground pepper to taste
1 beef tenderloin roast (about 4 pounds)

Mix all marinade ingredients in a large shallow baking dish. Pierce the roast all over on both sides with a sharp fork. Place the meat in the marinade, and turn to coat both sides. Cover, and refrigerate for 4–6 hours. Turn at least once during marinating.

When done, place roast on a rack in a shallow roasting pan. Roast in a 350° oven for 18–20 minutes per pound for approximately 1 hour 15 minutes. Baste with pan juices and any leftover marinade several times during roasting. Serves 6.

BASIC POT ROAST

Per serving:
369 calories
25 g protein
24 g fat
10 g carb.

Note: You may add other vegetables such as carrots or potatoes before cooking the roast. Make sure they are well covered with liquid.

1 bottom round, shoulder, chuck roast, or short ribs of beef (about 4 pounds)
2 cloves fresh garlic, pressed
1 tablespoon safflower oil
2 tablespoons low-sodium tamari (naturally fermented soy sauce)
1 teaspoon each dried marjoram and thyme
2 bay leaves
6 whole peppercorns
2 large onions, sliced
2 large tomatoes, chopped
2 sprigs fresh parsley, chopped
3 cups Meat Stock (page 43)
2 tablespoons whole wheat flour

Trim fat from meat. Rub with pressed garlic. Heat oil over the stove in a large roasting pan. Lightly brown roast on both sides in the pan, adding 1 tablespoon of tamari on each side. Add herbs, onions, tomatoes, parsley and Meat Stock. Cover, and simmer over a medium low heat, or place in a 325° oven for 1½ hours.

When done, let it cool down, and pour out liquid. Refrigerate to skim off any fat that congeals at the top. Blend flour in the meat juice, and return to the roasting pan. Cover, and simmer with the roast for several more minutes until juice is slightly thickened. Serves 6.

CELEBRATED MEALS

DOWNHOME DINNER

Green Salad with Slimming Blue Cheese Dressing
Basic Pot Roast
Creamed Parsnips in Sauterne
Swiss Chard Romano
Potato Onion Bread
Lattice Berry Pie
Red wine

ROAST LAMB ROLLED WITH APRICOT MINT CHUTNEY

Apricot Mint Chutney:

Per serving:
353 calories
19 g protein
18 g fat
31 g carb.

⅔ *cup boiling water*
1 cup dried apricots
½ *cup dates, pitted and chopped*
1 tablespoon raw honey
1 tablespoon cider vinegar
¼ *cup fresh mint, chopped*
⅛ *teaspoon each ground coriander and cardamom*
⅓ *cup unsalted cashews, chopped*
1 boneless lamb leg or shoulder (about 4 pounds)
Vegetable salt and cayenne pepper to taste

In a small bowl, add boiling water to apricots, and allow them to soften for about ½ hour. Drain, and chop them. Add dates, honey, vinegar, mint, and spices, and blend well. Mix in nuts.

If lamb is tied, cut strings, and lay it out flat. Pound if necessary to even the thickness. Spoon chutney lengthwise across the center. Jelly-roll it back together. Tie it with string, and season lightly all around with salt and cayenne pepper.

Place it on a rack in a roasting pan, fat side up. Roast in a 325° oven at 25 minutes per pound or for about 1 hour and 20 minutes. Baste with pan juices halfway through cooking. Slice, and serve. Serves 6.

MARINATED ROAST PORK
WITH RUM RAISIN SAUCE

Marinade:

Per serving:
326 calories
16 g protein
22 g fat
16 g carb.

1 tablespoon raw honey
2 tablespoons dark rum
2 tablespoons freshly squeezed lime juice
2 cloves fresh pressed garlic
2 teaspoons ground ginger
Vegetable salt and freshly ground pepper (optional)
1 boneless pork loin (about 5 pounds)

Mix marinade ingredients together in a large shallow baking dish. Lay roast out flat in the marinade, and turn it over several times to coat it thoroughly. Cover dish tightly, and refrigerate at least 4 hours or overnight. Turn once if possible.

When ready to cook, roll up the roast, and secure it with string. Place on a rack in a shallow roasting pan, and pour any remaining marinade over the top. Roast in a 325° oven at 30–35 minutes per pound until a meat thermometer registers 170°. Baste once during cooking.

Let the roast stand for 15–20 minutes, then cut it into ¼-inch slices and arrange on a serving platter. Serve with Rum Raisin Sauce.

Rum Raisin Sauce:

¼ cup seedless raisins
⅓ cup dark rum
2½ cups Poultry Stock (page 70)
Pan juices
1 tablespoon arrowroot
¼ cup freshly squeezed lime juice
2 tablespoons raw honey
¼ teaspoon ground cloves

Soak seedless raisins in rum until plump. Pour 2 cups of the stock into the baking pan with juices and mix together. Strain into a medium saucepan. Bring to simmer. Moisten arrowroot in remaining ½ cup of the stock, and stir into the saucepan until it begins to thicken.

Blend in lime juice, honey, cloves, and rum-soaked raisins, and remove from the heat. Spoon sauce over the sliced pork and serve. Serves 8.

ROAST VEAL STUFFED WITH VEAL KIDNEY

Per serving:
323 calories
37 g protein
17 g fat
2 g carb.

1 tablespoon butter
4 veal kidneys (about ¾ lb), chopped and with membrane removed
2 cloves fresh garlic, pressed
½ cup dry white wine
1 teaspoon dried savory
½ teaspoon each dried marjoram and tarragon
1 bunch fresh spinach leaves, chopped
Vegetable salt and freshly ground pepper to taste
1 boneless rolled veal shoulder roast (about 4 pounds)
1 clove garlic, halved

Melt butter in a large nonstick skillet. Add veal kidneys and garlic, and sauté, tossing frequently, until kidneys are partially cooked. Add wine and herbs, and simmer for several minutes. Add spinach and salt and pepper if desired, and continue to stir over a low heat until spinach is wilted and the liquid has evaporated. Set aside.

Roll out veal shoulder, making cuts as necessary to flatten it. Spoon in an even row of kidney stuffing. Roll it up, and tie with a string. Rub the outside with halves of garlic, and salt and pepper it to taste. Place the roast on the bottom of a shallow roasting pan. Roast in a 300° oven at approximately 30 minutes per pound or until a meat thermometer reaches 160°. Turn every half hour during cooking.

If you wish to make gravy to accompany the roast, blend ¼ cup plain nonfat yogurt and 2 tablespoons dry white wine with the fat-skimmed drippings. Serves 8.

ROAST PORK LOIN WITH MAPLE MUSTARD GLAZE

Per serving:
403 calories
16 g protein
30 g fat
19 g carb.

2 tablespoons Dijon mustard
2 tablespoons lemon juice, freshly squeezed
1 clove fresh garlic, pressed
⅓ cup pure maple syrup
2 tablespoons sesame oil
1 pork loin (about 3 pounds)
Vegetable salt and freshly ground pepper to taste

Blend mustard, lemon juice, garlic, maple syrup, and 1 tablespoon of the oil together, and set aside. Brush meaty sides of the pork loin with the remaining tablespoon of oil. Salt and pepper if desired.

Place roast, bone side down, in a shallow roasting pan. Spoon half of the glaze over the meat. Roast in a 325° oven at 30–35 minutes per pound until a thermometer reads 170° in the thickest part of the meat. Baste with pan juices once during roasting but before adding remaining glaze. Baste with remaining glaze 20–25 minutes before roast is done. Serves 4.

MUSCLE BURGERS

There's nothing wrong with good lean red meat. In fact, everything about it is right. It is and will always remain nature's greatest source of pure protein.

For optimum muscular growth, the cells in the body need nitrogen, which is derived almost entirely from the essential and nonessential amino acids found in meat. Even if bodybuilding isn't your raison d'être, remember that the body requires protein for more functions than just muscle building and maintenance. Also, red meat supplies all the important B vitamins, phosphorus, sulfur, potassium, copper, and iron.

Know the facts before you shortchange yourself. If you want to muscle up, you've got to have plenty of first-class protein. Research shows a daily need of 2.5 grams of protein per kilogram (2.2 pounds) of body weight for athletes wanting to gain muscle, and 1 gram of protein per kilogram of body weight just to maintain it. That is a lot greater than the previously touted requirement of .8 grams of protein per kilogram of body weight, regardless of muscle size and physical condition.

The key is to eat lean red meat, and with the exception of pork, eat it as rare as possible. Rare meat yields over 50 percent more assimilable protein than meat that is well done, since overcooking destroys the essential amino acids and enzymes. Therefore, the more utilizable the protein, the more it will go toward tissue building rather than toward fuel burning.

Get the point? Don't be a lightweight. Go for meat and try these Muscle Burgers made with the leanest ground beef. It's best to buy top sirloin or round steak and have it ground fresh, after all the visible fat is removed. Each one of these tempting, healthy recipes has a distinctly different taste with all the ingredients mixed right in with the meat. They're simple to make too, because all of them are made with five ingredients or fewer, not counting the meat. Serve them on 7 Grain Sprouted Wheat Buns (page 180) with lettuce, tomato, and natural-style condiments.

These recipes will make two medium-size burgers, or, one Olympic-size burger if you really want to pack in the protein. Broil or charbroil (not fry) them to medium rare for the fullest flavor, then discover the protein power of lean red meat. More muscle to ya!

Fat Buster: An ideal on-the-go, high-protein snack is baby food! Yes, all varieties of strained meats come in little ready-to-eat pop-top jars and are prepared with nothing but meat and water.

Note: Nutritional calculations given are for 1 burger based on 2 burgers per recipe without buns.

TRICEP BURGER

Per burger:
304 calories
40 g protein
17 g fat
0 g carb.

¾ pound lean ground sirloin
¼ cup fresh parsley, minced
1 clove garlic, pressed
½ teaspoon dried sage
¼ teaspoon freshly ground pepper

Combine all ingredients, and mix well. Form patties 1-inch thick, and broil several minutes on each side (medium rare). Makes 2 burgers.

BICEP BURGER

Per burger:
405 calories
48 g protein
25 g fat
1 g carb.

¾ pound lean ground sirloin
2 ounces aged Swiss cheese, grated
¼ cup fresh mushrooms, chopped
1 tablespoon onion, finely chopped
⅛ teaspoon liquid smoke

Combine all ingredients, and mix well. Form patties 1-inch thick, and broil several minutes on each side (medium rare). Makes 2 burgers.

DOUBLE BICEP BURGER

Per burger:
355 calories
44 g protein
20 g fat
1 g carb.

¾ pound lean ground sirloin
1 egg
1 green onion, finely chopped
1 clove fresh garlic, pressed
1 tablespoon low-sodium tamari
1 tablespoon sherry

Combine all ingredients, and mix well. Form patties 1-inch thick, and broil several minutes on each side (medium rare). Makes 2 burgers.

BRAWNY BURGER

Per burger:
365 calories
36 g protein
23 g fat
1 g carb.

⅔ pound lean ground sirloin
2 ounces Braunschweiger (liver sausage)
1 tablespoon plain nonfat yogurt
2 tablespoons onion, finely minced
1 teaspoon caraway seeds

Combine all ingredients, and mix well. Form patties 1-inch thick, and broil several minutes on each side (medium rare). Makes 2 burgers.

PEC BURGER

Per burger:
365 calories
43 g protein
22 g fat
1 g carb.

Note: Serve this one open faced with a little more Dijon mustard spread over the top of the meat.

¾ pound lean ground sirloin
1 ounce crumbled blue cheese
1 clove fresh garlic, pressed
2 teaspoons Dijon mustard
1 tablespoon dry white wine
¼ teaspoon freshly ground pepper

Combine all ingredients, and mix well. Form patties 1-inch thick, and broil several minutes on each side (medium rare). Makes 2 burgers.

MOST MUSCULAR BURGER

Per burger:
412 calories
48 g protein
25 g fat
4 g carb.

Healthy note: If you'd like to try Veggie Muscle Burgers, add one or more of the following ingredients to the meat: bean sprouts, grated zucchini or carrots, finely chopped celery, green pepper, cabbage, or broccoli florets, or any of your other favorite vegetables. They'll add a delightful flavor and crunchiness to the burgers.

¾ pound lean ground sirloin
2 ounces Monterey Jack cheese, shredded
1 can (4 ounces) chopped green chilies, drained
1 tablespoon medium hot salsa
1 teaspoon chili powder

Combine all ingredients, and mix well. Form patties 1-inch thick, and broil several minutes on each side (medium rare). Makes 2 burgers.

MEATY ENTREES

There's more to meat than steaks and chops. The following careful selection of recipes features leaner cuts of meats, such as loin cuts, variety meats, and meats that are ground lean. They're nutritionally superior to higher-fat "prime" cuts primarily because they provide more protein per calorie. Ounce for ounce, pound for pound, that results in more bodybuilding vitamins, minerals, and essential amino acids. So don't be taken by expensive cuts of meat that look good. Go for the pure protein meats, and you'll save money too. It's the best food value around.

VEAL AND VEGETABLE MARSALA

Per serving:
372 calories
33 g protein
21 g fat
7 g carb.

1 tablespoon butter
1 tablespoon olive oil
Vegetable salt and freshly ground pepper to taste
1 pound veal, thinly sliced or scaloppini, pounded thin
½ cup Marsala wine
½ cup Poultry Stock (page 70)
1 cup julienned carrots, cut into 2-inch lengths
1 cup celery, thinly sliced
1 small yellow onion, thinly sliced

Melt butter and olive oil in a large nonstick skillet. Salt and pepper veal slices to taste, and lightly brown them on both sides over a medium low heat. Add wine, stock, and vegetables. Partially cover, and simmer for about 10 minutes, turning veal once. Serves 4.

VEAL AND ZUCCHINI PARMESAN

Per serving:
377 calories
36 g protein
19 g fat
16 g carb.

2 cups Marinara Sauce (see page 142)
1 pound zucchini, sliced
1 pound lean ground veal
⅓ cup Parmesan cheese, freshly grated
2 tablespoons fresh parsley, snipped

Spoon a little sauce in the bottom of a 13 x 9-inch baking dish. Lay half the zucchini slices on the bottom. Crumble ground veal evenly over the top. Spoon over half the sauce and Parmesan cheese and 1 tablespoon of the parsley.

Layer the remaining zucchini over the veal. Cover with the rest of the sauce, and sprinkle with the remaining Parmesan cheese. Bake uncovered in a 350° oven for 40–45 minutes until zucchini is tender. Sprinkle with reserved tablespoon of parsley. Serves 4.

SCHNITZEL WITH GROUND VEAL

Per serving:
353 calories
34 g protein
21 g fat
6 g carb.

1 pound lean ground veal
1 tablespoon whole wheat pastry flour
¾ teaspoon paprika
2 tablespoons butter
1 cup Poultry Stock (page 70)
½ cup plain nonfat yogurt
¼ teaspoon Worcestershire sauce
⅛ teaspoon anchovy paste
4 lemon wedges
4 sprigs parsley

Shape the veal into 4 thin patties. Combine flour with paprika, and lightly dust patties on both sides. Melt butter in a large nonstick skillet. Over a medium heat, brown patties on both sides (you may have to cook two at a time, in which case use half the butter).

When done, pour ½ cup of the stock over all four patties, partially cover, and braise them over a medium low heat for 7 or 8 minutes, turning once. Mix remaining stock, yogurt, Worcestershire sauce, anchovy paste, and any pan juices together. Pour over the veal, and heat. Garnish with lemon wedges and parsley. Serves 4.

ITALIAN MEATBALL AND RISOTTO SKILLET

Per serving:
382 calories
30 g protein
16 g fat
32 g carb.

1 pound lean ground sirloin
1 clove fresh garlic, pressed
1 cup fresh parsley, chopped
Vegetable salt and freshly ground pepper to taste
1 tablespoon olive oil
1 yellow onion, chopped
1 pound Italian plum tomatoes, chopped
1 green bell pepper, diced
¾ pound yellow summer squash, diced
1 tablespoon each fresh basil and oregano, chopped
1½ cups cooked risotto (see Herb Risotto, page 192, for cooking method)
⅓ cup freshly grated Romano cheese

Mix ground sirloin, garlic, parsley, and salt and pepper together in a medium bowl. Form 12 meatballs. Heat oil in a large ovenproof skillet, and brown meatballs along with onion over a medium low heat. When done, add tomatoes, green pepper, squash, and herbs, and cook several minutes. Stir in risotto. Sprinkle the top with Romano cheese, and bake uncovered in a 350° oven for 15 minutes. Serves 4.

SOUTHERN BEEF AND OKRA CASSEROLE

Per serving:
421 calories
38 g protein
21 g fat
24 g carb.

Note: To cook
cornmeal mush,
bring 1⅓ cups water
and ⅓ cup stone-
ground yellow
cornmeal to a boil in
a small saucepan.
Add a pinch of salt
if desired. Simmer
covered for 25
minutes until
cornmeal becomes
thick.

1 pound lean ground sirloin
1 clove fresh garlic, pressed
1 yellow onion, finely chopped (reserve 2 tablespoons)
1 can (8 ounce) tomato sauce
1 pound fresh okra, sliced and simmered in 2 cups water for 10 minutes;
   or 2 packages frozen (10 ounces each)
1 package (10 ounce) frozen corn; or use fresh corn from 2 ears
1 teaspoon each fresh marjoram and thyme, minced
½ teaspoon ground cumin
½ teaspoon cayenne pepper
Vegetable salt to taste
4 eggs, separated
1 cup yellow cornmeal mush (see Note below for cooking method)
1 teaspoon chili powder
½ cup aged cheddar cheese, grated (optional)

In a large nonstick skillet, brown sirloin along with garlic and onion over a medium heat. Stir in tomato sauce, okra, corn, and seasonings. Transfer to a 3-quart casserole dish.

Blend egg yolks, cornmeal mush, and chili powder, and set aside. Beat egg whites until soft peaks form. Fold into egg yolk mixture. Spread evenly over the top of the casserole, and sprinkle with reserved onions. (If desired, omit onions and replace with grated cheddar cheese.)

Bake in a preheated 375° oven for 20–25 minutes until topping and onions are golden. Serves 4.

STUFFED FLANK STEAK

Per serving:
289 calories
36 g protein
13 g fat
5 g carb.

1 tablespoon butter
1 clove fresh garlic, pressed
¾ cup zucchini, shredded
½ teaspoon each dried rosemary, sage, and thyme
1 tablespoon fresh parsley, chopped
Vegetable salt and freshly ground pepper to taste
¼ cup whole wheat bread crumbs
½ cup part-skim Mozzarella cheese, shredded
2 pounds beef flank steak, butterflied

Melt butter in a medium nonstick skillet. Over a medium heat, sauté garlic with zucchini, herbs, and salt and pepper until zucchini is semisoft. Remove from heat. Toss in bread crumbs and Mozzarella cheese until well combined. Season both sides of the steak with salt and pepper if desired.

Spread stuffing across the center, and roll the steak up tightly, starting with the short end. Tie rolled-up steak with a string every 1½–2 inches. Then slice steak between strings into 6 pieces. Place steaks on a rack under a broiler about 6 inches from the heat. Broil 6–7 minutes on each side for rare. Remove strings before serving. Serves 6.

BAKED BRAINS PROVENÇALE

Per serving:
209 calories
14 g protein
15 g fat
5 g carb.

1 pound calf brains
¼ cup unseasoned rye crackers, finely crushed
¼ cup Parmesan cheese, freshly grated
½ teaspoon dried marjoram
2 cloves fresh garlic, pressed
1 tablespoon olive oil
Vegetable salt and freshly ground pepper to taste
2 sprigs fresh parsley, snipped

To prepare brains, peel off membrane, and cut off any excess connective tissue under cold running water. Drain. Place brains in a small casserole dish. Then combine crushed rye crackers, Parmesan cheese, and marjoram. Add garlic, olive oil, and salt and pepper. Work with fingers until well combined. Sprinkle mixture over the top of the brains.

Bake uncovered in a preheated 350° oven for 20–25 minutes until top is brown. Serve topped with snipped parsley. Makes 4 servings.

BEEF LIVER STROGANOFF

Per serving:
284 calories
26 g protein
11 g fat
15 g carb.

2 tablespoons butter
1 pound beef or calves liver
1 clove fresh garlic, pressed
1 white onion, sliced
1 cup fresh mushrooms, sliced
½ cup semidry white wine
1 cup Meat Stock (page 43)
1 cup plain nonfat yogurt
1 teaspoon Dijon mustard
1 tablespoon low-sodium tamari
1 teaspoon fresh dill, minced
Freshly ground pepper

Melt butter in a large nonstick skillet. Add liver with garlic, onions, and mushrooms, and sauté until liver is brown on both sides. Stir onions and mushrooms occasionally, using the wine as needed for braising. When onions are translucent, combine remaining ingredients, and stir into the skillet. Cover, and simmer liver in the Stroganoff for several more minutes. Serves 4.

LAMB AND BULGUR STUFFED EGGPLANT

Per serving:
453 calories
42 g protein
22 g fat
22 g carb.

Note: To cook bulgur, add ⅔ cup bulgur to 1⅓ cups water or stock in a small saucepan. Bring to a boil, and boil for 5 minutes. Reduce heat, cover tightly, and simmer approximately 15 minutes, or until fluffy.

2 small eggplants
1 pound lean ground lamb
4 shallots, minced
1 large tomato, chopped
½ teaspoon each ground cumin and dried oregano
⅛ teaspoon cayenne pepper
¼ cup fresh parsley, chopped
1½ cups cooked bulgur (see below for cooking method)
Vegetable salt to taste

Halve eggplants. Scoop out centers, leaving a ½-inch-thick shell. Dice eggplant flesh and set aside. Crumble lamb into a large nonstick skillet, and lightly brown with shallots over a medium heat. Add diced eggplant, and continue to cook until it is semitender. Remove from heat, and drain off any excess fat.

Add remaining ingredients, and toss until well combined. Spoon equal portions of the mixture into eggplant shells. Arrange them in a baking pan, and cover loosely with foil.

Bake in a preheated 350° oven for 25–30 minutes. Remove foil and bake another 5 to 10 minutes, or until eggplant shells are tender and top is brown. Serves 4.

HERB-BASTED LAMB CHOPS

Per serving:
560 calories
33 g protein
46 g fat
2 g carb.

4 loin lamb chops (about 1 pound)
1 tablespoon Dijon mustard
2 tablespoons sauterne
1 clove fresh garlic, pressed
½ teaspoon each dried rosemary and thyme
⅛ teaspoon freshly ground pepper
Vegetable salt to taste

Trim excess fat from the lamb chops. Blend remaining ingredients together, and brush on both sides of the chops. Broil 4 inches from the heat, 4–5 minutes on each side. Serves 2.

LUSCIOUS LAMB MEATLOAF

Per serving:
337 calories
25 g protein
25 g fat
6 g carb.

1½ pounds lean ground lamb
½ cup whole wheat bread crumbs
2 eggs
2 cloves fresh garlic, pressed
2 teaspoons each fresh sage, parsley, and baby chives, minced
1 teaspoon each fresh oregano and mint, minced
Vegetable salt and freshly ground pepper to taste
2 tablespoons tomato paste

In a large bowl, mix all ingredients together well except for tomato paste. Press into a 9 x 5-inch loaf pan. Spread the top with tomato paste, and bake loosely covered in a 350° oven for 45–50 minutes. Uncover the last 15 minutes of baking. Pour off any fat from the pan before cutting the meatloaf. Serves 8.

WINE-BRAISED LAMB KIDNEYS

Per serving:
347 calories
37 g protein
19 g fat
3 g carb.

2 tablespoons butter
1 clove fresh garlic, pressed
1 scallion, minced
1 pound lamb kidneys, chopped and with membrane removed
1 teaspoon each fresh chervil and oregano, chopped
Vegetable salt and freshly ground pepper to taste
½ cup semidry red wine

Melt butter in a medium nonstick skillet. Sauté garlic and scallions over a low heat for 1 minute. Add kidneys, raise heat to medium, and continue to sauté until they're brown all around. Add herbs, salt and pepper, and a little red wine as needed for braising until kidneys are cooked tender (about 5 minutes). When done, pour in any remaining wine, then remove from the heat. Serves 4.

SHERRIED LAMB SHANKS

Per serving:
557 calories
56 g protein
36 g fat
9 g carb.

Step-saving note:
You may also wrap the lamb shanks with marinade ingredients and onions tightly in foil, and bake in a 325° oven for 1–1½ hours, or until tender. This eliminates the marinating process and the need for oil.

4 lamb shanks (¾ pound each, holding a total of 6 ounces of meat)
⅓ cup sherry (reserve 2 tablespoons)
⅓ cup freshly squeezed orange juice
2 tablespoons low-sodium tamari
1 tablespoon raw honey
2 cloves fresh garlic, pressed
1 tablespoon peanut oil
1 yellow onion, sliced
Freshly ground pepper

Pierce lamb shanks all over with the tines of a sharp fork. Mix all but 2 tablespoons of sherry, orange juice, tamari, honey, and garlic in a large bowl or pan. Place shanks in the marinade, and turn them all around to coat. Marinate them at least 6 hours, turning several times.

Heat oil in a large skillet. Slowly brown the shanks on all sides over a medium low heat. Add onions with the remaining marinade and pepper to taste, and stir. Cover, and simmer for about 1 hour or until shanks are tender. When done stir in the reserved 2 tablespoons of sherry. Serves 4.

APPLE-STUFFED PORK CHOPS
WITH APPLESAUCE MUSTARD

Pork Chops:

Per serving:
399 calories
20 g protein
28 g fat
18 g carb.

2 medium apples, cored, peeled, and cut into chunks
¼ cup unfiltered apple juice
1 teaspoon freshly squeezed lemon juice
Pinch of allspice
¼ cup whole wheat bread crumbs
2 tablespoons onion, finely chopped
¼ teaspoon dried sage
Vegetable salt and freshly ground pepper to taste
4 rib pork chops (¾ inch thick, about 6 ounces each)

Put apples, juices, and allspice in a small saucepan with a tight-fitting lid. Simmer for about 10 minutes until apples are tender and most of the liquid has been absorbed. Mash them up with a fork. Set aside ½ cup of the applesauce. Combine bread crumbs, onions, sage, and salt and pepper with the rest of the applesauce.

Cut evenly sliced pockets along the meat side of each pork chop, lengthwise to the bone. Spoon one quarter of the stuffing into each pocket. Close with string or wooden toothpicks.

Applesauce Mustard:

½ cup reserved applesauce
1½ tablespoons Dijon mustard
½ teaspoon prepared horseradish
Vegetable salt and freshly ground pepper to taste

Puree all ingredients in a blender. Brush pork chops generously on both sides with applesauce mustard, reserving some for a final basting. Place them in a shallow baking pan, and cook them for 45 minutes in a preheated 325° oven. Ten minutes before they're done baking, baste them on the top side with the remaining applesauce mustard. Serves 4.

SWISS STYLE PORK CHOPS

Per serving:
417 calories
25 g protein
28 g fat
13 g carb.

4 blade-cut pork chops (about 6 ounces each)
1½ cups Poultry Stock (page 70)
2 large tomatoes, diced
1 large onion, sliced
12 ounces brussels sprouts, trimmed and halved
1 clove fresh garlic, pressed
½ teaspoon each dried basil and savory
Dash of Worcestershire sauce
Freshly ground pepper

Place pork chops in a large nonstick skillet. Add a small amount of stock for liquid. Partially cover, and cook pork chops over a medium low heat for about 5 minutes on each side until liquid has evaporated and pork chops are slightly brown. Drain off any fatty liquid, then stir in the rest of the stock along with the remaining ingredients. Lower heat, and simmer partially covered for 15–20 minutes until brussels sprouts are tender-crisp. Serves 4.

PORK CHOPS
WITH FRESH TOMATO CORIANDER SALSA

Per serving:
397 calories
21 g protein
27 g fat
24 g carb.

4 large loin pork chops (about 6 ounces each)
4 thick round slices of sweet yellow onion
4 tomatoes, seeded, peeled, and chopped
½ red bell pepper, seeded and chopped
1 large rib celery, chopped
¼ cup cilantro (coriander leaves), chopped
¾ teaspoon ground coriander
¼ teaspoon ground cumin
Vegetable salt to taste

Place pork chops in a shallow baking dish, and top each with a slice of onion. Cook uncovered in a 350° oven for 35–40 minutes. Place remaining ingredients in a blender, and blend to a thick chunky consistency. Warm coriander salsa slightly. When pork chops are done, spoon one quarter of the salsa over each chop, and serve. Makes 4 servings.

PORK-STUFFED WHOLE CABBAGE

Sauce:

Per serving:
337 calories
20 g protein
23 g fat
12 g carb.

2 cans (8 ounces) tomato sauce
½ pound ripe tomatoes, finely chopped
1 tablespoon low-sodium tamari
1 teaspoon raw honey
Pinch of allspice

Simmer all ingredients in a large covered saucepan for 20 minutes.

Stuffed Cabbage:

Note: To cook rice, add ⅓ cup rice to ⅔ cup water or stock in a small saucepan. Bring to a boil and boil for 5 minutes. Reduce heat, cover tightly, and simmer for approximately 40 minutes, or until rice is tender and fluffy.

1 large head green cabbage
1 pound lean ground pork
1 clove fresh garlic, pressed
1 white onion, diced
1 teaspoon each dried sage and savory
½ teaspoon caraway seeds
¼ teaspoon celery seeds
Vegetable salt and freshly ground pepper to taste
1 cup cooked brown rice (see below for cooking method)

Cut stem out of whole cabbage, and scoop out center, leaving about 1 inch of shell all around. Use a small ice cream or melon ball scoop to do this. Remove tough outer leaves, saving 2 large ones.

Chop 1 cup of the inside cabbage. In a large nonstick skillet, brown pork with garlic over a medium heat. Pour off any excess fat. Then add onions, seasonings, and 2 cups of cabbage, and continue to cook about 10 minutes, partially covered, until cabbage is semitender. Stir in rice and 1 cup of the sauce, and remove from heat.

Fill cabbage shell with pork mixture. Place outer cabbage leaves over the openings of the stuffed cabbage, tying with string if necessary. Set it in a 5-quart Dutch oven with the leaf-covered opening down. Pour remaining sauce over the top. Heat Dutch oven to high, cover, then reduce heat to low. Simmer for about 1¼ hours, basting occasionally, until cabbage shell is tender-crisp. Place stuffed cabbage in a serving dish, and cut wedges from the center to serve. Makes 6 servings.

HEARTY SOUPS AND STEWS

Fat Buster: To enrich a clear broth without making it creamy (and fattening), beat 2 eggs and 1 teaspoon of whole wheat flour to make a smooth batter. Pour it slowly through a sieve or slotted spoon into 1 quart boiling stock and simmer about 5 minutes. This will also add an extra 13 grams of protein.

Skip the skimpy fare for a change and whip up a hearty kettle of healthy meats and vegetables in a natural savory stock. They're free of starches, thickeners, and creams, so you still stay on the diet track while you belly up to these extravagant one-pot meals. Although these stews call for ingredients prepared from scratch, they can be made with leftover cooked meat (charbroiled is especially good) or vegetables. Since you don't want to overcook the food, your preparation will be cut down to heating time. You may use canned broth or stock (low sodium, of course) for the base, but a homemade stock is the key to a truly stew-pendous stew.

MEAT STOCK
(Brown Stock)

Per cup:
32 calories
5 g protein
0 g fat
3 g carb.

3 pounds marrow bones (or cooked beef, lamb, veal, or pork with bones)
3 quarts water
1 onion, chopped
3 ribs celery with leaves, sliced
1 carrot, sliced
2 large tomatoes, chopped
2 sprigs parsley
1 bay leaf
½ teaspoon dried thyme
1 clove garlic, chopped
6 black peppercorns

Place all ingredients in a large kettle or stockpot. Bring to a boil, reduce heat, and simmer uncovered for approximately 2 hours, or until liquid is reduced by half. Remove large bones, and strain stock through a fine sieve or colander lined with a paper towel. Chill to remove any fat that solidifies at the top. Makes about 6 cups of stock.

CURRIED LAMB STEW

Per serving:
400 calories
43 g protein
25 g fat
8 g carb.

1 tablespoon butter
2 cloves fresh garlic, pressed
1 large yellow onion, chopped
1½ pounds lean boneless lamb chunks
4 cups Poultry Stock (page 70)
2 large carrots, sliced into ½-inch rounds
1 cup fresh-shelled peas
½ cup fresh parsley, chopped
2 teaspoons curry powder
Vegetable salt and freshly ground pepper to taste
½ cup plain nonfat yogurt
½ cup nonfat milk

In a large kettle or stockpot, melt butter over a low heat, and sauté garlic, along with the onions, until they are translucent. Add the lamb chunks, and toss until they're lightly browned all around. If liquid is needed, add a dash of the stock, and braise until the lamb is done.

Pour in all the stock, and add the carrots, peas, parsley, and seasonings. Bring to a boil, and simmer covered over a low heat for approximately 20–25 minutes.

When vegetables are tender-crisp, blend the yogurt and the milk together, and stir in to the stew. Continue to cook to heat the stew through, but do not boil. Serve at once. Makes 6 servings.

BURGUNDY VEAL STEW

Per serving:
331 calories
32 g protein
17 g fat
8 g carb.

1 tablespoon olive oil
2 cloves fresh garlic, pressed
4 veal shanks (about 1 pound each with 8 ounces of meat)
6 cups water
1 pound green beans, cut into 1-inch diagonal slices
2 pounds Italian plum tomatoes, chopped
8 fresh mushrooms, sliced
4 shallots, chopped
1 bay leaf
1 teaspoon each dried basil and rosemary
Vegetable salt and freshly ground pepper to taste
½ cup Burgundy wine

Heat oil in a large kettle or stockpot. Add garlic and veal shanks. Over a medium low heat, turn shanks on all sides to brown them in the garlic. Add water, and bring to a boil. Lower heat, and simmer uncovered for about 1 hour or until veal is tender.

When done, turn off the heat, take the shanks out of the pot, and remove the meat from the bone. Put the meat back into the pot of stock, and add green beans, tomatoes, mushrooms, shallots, and seasonings. Raise the heat, cover, and continue to cook over a medium heat, stirring occasionally to break up the tomatoes. Cook for 15–20 minutes or until green beans are tender-crisp. When done, stir in Burgundy wine, simmer for a minute or two, and serve. Makes 8 servings.

SLOW BEEF STEW

Here's a dandy recipe for Crockpot cooking. The slow method allows you to leave the stew all day, come back later, and have a healthy, perfectly cooked meal waiting for you.

Actually, any of these stew recipes are adaptable to Crockpot cookery. Just be sure there is enough liquid to cover all the ingredients. Put the potatoes and the vegetables at the bottom, since they take longer to cook than meats. And don't forget to skim off any fat that forms at the top. Cooling the stew a bit first will make this easier to do.

Per serving:
310 calories
42 g protein
9 g fat
19 g carb.

4 cups Meat Stock (page 43); or water
¼ cup fresh parsley, chopped
1 bay leaf
½ teaspoon each dried marjoram and thyme
1 clove fresh garlic, pressed
Vegetable salt and freshly ground pepper to taste
2 large potatoes, peeled and cut into large chunks
2 carrots, cut into chunks
2 medium stalks broccoli, cut into chunks
12 tiny white onions
1½ pounds lean boneless beef chunks

Add all the ingredients in the order listed in a large Crockpot. Cover and cook on low for 8–12 hours or on high for 4–6 hours. No stirring is necessary.

The stew will be quite brothy. If you wish a thicker stew, mash up several of the potato chunks, and blend them into the stock, or take the cover off, and cook the stew on high until some of the liquid is reduced, perhaps for an hour or more. Makes 6 servings.

MEDITERRANEAN LAMB STEW

Per serving:
355 calories
26 g protein
25 g fat
8 g carb.

Delicious suggestion:
This is sensational
topped with freshly
grated Parmesan
cheese.

1½ pounds lean ground lamb
1 clove fresh garlic, pressed
¼ cup fresh parsley, chopped
½ teaspoon anise seed
Vegetable salt and freshly ground pepper to taste
1 tablespoon olive oil
4 cups Meat Stock (page 43)
1 large eggplant, peeled and cut into 1-inch cubes
1 green bell pepper, cut into ½-inch strips
2 large zucchini, sliced into 1-inch rounds
1 pound Italian plum tomatoes, coarsely chopped
1 teaspoon each dried basil and chervil
½ teaspoon dried oregano

Mix lamb, garlic, parsley, anise seed, and salt and pepper together well, and form 12 meatballs. Heat oil in a large kettle or stockpot, and lightly brown meatballs on all sides over a low heat.

When done, pour off any fat, and add stock, eggplant, green pepper, zucchini, tomatoes, and seasonings. Salt and pepper to taste if desired. Bring to a boil, partially cover, and simmer 20–25 minutes until vegetables are semitender. Serves 8.

YOSEMITE STEW

Born of necessity, this makes a great camp-out (or eat-in) goulash. It's best served with slices of delicious whole grain bread.

Per serving:
340 calories
28 g protein
10 g fat
35 g carb.

1½ pounds lean ground beef
4 cups Marinara Sauce (page 142); or 1 jar (32 ounces)
    of natural-style marinara sauce
4 large russet potatoes
1 pound zucchini, sliced ½-inch thick
1 large onion, quartered

Crumble generous chunks of ground beef into a large kettle or stockpot over a medium heat. Toss the meat to brown it. When done, drain off any fat, and add the Marinara Sauce. Bring to a slow boil, adding a little water if necessary to thin it. Add the potatoes, cover, and cook for about 15–20 minutes over a medium heat.

Toss in the zucchini and onion, making sure they're completely covered with sauce. Lower the heat, cover, and continue to simmer another 10–15 minutes, or until potatoes and zucchini are semitender. Serves a gang of 6.

SWEET AND SPICY PORK STEW

Per serving:
428 calori...
23 g prot...
28 g fat
24 g car...

...an ground pork
...ion, minced
...h garlic, pressed
...dried sage
...allspice
...n vegetable salt
...ultry Stock (page 70)
...otatoes, peeled and cut into ¾-inch slices
...lery, cut into 1-inch diagonal pieces
...pears, peeled, cored, and cut into 1-inch chunks
...oon dried savory
...poon paprika

...onion, garlic, sage, allspice, and salt together well. Form meatballs ...nch in diameter. In a large kettle or stockpot, slowly cook meatballs ...them on all sides. Usually ground pork has enough fat in it so that ...begins to cook, no oil is needed. Use the stock as needed for liquid to ...arted.

...hen done, after about 10–15 minutes of cooking, drain off any fat, then add remaining stock, sweet potatoes, and celery. Bring stock to a boil, lower heat, and simmer covered for about 20 minutes. Add pears, seasonings, and salt to taste if desired. Continue to simmer partially covered for another 10 minutes or until sweet potatoes are tender. Serves 8.

BEEF HEART AND BARLEY SOUP

Per serving:
270 calories
17 g protein
12 g fat
22 g carb.

6 cups Meat Stock (page 43); or water
2 cloves fresh garlic, pressed
1 leek (bulk only), chopped
¼ cup fresh parsley, chopped
1 bay leaf
6 whole peppercorns
1 pound beef heart, cut into small chunks and visible fat removed
1 cup pearl barley
2 carrots, diced
2 ribs celery, diagonally sliced
1 cup fresh mushrooms, sliced
Vegetable salt to taste

Combine stock, seasonings, beef heart, and barley in a large kettle or stock-pot. Bring to a boil, then immediately lower the heat. Partially cover, and simmer slowly for 1 hour. Add vegetables, and continue to simmer another ½ hour until vegetables are tender but crunchy. Makes about 10 cups of soup.

5
POULTRY

FEASTS OF FOWL

Roasting fowl, unlike meat, is a bit less of a challenge, but every bit as rewarding. As long as you cook it according to the prescribed temperature and cooking time, it will come out well cooked yet juicy.

To prepare a bird, first remove any giblets and inner wads of fat. If it has stray feathers, singe them off or pluck them out when the bird is at refrigerator temperature. Rinse it off and pat it dry with a paper towel. If you wish to season the inside, do so at this time.

Fowl is best cooked at 350° and no less. The average cooking time for birds over 3 pounds is 20 minutes per pound, 18 minutes for very large birds such as turkey. When a fowl is done, a meat thermometer inserted into the meatiest section of the bird should register 180°. For stuffed poultry, add 15 minutes to the prescribed overall cooking time. Frozen poultry takes just about twice as long to roast as fresh or thawed. Always cook poultry with the skin on, to keep it from drying out, but prick the skin of fatty birds like goose and duck, especially around the bottom, to allow the fat juices to run out during cooking.

Roast birds on a rack in a shallow roasting pan to keep them out of the fat. To be assured of more uniform cooking and even browning, truss a bird by tying the wings and legs close to the body with a string. Baste every half hour if you wish. Place a loose tent of foil over the top of birds if they get too brown. Let small birds stand for 15 minutes before carving and large birds 15 to 30 minutes.

Don't get into a flap about leftovers. Follow these tips. If possible, wrap leftover fowl tightly in foil and refrigerate it while it's still warm. This method of storage helps keep it moist. Leftover fowl has a tendency to dry out, so it's best not to reheat it more than once. If you're warming large birds such as turkey, just cut off what you're going to eat. For smaller fowl remove any legs or wings and meat from the carcass. Wrap it in foil and heat it in a 275° to 300° oven until it is palatably hot. Microwaving it is all right (seal it in plastic wrap), but it will make the meat a little tougher. If you have some

Note: All of the nutritional calculations are based on 4 ounces of equal amounts of light and dark meat, combined with the recommended servings of dressing.

49

leftover juice or gravy, pour it over the meat first. It will make it juicier. Of course there's nothing like slices of cold chicken or turkey in a sandwich or salad with Swiss cheese for the ultimate deli treat.

Any way you slice it, fowl is as nutritious as it is delicious. Boasting 37 grams of protein per 4 ounces of white meat, poultry is one of the best sources of pure protein for the calories that money can buy.

GOLDEN ROASTED CHICKEN

Per serving:
478 calories
39 g protein
9 g fat
67 g carb.

2 tablespoons butter
¼ cup yellow onion, chopped
2 tablespoons fresh parsley, chopped
Chicken giblets (no liver), chopped
⅔ cup uncooked bulgur
1⅓ cups Poultry Stock (page 70); or water
1 cup golden apples, chopped
½ cup golden seedless raisins
½ teaspoon curry powder
Pinch of nutmeg
1 roasting chicken (3½ to 4 pounds)
Vegetable salt and freshly ground pepper to taste

Melt butter in a large nonstick skillet. Sauté onions and parsley until onions are translucent. Add giblets, and continue to sauté. Add bulgur, and mix over a low heat until it's thoroughly coated and golden. Pour in stock, and bring to a boil for 1 minute. Lower heat, and add apples, raisins, and spices.

Cover, and simmer for 12–15 minutes or until all liquid is absorbed. Spoon bulgur into the cavity of the chicken. Close opening with skewers. Salt and pepper the chicken if desired. Place chicken on a rack in a shallow roasting pan, and roast in a preheated 375° oven for 15 minutes. Lower heat to 350°, and continue to cook for approximately 1 hour 15 minutes more. Makes 4 servings.

BOURBON-BASTED GOOSE WITH MINCEMEAT STUFFING

Per serving:
697 calories
26 g protein
45 g fat
48 g carb.

½ cup each bourbon and apple cider
½ cup each chopped pitted prunes, currants, seedless raisins, and dried apples
1 tablespoon butter
1 small yellow onion, finely chopped
1 goose liver, chopped
1 teaspoon each orange and lemon rind
¼ teaspoon each ground cloves, cinnamon, mace, and nutmeg

½ cup walnuts, chopped
Vegetable salt and cayenne pepper
1 goose (6 to 7 pounds)
1 cup Poultry Stock (page 70)

Combine bourbon and apple cider. Soak dried fruits in 1 cup of the mixture for 1 hour. Reserve other cup. Melt butter in a medium nonstick skillet, and sauté onions until they are translucent. Add goose liver, and continue to sauté several minutes until cooked.

Combine with dried fruits, and mix in orange and lemon rinds, spices, and walnuts. Add salt and cayenne pepper to taste. Spoon filling into cavity of goose. Close opening by sewing with a string or securing it with skewers. Truss by tying legs together close to the body.

Place goose on a rack in a shallow roasting pan. Pour half of the reserved bourbon and cider mixture over the top. Salt and pepper skin if desired. Roast in a preheated 350° oven for about 2½–3 hours.

Prick the skin of the goose several times during cooking. Half an hour before goose is done, untie legs to allow them to brown evenly, and baste with remaining bourbon and cider mixture. Pour off the fat, and add stock to the roasting pan to make a gravy with the juices. Makes 6 servings.

OLA'S ROSEMARY CHICKEN

My Aunt Ola, who helped kitchen-test the recipes in this book, created this delicious way to roast chicken.

Per serving:
135 calories
28 g protein
2 g fat
0 g carb.

1 whole roasting chicken (3½ to 4 pounds)
4 cloves garlic, peeled and split into quarters
Freshly ground pepper to taste
1 sprig rosemary
1 sprig thyme
Vegetable salt

With a small sharp knife, make slits all around the meaty part of the chicken, and slip in slivers of garlic just under the skin. Pepper the cavity, and insert a sprig of rosemary and thyme and several reserved slivers of garlic. Salt and pepper the skin of the chicken if desired.

Place it, breast up, on a rack in a shallow roasting pan, and roast in a 350° oven for approximately 1¼–1½ hours until the skin is golden brown. When done, the joints should move easily. Let it stand 15–20 minutes before carving. Makes 4 servings.

TARRAGON ROAST DUCK WITH LIME SAUCE

Per serving:
491 calories
19 g protein
33 g fat
25 g carb.

6 whole black peppercorns
1 small onion, quartered
2 sprigs fresh tarragon
1 duck (about 5 pounds)
1 large lime
Vegetable salt and freshly ground pepper
½ cup raw honey
1 teaspoon arrowroot, moistened in 1 tablespoon water

Place peppercorns, quartered onions, and 1 sprig of the tarragon in the cavity of the duck. Grate 1 teaspoon of peel from the whole lime, and save. Cut the lime in half, juice both halves, and set juice aside. Then put the rind of half the lime in the cavity of the duck, saving the other half for grating.

Salt and pepper the outside of the duck if desired. Place the duck on a rack in a shallow roasting pan, and prick the skin all over with a sharp fork. Roast in a preheated 350° oven for about 1 hour and 45 minutes. Baste with pan juices, and prick the skin with a fork several more times during cooking.

Meanwhile, finely chop remaining sprig of tarragon, and grate the rind of the remaining lime half. Combine them with raw honey and reserved lime juice in a small saucepan. Cook it over a simmering heat until raw honey dissolves. Whisk in moistened arrowroot until it thickens, then remove from heat. Spoon the sauce over the top of the carved duck arranged on a serving platter, or serve it on the side in a cruet. Makes 4 servings.

VINEYARD ROAST CHICKEN

Per serving:
311 calories
32 g protein
11 g fat
18 g carb.

2 cups fresh seedless Thompson or red flame grapes, halved
½ cup pine nuts (pignolias)
1 sprig thyme, minced
½ cup Marsala wine
1 whole roasting chicken (3½ to 4 pounds)
Freshly ground white pepper to taste

Toss grapes, pine nuts, and thyme with ¼ cup of the wine, and stuff them tightly into chicken cavity. Sew opening with strings or close with skewers. Then tie the end of the drumsticks together close to the body.

Place chicken, breast side up, on a rack in a shallow roasting pan. Pour remaining ¼ cup of wine over the top of the chicken. Sprinkle with white pepper. Roast in a 350° oven for 1¼–1½ hours, basting with pan juice several times during the roasting. Serves 4.

GINGER GLAZED DUCK

Per serving:
433 calories
20 g protein
33 g fat
17 g carb.

Juice of ½ grapefruit (save the rind)
3 tablespoons raw orange blossom honey
1 tablespoon low-sodium tamari
2 cloves fresh garlic, pressed
1 teaspoon fresh ginger, finely minced
1 teaspoon dried mustard
⅛ teaspoon crushed red pepper
1 duck (4 to 5 pounds)
Small piece of fresh gingerroot

Blend all ingredients together except for duck and gingerroot. Place duck on a rack breast side up in a shallow roasting pan. Pierce the skin all around with a sharp fork to allow fatty juices to run out during roasting. Place a small piece of grapefruit rind and gingerroot inside the cavity. Pour half the glaze over the duck.

Roast in a preheated 350° oven for approximately 1¾ hours. Prick with a fork, and baste with drippings several times during cooking. Then 20 minutes before it's done (test by moving a leg; it should move easily), pour remaining glaze over the top and finish roasting. Serves 4.

ORANGE-ROASTED CORNISH HENS

Per serving:
189 calories
28 g protein
2 g fat
11 g carb.

4 cornish hens (1 pound each)
2 oranges
12 whole cloves
1 large fresh peach, peeled, pitted, and pureed
¼ cup Madeira wine
1 tablespoon raw honey
2 tablespoons onion, finely minced
Vegetable salt and freshly ground pepper to taste

Place hens evenly apart on a flat rack in a shallow roasting pan. Quarter 1 whole orange. Stick 3 cloves in each quarter, and place one in the cavity of each hen. Salt and pepper to taste. Roast in a preheated 325° oven for 45–50 minutes. Baste once during cooking.

Meanwhile, juice 1 orange, and mix with peach puree, wine, raw honey, and onion. Then, 15 minutes before cooking is done, dribble half the peach-orange sauce over the hens. When done, pour remaining sauce over the individual hens before serving. Makes 4 servings.

CORNISH HENS STUFFED WITH EGGS AND OYSTERS

Per serving:
431 calories
51 g protein
22 g fat
11 g carb.

Note: For
convenience, you
may replace the
oysters with giblets
from the bird.

3 tablespoons butter
4 shallots, finely chopped
½ pint shucked oysters, chopped and the liquor reserved (see below)
⅔ cup fresh mushrooms, sliced
3 tablespoons dry sherry
¼ cup fresh parsley, chopped
6 eggs, beaten
1 teaspoon each fresh marjoram and savory, chopped
Vegetable salt and freshly ground pepper to taste
4 cornish hens (1 pound each)

Melt 1 tablespoon of the butter in a large nonstick skillet. Over a low heat, sauté shallots for 1 minute. Add oysters, and quick-cook them for about another minute. Toss in mushrooms, 2 tablespoons sherry, and parsley, and continue to sauté. Add reserved oyster liquid, and cook until mushrooms darken slightly and liquid has evaporated. Set aside.

Melt 1 tablespoon of butter in a medium nonstick skillet, and lightly scramble eggs with herbs until they're set but moist. Add oyster mixture and toss everything together well. Salt and pepper to taste.

Spoon equal portions of the egg and oyster stuffing into each hen. Seal off the cavity with a string or skewers. Space the hens on a rack in a shallow roasting pan. Melt last tablespoon of butter, and mix with remaining tablespoon of sherry. Brush over the top of the hens.

Roast in a 325° oven for 50–60 minutes. Baste several times with pan juices if desired. Makes 4 servings.

ROAST CAPON WITH HARVEST DRESSING

Here's a traditional bread dressing with a new twist—a portion of bread is replaced with butternut squash, giving the dressing a tasty moistness while cutting down on calories.

Per serving:
301 calories
35 g protein
14 g fat
12 g carb.

2 tablespoons butter
1 small onion, chopped
½ cup celery with leaves, chopped
3 ounces giblets (liver optional), chopped
1½ teaspoons poultry seasoning
1½ cups whole wheat bread cubes
⅔ cup butternut squash, steamed and mashed; see Acorn Squash Filled with
    Festive Fruits (page 136) for cooking method
½ cup pecans, chopped

1 cup Poultry Stock (page 70)
Vegetable salt and freshly ground pepper
1 capon (6 to 8 pounds)
Ground sage

Melt butter in a medium nonstick skillet. Sauté onion and celery until they are translucent. Add giblets, and sauté several more minutes. Stir in poultry seasoning, and set aside. Combine bread cubes, squash, and pecans in a large bowl. Add sauté mixture, and blend well. Add stock as needed for moistness. Season with salt and pepper to taste.

Spoon dressing into capon cavity. Close opening with string or skewers. Dust skin with ground sage and salt and pepper if desired. Place bird on a rack in a shallow roasting pan. Roast in a 350° oven for 2½ hours. Baste occasionally with pan drippings during roasting. Add remaining stock to fat-skimmed pan juices to make gravy. Dressing makes 6 servings.

CLASSY CHICKEN

What's the latest word on the well-bred chicken? They're saying you can dress it up or dress it down—you can even take it out. It absolutely promises to be low in calories yet high in protein, elegant yet economical, sophisticated yet simple. It's hearty, it's handy, and it's healthy.

Most of these recipes call for breasts, because white meat is virtually fat free. Four ounces of chicken breast sans skin has only 120 calories. But you can use white or dark meat for any of these dishes. Nutritionally, both are excellent.

When broiling or baking chicken without a sauce or a baste, leave the skin on to keep it from drying out. Discard it after cooking. Remember, the skin is very high in fat. Unfortunately, it's hard to obtain the full flavor of the seasonings when chicken is cooked with the skin on, so these recipes offer you some fabulously saucy ideas. And when you don't feel like fussing with that bird, add this to your repertoire: Slit the skin of the chicken and slip underneath it slivers of garlic, twists of lemon or orange peel, whole cloves or peppercorns, fresh herbs, or even chopped fruits.

Make a splashy showing with these new chicken creations or keep it simple with a pinch of spice. The word is out. Any way you cook it, chicken is a class act.

Fat Buster: Keep skinless chicken juicy while cooking by wrapping it tightly in foil with your favorite herbs or spices. This method of baking *en papillote* allows chicken to remain moist and flavorful, yet fat free.

Tidbit: To peel and seed a tomato as called for in a recipe, plunge the tomato in boiling water for 10 seconds, then immediately in cold water to cool. With a sharp paring knife cut it in half crosswise and squeeze out the seeds, then peel off the skin.

NECTARINE AND CHICKEN CREPES

Per serving:
411 calories
31 g protein
15 g fat
40 g carb.

3 large ripe nectarines
1½ cups plain nonfat yogurt
3 tablespoons rice vinegar
½ teaspoon ground ginger
2 cups cooked white meat of chicken, diced
½ cup celery, finely chopped
2 green onions, finely chopped
½ cup walnuts, chopped
8 Whole Wheat Dessert Crepes (page 208)

Peel, pit, and chop 2 nectarines. Mix in a blender with yogurt, rice vinegar, and ginger until smooth. Coarsely chop remaining nectarine. Toss with chicken, celery, onions, and walnuts, and stir into half of the yogurt mixture. Spoon equal amounts of the filling into each crepe, and fold to overlap. Top crepes with remaining yogurt mixture. You may serve these warm or cold. Serves 4.

CHICKEN AND CHEESE STUFFED PEPPERS

Per serving:
261 calories
34 g protein
5 g fat
19 g carb.

4 red bell peppers
2 cups cooked chicken, finely chopped
1 cup cooked brown rice (see Pork Stuffed Whole Cabbage, page 42,
*   for cooking method)*
1 yellow onion, finely chopped
½ cup Monterey Jack cheese, grated
¼ cup fresh parsley, chopped
1 tablespoon low-sodium tamari
¼ teaspoon each ground cumin, turmeric, and crushed red pepper
Paprika to taste

Cut tops off bell peppers, and hollow out cavity. Place them in boiling water for 2 minutes and then cold water to cool. Then turn them upside down to drain dry. Toss remaining ingredients together and fill each pepper full. Sprinkle the tops with paprika.

Place them snugly in a baking dish with water halfway up the sides of the peppers. Cover, and bake for about 40 minutes in a 350° oven. Remove lid, and bake another 15–20 minutes until the tops are golden brown. Serves 4.

CAJUN-STYLE CHICKEN CUTLETS

Per serving:
222 calories
27 g protein
12 g fat
0 g carb.

Popular note:
This is the basic
recipe for making
''blackened'' fish
filets or steaks.

¼ cup sweet butter
1 tablespoon freshly squeezed lemon juice
¼ teaspoon dried thyme, crushed
¼ teaspoon dried oregano, crushed
¼ teaspoon cayenne pepper
¼ teaspoon finely ground fresh black pepper
Vegetable salt
4 boneless skinned chicken breasts (4 ounces each), pounded thin

Melt butter in a small saucepan over a low heat. Add lemon juice, herbs, black pepper, and salt to taste. Continue to cook for several minutes over a low heat until herbs soften.

Heat a large cast-iron skillet to high. Coat both sides of the cutlets well with the butter mixture. Cook the cutlets for several minutes on each side. When done, they will be black on the outside and tender and juicy on the inside. Serves 4.

CHICKEN BREAST REMOULADE

Per serving:
223 calories
24 g protein
13 g fat
3 g carb.

4 half chicken breasts, skinned
½ cup Low-Cal Mayonnaise I (see below)
1 teaspoon Dijon mustard
1 clove fresh garlic, pressed
2 teaspoons fresh tarragon, minced
2 teaspoons freshly squeezed lemon juice
½ teaspoon lemon rind, grated
⅛ teaspoon freshly ground pepper
Vegetable salt to taste

Place chicken breasts, meaty side up, on a broiling rack. Mix remaining ingredients together, and coat the top of the breasts generously with the mixture. Reserve a little for a final coating. Cover breasts loosely with foil.

Bake in a 350° oven for about 35 minutes. Remove foil, coat once more with remoulade, baste, and place under a broiler about 6 inches from the heat. Broil 6–7 minutes until breasts are brown. Serves 4.

LOW-CAL MAYONNAISE I

Per tablespoon:
54 calories
0 g protein
6 g fat
0 g carb.

Equal parts plain nonfat yogurt and safflower oil mayonnaise

Blend together well.

CHICKEN ARMANDA

Per serving:
182 calories
26 g protein
5 g fat
6 g carb.

Serving Suggestion:
Serve over cooked
brown rice or Whole
Wheat Pasta.

1 tablespoon safflower oil
1 clove fresh garlic, minced
¼ cup celery, finely chopped
2 whole boneless, skinless chicken breasts, cut into large chunks
½ cup plain nonfat yogurt
½ cup Poultry Stock (page 70)
1 pound Italian plum tomatoes, peeled, seeded, and sliced
½ teaspoon dried marjoram
1 small bay leaf
Vegetable salt and freshly ground pepper to taste
¼ cup Chianti or rosé wine

Heat oil in a large nonstick skillet. Lightly sauté garlic, then add celery and chicken. Continue to sauté until chicken pieces are slightly browned all around. Stir in remaining ingredients, except for Chianti. Cover, and cook over a low heat for about 25 minutes, stirring occasionally. Just before serving, remove bay leaf and stir in wine. Serves 4.

CHAMPAGNE CHICKEN

Per serving:
240 calories
31 g protein
8 g fat
7 g carb.

2 tablespoons butter
2 cloves fresh garlic, pressed
1 tablespoon fresh chervil, chopped
4 boneless, skinless half chicken breasts
2 cups champagne
⅓ cup scallions, minced
6 fresh mushrooms, sliced
½ cup part-skim ricotta cheese
½ cup nonfat milk
Vegetable salt and freshly ground white pepper

In a large nonstick skillet, melt butter over a medium low heat. Stir in garlic and chervil. Add chicken breasts, and sauté lightly on both sides until just browned. Remove chicken, and set aside.

To the same skillet, add champagne, scallions, and mushrooms, and simmer about 5 minutes, until mushrooms are tender. Blend ricotta and milk together until creamy, and add to the skillet. Salt and pepper to taste. Add the chicken breasts to the champagne sauce, cover the skillet, and simmer about 20 minutes more, until done. Serves 4.

CHICKEN BREASTS WITH A CREAMY PIQUANT SAUCE

Per serving:
144 calories
25 g protein
3 g fat
2 g carb.

1 tablespoon butter
⅔ cup buttermilk
½ teaspoon each Dijon mustard and prepared horseradish
1 teaspoon Worcestershire sauce
1 clove fresh garlic, pressed
½ teaspoon capers
1 teaspoon each fresh basil, parsley, and tarragon, finely minced
⅛ teaspoon freshly ground white pepper
4 half chicken breasts

Melt butter in a small saucepan. Add remaining ingredients except chicken and stir until hot. Set aside. Bake chicken breasts with the skin on in a preheated 350° oven for 35–40 minutes. When done, skin the breasts, and arrange them on a serving platter. Serve them with warm sauce spooned over the top. Serves 4.

CHICKEN LIVERS, ITALIAN STYLE

If you're a chicken liver lover, try this recipe solo, in an omelet, or in a tomato sauce over potatoes, pasta, or polenta (cornmeal mush).

Per serving:
265 calories
31 g protein
12 g fat
7 g carb.

2 tablespoons olive oil
2 cloves fresh garlic, pressed
1 large white onion, sliced
1 green pepper, julienned
1 pound chicken livers, cut up
¼ cup fresh parsley, chopped
Vegetable salt and freshly ground pepper to taste

Heat olive oil in a large nonstick skillet. Add garlic, onion, and peppers, and sauté over a medium heat for several minutes. Cover the skillet, lower heat, and cook about 20–25 minutes, stirring occasionally. When peppers are tender-crisp, add chicken livers, raise the heat to medium, and sauté for about 3–4 minutes. Stir in parsley and salt and pepper, and cook several minutes more. Serves 4.

STUFFED CHICKEN WITH APRICOT MUSTARD

Chicken:

Per serving:
386 calories
27 g protein
18 g fat
26 g carb.

Note: This recipe
needs to be baked
above (not in) its
juices, so I put the
breasts on a broiler
rack but bake in the
oven.

1 tablespoon butter
2 tablespoons almonds, sliced
4 fresh apricots, peeled and chopped
2 teaspoons raw honey
1 teaspoon cider vinegar
2 boneless half chicken breasts

Melt butter in a nonstick sauté pan. Add almonds, and toss to coat. Add apricots, and stir them over a low heat with raw honey and vinegar until raw honey has melted. Remove from heat.

Lay the chicken breasts out flat, skin side down. Flatten them by pounding with a mallet if necessary. Spoon half of the filling in a strip along the center of each breast. Roll up carefully, and tie with string or secure with a skewer. Place them on a broiler rack (see below), loosely cover with foil, and bake them in a 350° oven for about 35–40 minutes.

Apricot Mustard:

2 fresh apricots, halved and pitted
2 tablespoons freshly squeezed orange juice
2 teaspoons Dijon mustard
1 teaspoon raw honey
Sea salt and freshly ground pepper

Puree all ingredients together in a blender. Brush the rolled chicken breasts with a little of the apricot mustard, and place them under the broiler for about 1 minute. Serve spread with the remaining mixture. Serves 2.

MELON CHICKEN

Per serving:
251 calories
29 g protein
8 g fat
11 g carb.

2 tablespoons butter
4 whole chicken legs, skinned
1 small white onion, thinly sliced
1 cup semidry white wine
1 teaspoon arrowroot, moistened with 1 tablespoon water
1 cup honeydew melon balls or pieces
1 cup Cranshaw melon balls or pieces
1 tablespoon fresh mint, snipped
Pinch of freshly ground white pepper
Sea salt

Over a medium heat melt butter in a large nonstick skillet or wok. Add chicken legs, and cook about 5 minutes on each side. Add the onion and ½ cup of the wine. Partially cover the skillet, and lower the heat to a simmer.

Cook about ½ hour more, turning the chicken legs once halfway through cooking. When done, add remaining ½ cup of wine mixed with moistened arrowroot, melon balls, mint, and white pepper. Season with salt to taste if desired. Stir for about 1 minute over a low heat. Serves 4.

CHICKEN AND ARTICHOKE HEARTS SAUTÉED IN GARLIC AND HERBS

Per serving:
212 calories
27 g protein
9 g fat
6 g carb.

1 tablespoon butter
1 tablespoon olive oil
2 cloves fresh garlic, pressed
2 whole boneless, skinless chicken breasts, cut into ½-inch-thick strips
½ pound artichoke hearts, cooked and quartered
1 tablespoon each fresh basil and parsley, chopped
¼ cup Parmesan cheese
¼ cup Poultry Stock (page 70)
2 tablespoons dry white wine
Vegetable salt and freshly ground pepper

In a large nonstick skillet, heat butter and olive oil. Add garlic and chicken, and sauté over a medium heat until chicken turns white. Add artichoke hearts and herbs, and continue to toss over a medium heat until heated through. Reduce heat.

Mix Parmesan cheese, stock, and wine, and pour into skillet. Toss for 1–2 minutes until chicken and artichokes are thoroughly coated with the sauté. Salt and pepper to taste. Serves 4.

ORANGE-BASTED HERB CHICKEN

Per serving:
151 calories
37 g protein
1 g fat
4 g carb.

4 large half skinless chicken breasts
Juice of one large orange
2 tablespoons each fresh savory and thyme, minced
1 tablespoon fresh tarragon, minced
Sea salt and freshly ground pepper
4 orange slices

Arrange chicken breasts, meaty side up, in a baking dish. Dribble orange juice over the top, and evenly sprinkle with minced herbs. Salt and pepper to taste, and top each with an orange slice.

Cover the baking dish loosely with foil, and bake in a 350° oven for approximately 35–40 minutes. Baste breasts several times during baking with orange juice drippings. When serving, spoon a little of the drippings over each breast. Serves 4.

WHEAT GERM CHICKEN

Per serving:
385 calories
60 g protein
10 g fat
15 g carb.

Note: Nutritional calculations are based on 8 ounces each of white and dark meat per person.

1 frying or roasting chicken (3½ to 4 pounds), cut up and skinned
2 tablespoons safflower oil, mixed with 2 tablespoons water
½ cup wheat germ
½ cup whole wheat flour
½ teaspoon poultry seasoning
Vegetable salt and freshly ground pepper to taste

Brush chicken pieces with oil and water mixture. Set them on a rack for several minutes to drain. In a plastic bag, shake wheat germ, flour, and seasonings to mix. Then shake each piece of chicken in the plastic bag until coated with the wheat germ mixture. Place them evenly apart on a baking rack, and bake them in a 375° oven for 45–50 minutes. Makes enough for 4 people.

TACKLING A WILD TURKEY

Is there life after turkey? Well, let's see. There's Monday, turkey, Wednesday, turkey, Friday, Saturday, turkey, turkey, turkey. Oh, yes, you can be a slave to your leftovers, or you can be brave and make your turkey taste different every day.

How? By whipping up any of these wild new recipes. They're best made with leftover, preroasted meat so there's a minimum of preparation. All portions of the turkey are used too, so there's nothing left to waste.

Tackling a leftover turkey, as you know, is no easy task, but if you don't, it's bound to be an even bigger problem. Let's face it, it's hard enough finding room in the refrigerator for that big bird without a hill of withered turkey remains haunting you too.

So don't let a turkey get you down. Get wild and put that fowl in a mold, a casserole, a pâté, or light it on fire *à la flambée*.

ROAST TURKEY WITH SLIM COUNTRY GRAVY

Yes, there is life after turkey, but first you start with the roast.

Allow about 1 pound of turkey per person, to make sure there is enough white and dark meat for everyone. Rinse it thoroughly and pat it dry. Place it on a rack in a large roasting pan. Roast it uncovered at 300° at approximately 20 minutes per pound or until a meat thermometer inserted into the breast registers 180° to 185°. Baste occasionally during roasting.

If the skin of the turkey should become too brown, place a loose tent of foil over the top of it. (About the giblets: If you're going to eat the giblets, rinse them and put them back into the cavity of the turkey while roasting so that they cook in moist flavorful heat.) Let the turkey stand ½ hour before carving.

To make Slim Country Gravy, skim the fat off the drippings. Dissolve 2 tablespoons of whole wheat pastry flour into equal parts of nonfat milk and Poultry Stock or water. Stir it into the pan with the drippings over a medium heat, adding more of the liquid mixture as needed. Season if desired. Simmer, stirring constantly, until gravy thickens.

CELEBRATED MEALS

SEASONED GREETINGS

Roast Turkey with Slim Country Gravy
Cornbread Dressing
Vegetable Medley with Tangy Cheese Sauce
Cranberry Gelatin Salad
Pumpkin Yogurt Chiffon Pie
Ginger Spice Tea

TURKEY CANNELONI

Now here's what you can do with an abundance of white meat.

Per serving:
442 calories
42 g protein
21 g fat
17 g carb.

8 ounces part-skim ricotta cheese
1 egg, beaten
1 cup fresh parsley, chopped
Vegetable salt to taste
8 slices (2 ounces each) turkey breast, uniformly sliced
2 cups Marinara Sauce (page 142)
8 slices (1 ounce each) part-skim Mozzarella cheese
Parmesan cheese

In a small bowl mix ricotta, egg, parsley (reserve a small amount for garnish), and salt. Lay each slice of turkey out flat. Place 3 tablespoons of the ricotta filling in the center of the turkey, and roll it up, securing it with a wooden toothpick. (If the turkey slices are dry and unflexible, soak them first for several minutes in a little warm turkey juice or stock.) Repeat with each piece of turkey, and place them, overlapping side down, in a shallow baking dish.

Spoon an ample amount of the sauce over the rolls, and top each one with a slice of Mozzarella cheese. Bake loosely covered in a 325° oven for 25 minutes. Top with any leftover Marinara Sauce and reserved parsley. Sprinkle with Parmesan cheese if desired. Serves 4 people, 2 rolls each.

TURKEY AND VEGETABLES IN DIJON CREAM

Per serving:
417 calories
48 g protein
16 g fat
22 g carb.

1 tablespoon butter
1 shallot, finely minced
½ cup nonfat milk
4 ounces Neufchâtel cheese
1½ tablespoons Dijon mustard
2 tablespoons vermouth
⅛ teaspoon freshly ground pepper
Vegetable salt
1 pound turkey breast, sliced and warmed
1 bunch (about ½ pound) tiny carrots, tops clipped, steamed
½ pound snap peas, steamed
8 tiny potatoes, steamed and sliced
2 tablespoons fresh parsley, snipped

Melt butter over a low heat in a small nonstick sauté pan. Add shallot, and toss for about 30 seconds. Pour in milk, add Neufchâtel cheese, and continue to stir over a low heat until it becomes creamy. Stir in mustard, vermouth, pepper, and salt to taste if desired. Set the resulting Dijon Cream aside but keep warm.

Arrange turkey slices, carrots, snap peas, and potatoes on a serving platter, and pour Dijon Cream over the top. Sprinkle with snipped parsley. Serves 4.

APPLE AND CHEESE TURKEY BAKE

Here are some interesting fixings when you're left with both white and dark meat.

Per serving:
265 calories
40 g protein
8 g fat
8 g carb.

2 pounds white and dark meat turkey, sliced
⅔ cup Poultry Stock (page 70)
2 large red apples, cored and cut into ¼-inch slices
⅓ cup apple cider
⅛ teaspoon each nutmeg and cloves, freshly ground
1 cup shredded aged cheddar cheese

Arrange turkey slices in a large baking dish. Pour stock slowly over the top until all the liquid is absorbed into the meat. Arrange very thin apple slices evenly over the turkey, then pour the apple cider over them. Sprinkle with spices, and spread the grated cheese over the apples. Loosely cover with foil, and bake in a 350° oven for 30–40 minutes, or until apples are semitender. Serves 8.

TURKEY PAPAYA FLAMBÉ

Per serving:
413 calories
40 g protein
4 g fat
54 g carb.

Note: If papaya is
not available,
cantaloupe works
very well as a
substitute.

1 large ripe papaya (see below)
1 medium ripe banana
Juice of one orange
2 tablespoons raw honey
1 tablespoon low-sodium tamari
1 teaspoon fresh ginger, grated
¼ teaspoon dry mustard
1 tablespoon sesame seeds
8 ounces turkey breast, diced into ½-inch chunks
Sprigs of watercress
4 ounces light rum
Raw sugar

Halve and seed papaya. Carefully scoop out fruit, leaving the shell intact. In a medium bowl, dice fruit into ½-inch chunks. Slice in banana. Blend orange juice, raw honey, tamari, ginger, and mustard together, and stir into fruit. Add sesame seeds and turkey chunks, and carefully mix everything together well.

Fill each papaya shell with equal amounts of the mixture. Place each papaya half in an individual dessert-size ovenproof dish. Keep them room temperature until ready to ignite.

Heat rum, but not to boiling. Before serving, sprinkle a little raw sugar over the papaya mixture. Place sprigs of watercress on the sides for garnish. The moment you are ready to serve, pour 2 ounces of the hot rum over the entire top of each papaya, and ignite by touching the edge of the papaya with the flame of a long-handled match or candle. Then stand back, and watch the show. Each papaya half serves 1.

WILD TURKEY ROUNDUP

Here's another holiday special, only this recipe includes *all* the leftovers.

Per serving:
392 calories
34 g protein
16 g fat
21 g carb.

2 cups turkey dressing, moistened with stock or gravy if necessary (or see
    Cornbread Dressing, page 194)
2 pounds white and dark meat of turkey, diced
1½ cups carrots, sliced and cooked; or baked yams
1 cup cooked peas
1 cup turkey gravy; or Poultry Stock (page 70)
1½ cups mashed potatoes, liquefied with ½ cup nonfat milk
Freshly grated nutmeg

In a large baking dish or roasting pan, layer, in order, turkey dressing, turkey, carrots, and peas. Dribble gravy over the top. Then spread a layer of mashed potatoes over that to form a crust. Sprinkle with grated nutmeg. Bake in 350° oven for about 30 minutes, or until it's heated through. Makes 10 servings.

TURKEY AT THE WALDORF

Per serving:
440 calories
43 g protein
14 g fat
35 g carb.

2 packets unflavored gelatin
2½ cups white grape juice
1 pound turkey breast, cut into ¾-inch chunks
1 rib celery, finely sliced
⅓ pound seedless red grapes, halved
1 red apple, shredded with the skin on
1 cup walnuts, chopped
½ cup low-fat cottage cheese
½ cup Low-Cal Mayonnaise II (below)

In a medium saucepan, mix gelatin into 1 cup of the grape juice. Stir over a medium heat until gelatin is completely dissolved. Remove saucepan from heat and add remaining grape juice. Let it cool, then refrigerate mixture until it becomes semigelled. Then fold in turkey, celery, grapes, shredded apple, and half of the chopped walnuts.

Pour into a 1-quart decorative ring or mold. Chill about 2 or 3 hours until set. Unmold onto a chilled serving platter. Before serving, whir the cottage cheese and mayonnaise together in a blender. Stir in the remaining half of the walnuts, and pour mixture around the top of the mold. Serves 4.

LOW-CAL MAYONNAISE II

Per tablespoon:
40 calories
0 g protein
4 g fat
1 g carb.

⅔ cup plain nonfat yogurt
⅓ cup safflower oil mayonnaise

Blend ingredients together well.

TURKEY AND CRANBERRY STIR-FRY

Try this new recipe idea for holiday leftovers.

Per serving:
358 calories
30 g protein
12 g fat
33 g carb.

Note: If you are
using Cranberry
Gelatin Salad recipe,
omit walnuts and
orange rind.

⅔ cup freshly squeezed orange juice
2 tablespoons low-sodium tamari
2 tablespoons rice vinegar
12 ounces turkey breast, julienned
1 tablespoon peanut oil
2 ribs celery, diced
2 green onions, chopped
1 cup whole cranberry relish (or see Cranberry Gelatin Salad, page 173)
1 tablespoon grated orange rind
¼ cup chopped walnuts

Combine orange juice, tamari, and vinegar in a large bowl. Marinate turkey pieces in the mixture for 1 hour. Heat oil in a wok or large nonstick skillet. Stir-fry celery and green onions until celery is tender-crisp. Add turkey, and toss until hot. Stir in cranberry relish, orange rind, and walnuts. Add any remaining marinade, and stir quickly over a medium high heat until most of the liquid has evaporated. Serves 4.

TURKEY HASH

Here's what to do when that dark meat includes the neck, back, and other obscure portions of the turkey.

Per serving:
310 calories
36 g protein
13 g fat
14 g carb.

Serving suggestion:
Top each portion
with a poached egg
for a protein boost,
and serve with your
favorite salsa on the
side.

1 tablespoon safflower oil
1 large white onion, chopped
1 clove fresh garlic, pressed
½ red bell pepper, finely diced
2 medium potatoes, peeled and cut into ½-inch cubes
1 pound turkey pieces, chopped
Dash of Worcestershire sauce
Pinch of cayenne pepper
Vegetable salt to taste

Heat oil in a large nonstick skillet, and sauté onion, garlic, and bell pepper until semisoft. Add potatoes and toss over a medium heat for 8–10 minutes until potatoes are done and slightly browned. Add turkey and seasonings, and stir for several minutes more until heated through. Serves 4.

TURKEY PATTIES ROQUEFORT

Per patty:
292 calories
38 g protein
14 g fat
1 g carb.

1½ pounds cooked turkey, coarsely ground
½ cup Roquefort cheese, crumbled
2 tablespoons fresh parsley, chopped
Dash of low-sodium tamari
½ teaspoon poultry seasoning
¼ teaspoon freshly ground pepper
2 eggs, beaten

Interesting idea: You may also bake this as a meat loaf for 25–30 minutes.

Combine all ingredients together in a large mixing bowl. Form 6 patties. Place them in a large aluminum baking pan. Bake them for 15 minutes in a 375° oven or until hot and golden brown. Serves 6.

WILD, WILD WINGS

For things like wings, drumsticks, or thighs, try this.

Per serving:
480 calories
57 g protein
16 g fat
28 g carb.

8 ounces plain nonfat yogurt
2 cans (8 ounces each) tomato sauce
2 tablespoons prepared yellow mustard
2 tablespoons raw honey
1 tablespoon red wine vinegar
2 tablespoons low-sodium tamari
1 tablespoon chili powder
1 tablespoon onion, finely grated
1 clove fresh garlic, pressed
½ teaspoon liquid smoke
Dash of Tabasco sauce
2 ears fresh corn
Turkey wings, drumsticks, or thighs

Note: Serve skewers with the corn for those guests who dislike getting their fingers sauced up.

Note: Nutritional calculations are based on a 6-ounce serving of dark turkey meat per person.

Blend all of the ingredients together, except for corn and turkey, to make a sauce. Halve each ear of corn, and parboil for 5 minutes. Arrange the turkey and corn in a deep baking dish. Pour enough of the sauce over the top to cover them adequately. Cover loosely with foil, and bake in a 350° oven for 25 minutes. Two wings and 2 large drumsticks or thighs will serve 4 people.

TURKEY LIVER AND PISTACHIO PÂTÉ

If you can think of fifty ways to leave your liver uneaten, here's one that might change your mind.

Per serving:
95 calories
10 g protein
4 g fat
6 g carb.

6 ounces cooked turkey liver
½ cup low-fat cottage cheese
1 hard-boiled egg
¼ cup champagne
1 tablespoon port wine
1 shallot, chopped
½ teaspoon dried sage
¼ teaspoon each dried savory and thyme
Pinch of freshly ground white pepper
Vegetable salt to taste
¼ cup unsalted pistachio nuts, shelled

Nosh note: Go creative. Before chilling, fill a pastry tube with the pâté mixture. Squeeze florets of the pâté on crackers, cucumber, or zucchini rounds, or line ribs of celery or split snow peas with a lacy filling.

In a food processor, combine all of the ingredients except for pistachios, and process. Add pistachios, and continue processing, just until they retain a slightly coarse texture. Spoon mixture into a small terrine, and chill about 1 hour. Serve with whole grain crackers or veggies. Makes about 2 cups, enough for 8 appetizer servings.

POULTRY STOCK

Here's what to do when you're down to the bones.

Per cup:
33 calories
4 g protein
1 g fat
2 g carb.

1 turkey carcass (about 3 pounds)
3 quarts water
1 large onion, chopped
3 ribs celery with leaves, chopped
1 carrot, chopped
1 bay leaf
1 clove garlic, minced
6 white peppercorns

Note: You may also use this recipe to make a chicken stock. Reduce the ingredients proportionately to the weight of the chicken pieces used.

Break up the turkey carcass into small parts. Leave on any scraps of meat or skin to give the stock more flavor. Place it in a large kettle or stockpot with water and remaining ingredients. Simmer uncovered for 2½ hours. Strain stock through a fine sieve or colander. Chill to remove any fat that solidifies at the top. Makes about 5 cups of stock.

SAUCY SOUPS AND STEWS

What's the well-bred bird into these days? Soups and stews, of course. And if you think chicken and turkey look good in an entree, you should see them in a wonderfully rich base surrounded by gorgeous grains and vegetables.

These country-style soups and stews are homey and wholesome, yet elegant enough to be served at the snootiest affair. Complement any of them with an oak-aged chardonnay or a crisp sauvignon blanc, and *voilà*! They're classy, they're sassy—and they're haute!

Fat Buster: For extra protein and calcium without extra fat, add 1 to 2 tablespoons of powdered nonfat milk per cup of liquid to enrich cream soups and stews. One tablespoon has only 16 calories. Be sure to use the noninstant powdered milk produced with the smallest amount of processing. It can be found in health food stores.

Tidbit: For a fuller flavored soup or stew, use stock instead of water for a base.

Per serving:
214 calories
28 g protein
5 g fat
18 g carb.

Note: Nutritional calculations are based on a 3-ounce serving of dark turkey meat per person.

TURKEY VEGETABLE GUMBO

1½ pounds meaty turkey pieces with bones, cooked or uncooked
6 cups water
2 cloves garlic, peeled
2 bay leaves
1 medium onion, chopped
2 large ripe tomatoes, peeled, seeded, and chopped
1 cup fresh or frozen corn
1½ cups fresh or frozen okra, sliced
¼ cup fresh parsley, chopped
1 teaspoon each dried marjoram and thyme
¼ teaspoon red pepper flakes
Vegetable salt to taste

Put turkey pieces, water, garlic, and bay leaves in a large kettle or stockpot and bring to a boil. Lower heat, partially cover, and simmer about 1–1½ hours until turkey meat begins to fall from the bones. Strain broth, and reserve turkey pieces. Chill, and skim any fat off the top.

Pour stock back into the pot with remaining ingredients. Simmer covered for 10 minutes. Remove turkey from bones, and discard any skin. Cut turkey chunks into bite-size pieces, and add to the gumbo. Simmer 5 more minutes. Serves 6.

CURRIED CHICKEN AND RICE SOUP

Per serving:
205 calories
30 g protein
2 g fat
16 g carb.

Note: Nutritional calculations are based on a 3-ounce serving of equal amounts of white and dark meat per person.

Creamy option: If you want a creamy curry, stir in ½ cup of plain nonfat yogurt with ½ cup of low-fat milk.

1 frying or roasting chicken (3½ to 4 pounds), cut up and skinned
10 cups water
2 cloves garlic, peeled
2 carrots, chopped
2 ribs celery with leaves, chopped
1 bay leaf
1 teaspoon dried thyme
1 sprig parsley
1 cup uncooked short-grain brown rice
1 medium onion, diced
1 tablespoon curry powder
1 teaspoon Dijon mustard
Vegetable salt and freshly ground pepper to taste

In a large kettle or stockpot bring chicken, water, garlic, carrots, celery, and herbs to a boil. Lower heat, and simmer partially covered for 45–50 minutes. Strain broth, and chill to remove congealed fat. Remove chicken from bones, cut it into small pieces, and set aside.

Pour stock back into pot, and add rice. Bring to a boil for 5 minutes. Lower heat, add onion, and simmer covered for 35–40 minutes until rice is tender. Stir in reserved chicken pieces, curry powder, mustard, and salt and pepper. Simmer soup another 5 minutes. Serves 12.

CREAM OF CHICKEN AND CAULIFLOWER SOUP

Per serving:
81 calories
12 g protein
1 g fat
8 g carb.

6 cups water
2 half chicken breasts, skinned
1 clove garlic
1 medium onion, chopped
2 ribs celery with leaves, chopped
1 carrot, chopped
½ teaspoon each dried marjoram and thyme
2 cups cauliflower florets
1 cup nonfat molk
3 tablespoons powdered nonfat milk
1 tablespoon Parmesan cheese
Vegetable salt and freshly ground pepper to taste
¼ cup fresh parsley, snipped

In a large kettle or stockpot, bring water, chicken breasts, garlic, onion, celery, carrots, and herbs to a boil. Lower heat, and simmer partially covered for 40–45 minutes. Strain broth, and pour it back into the pot. Bring it to a boil again, and add cauliflower.

Lower heat, and simmer covered for about 15–20 minutes until cauliflower is tender. Stir in milk, powdered milk (dissolved in the liquid milk), and Parmesan cheese during the last several minutes of cooking. Then puree it in a blender or food processor (reserve some of the cauliflower pieces for a chunkier texture if you wish).

Meanwhile, remove bones from chicken, and cut breasts into small chunks. Add cauliflower and chicken back to the pot, and simmer until just hot. Season with salt and pepper if desired. Serve sprinkled with snipped parsley. Makes 6 servings.

CHICKEN POTAGE

Per serving:
422 calories
59 g protein
7 g fat
25 g carb.

Note: Nutritional calculations are based on a 6-ounce serving of equal amounts of white and dark meat per person.

2 cloves fresh garlic, pressed
2 large onions, quartered
1 tablespoon olive oil
1 frying or roasting chicken (3½ to 4 pounds), cut up and skinned
6 cups water
6 red skinned potatoes, quartered
½ cup fresh parsley, chopped (reserve ¼ cup for garnish)
2 bay leaves
1 tablespoon fresh thyme, chopped
1 lemon slice
Vegetable salt and freshly ground pepper to taste
½ cup dry white wine

In a medium nonstick skillet, sauté garlic and onions in olive oil until golden brown. Set aside. Put chicken into a large kettle or stockpot, and add 6 cups of water. Bring to a boil, cover, and simmer for about 45 minutes, or until chicken falls readily from the bone. When done, strain the stock, and set aside.

Remove the chicken from the bones, and put the chicken pieces and the stock back into the pot. Add remaining ingredients, except for the wine, and continue to simmer covered for approximately ½ hour, or until potatoes are tender.

Remove the bay leaves and lemon slice. Mash up several of the potatoes in the pot to give the stock a thick, creamy consistency. Add garlic and onion sauté along with the wine. Stir well, and serve topped with the remaining chopped parsley. Serves 6.

TURKEY AND RICE CHILI POT

Per serving:
348 calories
42 g protein
8 g fat
29 g carb.

Delectable suggestion: Top each serving with shredded Jack cheese, sliced avocado, or fresh chopped chives. It is also excellent with hot cornbread on the side.

1 tablespoon olive oil
1½ pounds fresh ground turkey
1 clove fresh garlic, pressed
1 large yellow onion, diced
3 cans (8 ounces each) tomato puree, plus 3 cans water
½ pound tomatillos, peeled and chopped
2 ribs celery, diced
2 sprigs cilantro, chopped
½ cup uncooked brown rice
2 tablespoons rice vinegar
1½ tablespoons chili powder
2 teaspoons ground cumin
¼ teaspoon cayenne pepper
Vegetable salt to taste

Heat oil in a large kettle or stockpot. Crumble in the turkey, and brown it along with the garlic and onion. Stir in remaining ingredients. Bring pot to a slow boil, and continue to cook for 4–5 minutes. Lower the heat, cover, and simmer for another 35–40 minutes, or until rice is tender. Makes 6 servings.

CREAM OF TURKEY SOUP

Per serving:
74 calories
5 g protein
2 g fat
10 g carb.

Note: To cook wild rice, add ¼ cup rice to ¾ cup water in a small saucepan. Bring to a boil, and boil for 5 minutes. Reduce heat, cover tightly, and simmer for 45 minutes or more until rice is fluffy.

4 cups Poultry Stock (page 70)
¼ cup celery with leaves, finely chopped
8 fresh mushrooms, sliced
⅔ cup cooked wild rice (see below for cooking method)
1 cup low-fat milk
1½ tablespoons arrowroot, moistened with ¼ cup stock
½ teaspoon ground sage
Vegetable salt and paprika to taste
2 sprigs parsley, snipped

In a medium kettle or stockpot, simmer stock, celery, and mushrooms uncovered for about 5 minutes until vegetables are tender. Add rice, milk, moistened arrowroot, and sage. Heat soup through, stirring constantly until thick. Do not boil. Add salt and paprika to taste. Serve sprinkled with snipped parsley. Makes 6 servings.

CHICKEN WITH WHOLE WHEAT HERB DUMPLINGS

Chicken:

Per serving:
437 calories
62 g protein
6 g fat
31 g carb.

Note: Nutritional calculations are based on a 6-ounce serving of equal amounts of white and dark meat per person.

6 cups water
1 frying or roasting chicken (3½ to 4 pounds), cut up and skinned
2 ribs celery with leaves, sliced
2 carrots, sliced
1 leek, chopped
1 sprig parsley
1 bay leaf
Vegetable salt to taste

Place all ingredients in a large kettle or stockpot with water. Bring to a boil. Lower heat, and simmer uncovered for 1 hour. Strain stock, and remove chicken from the bones. If you wish, save the celery and carrots to put back into the stew when it's done.

Dumplings:

2 cups whole wheat flour
1 tablespoon baking powder
2 tablespoons butter
2 tablespoons each fresh chives and parsley, minced
1 cup nonfat milk, plus 2 tablespoons

In a medium bowl combine flour and baking powder. With a fork or pastry blender, cut butter into the flour until it's fine and crumbly. Mix in chives and parsley. Add milk, and stir just enough to blend everything together. Put the pieces of chicken meat back into the pot with the stock, and bring to a slow boil.

With a tablespoon, drop 12 equal-sized dollops of dumpling batter into the pot. Don't stir. Simmer for 10 minutes uncovered, then cover the pot, and simmer another 10 minutes. When done, the dumplings should be dry and fluffy on the inside and soft and mushy on the outside in a gravylike stock. Serve pieces of chicken and 2 dumplings each to 6 people.

6
SEAFOOD

LIGHT AND LIVELY FISH

Fish is the perfect bodybuilding food. Gram for gram, it is one of nature's best sources of protein for the least amount of fat and calories. It is also high in polyunsaturated fatty acids and contains many valuable nutrients. Minerals include iodine, potassium, magnesium, phosphorus, iron, copper, and zinc to name a few, with A and D high on the list of vitamins.

Cooking fish healthfully is a key factor in retaining its optimum nutrition. Never overcook fish. For baking, broiling, grilling, or barbecuing fish steaks and filets, cooking should usually take 8–10 minutes per inch of thickness. Poaching or steaming takes slightly less time, and whole fish need to cook a little more. Frozen fish take about 2–3 minutes longer to cook per inch of thickness. An average cooking temperature would be 350–400°, depending on thickness and consistency. When poaching, steaming, or moist-cooking fish, you can microwave it. Place the fish uniformly (small filet ends should be tucked under the larger portion to avoid overcooking) in a covered baking dish. Cook it approximately 4 minutes per half pound of fish. Rearrange it halfway through cooking to assure even doneness. Let it stand 4–5 minutes after cooking. When fish is done just right, it will be flaky yet moist and retain a little of its opaqueness. Never fry fish, unless of course it's freshly caught and over an open campfire.

Although fish prices are often high, pound for pound fish makes good sense. There is practically no waste, and it is a great entree to serve company, since it always lends elegance to a meal.

Break away from the usual plain broiled fish and try these light and lively fish recipes. They are marvelous for summer entertaining as well as everyday dining. In the Muscular Gourmet style, they are fancy but not overly fussy, and as always, they are calorie trimmed and prepared in the most nutritious way.

Fresh fish, if you can get it, is a must. If you do use frozen fish, however, thaw it out at room temperature first. Never thaw fish in a microwave, then cook it with oven heat. It breaks down the texture and destroys many valuable nutrients. If you're in a hurry, thaw it and cook it in the microwave; if you have more time, thaw it and cook it in the oven. For micro-cooking frozen fish, rinse it under cold water first and add one extra minute per half pound of fish to the prescribed cooking time. Check it halfway through cooking.

These particular recipes call for fish steaks and filets. They will vary in size, but allow approximately 6–8 ounces of fish per person.

Fat Busters: Here is a list of the high and low fat content of various fish and shellfish. Although the fattier fish are higher in calorie, they also contain higher amounts of omega-3 fatty acids, a group of polyunsaturated fats that change the ratio of cholesterol types in the blood. They lower the "bad" cholesterols—the LDL (low density lipoproteins) and the VLDL (very low density lipoproteins) that put cholesterol and triglycerides into the body and contribute to the buildup of fat on artery walls—in relation to the "good" cholesterols—the HDL (high density lipoproteins). Omega-3 also helps lower triglyceride levels or blood fat that is linked to heart disease, especially in women. Although higher fat fish such as the ones listed here are highest in omega-3, most cold water fish and salt water fish generally contain higher amounts of omega-3 than the warm water or fresh water types.

Over 5 percent fat: lake and rainbow trout, whitefish, butterfish, yellow-tail, salmon, mullet, eel, herring, mackerel, pompano, sardines, sablefish, shad.

Less than 5 percent fat: Atlantic and Alaskan pollock, Atlantic and Pacific cod, flounder, grouper, haddock, halibut, oysters, smelts, monkfish, lobster, scallops, shrimp, squid, tilefish, shark, kingfish, grunt, hake, ocean catfish, white and yellow perch, ocean perch, orange roughy, sea bass, sea trout, sole, buffalo, croaker, mahimahi (dolphin fish), halibut, roe, swordfish, tuna, turbot, clams, rockfish, scrod, dabs, lingcod, skate, fluke, cusk, frogs' legs, crappie, barracuda, blackfish, carp, porgy, muskellunge.

MARINATED SWORDFISH WITH AVOCADO BUTTER

4 swordfish steaks (approximately 1 inch thick)

Marinade:

Per serving:
281 calories
50 g protein
17 g fat
4 g carb.

¼ cup low-sodium tamari
¼ cup freshly squeezed lime juice
½ teaspoon lime peel, grated
1 clove fresh garlic, pressed

Blend ingredients in a large shallow dish. Turn each steak several times in the marinade to coat. Refrigerate steaks several hours in the marinade, turning occasionally. Grill or broil fish about 4 minutes on each side, 6 inches from the heat, basting with leftover marinade.

Avocado Butter:

> ½ cup ripe avocado, mashed
> ¼ cup buttermilk
> 3 tablespoons freshly squeezed lime juice
> 1 tablespoon fresh parsley, minced
> 1 clove fresh garlic, pressed
> Sea salt to taste

Combine all ingredients and blend until smooth. Top each steak with one quarter of the avocado butter, and garnish with a wedge of lime if desired. Serves 4.

GRILLED YELLOWTAIL WITH ORIENTAL VEGETABLES

Vegetables:

Per serving:
312 calories
48 g protein
6 g fat
9 g carb.

> ⅓ cup sake
> 2 tablespoons low-sodium tamari
> 2 cloves fresh garlic, minced
> 6 green onions, chopped
> 1 cup each carrots, broccoli, celery, and mushrooms, thinly sliced
> 1 teaspoon fresh ginger, minced
> 1 teaspoon lemon peel, grated

Combine all ingredients in a large nonstick skillet or wok. Cover, and steam vegetables slowly, stirring occasionally. Add water as necessary to keep vegetables moist. When they are slightly crunchy, remove vegetables from skillet, and transfer to a large ovenproof platter, and keep them warm in a low oven.

Fish:

> 4 yellowtail steaks (approximately 1 inch thick)
> Low-sodium tamari

Brush steaks on both sides with tamari. Grill or barbecue 6 inches from the heat, approximately 4 minutes on each side. Serve steaks arranged on top of vegetables. Garnish with lemon wedges if desired. Serves 4.

POACHED HALIBUT FLORENTINE

Per serving:
259 calories
49 g protein
6 g fat
2 g carb.

2 bunches spinach
2 shallots, finely chopped
4 halibut steaks (approximately 1 inch thick)
Freshly ground nutmeg to taste
Freshly ground white pepper to taste
4 tablespoons Parmesan cheese, freshly grated
1 hard-boiled egg, grated

Wash spinach leaves, and remove stems. Arrange leaves and shallots in a large baking dish. Place halibut steaks on top, and sprinkle with nutmeg and white pepper. Cover with foil, and bake in a preheated 400° oven for 10 minutes.

Open oven door, uncover fish, and let it stand for several minutes. Remove steaks, and drain off any excess liquid from spinach. Arrange steaks on a platter, and top with equal portions of spinach. Sprinkle each with a tablespoon of Parmesan cheese, some grated egg, then a final dash of nutmeg. Makes 4 servings.

RED SNAPPER IN GREEN SALSA

Per serving:
200 calories
36 g protein
2 g fat
9 g carb.

Note: Using canned chilies is a step-saver. You can roast your own fresh chilies by holding them with a fork over a gas flame or electric burner until the skin is charred and easy to peel. Or you may use 4 cans (4 ounces each) of chilies and omit the tomatillos.

2 cloves garlic, peeled
1 small white onion, quartered
1 tablespoon freshly squeezed lime juice
½ teaspoon sea salt
3 cans (4 ounces) chopped green chilies (see below)
4 tomatillos, husked and peeled
2 sprigs cilantro
2 pounds red snapper filets

One by one, put all ingredients, except fish, into a blender or food processor, using a metal blade, and chop until salsa is liquid but chunky. Makes about 2½ cups.

Place fish filets in a flat casserole dish. Pour salsa over the top to cover the fish. Cover tightly, and bake in a preheated 400° oven for 10 minutes. Serve garnished with extra sprigs of cilantro. Makes 4 servings.

ORANGE ROUGHY WITH GRAPE TARRAGON SAUCE

Fish:

Per serving:
200 calories
35 g protein
2 g fat
8 g carb.

2 pound orange roughy filets
4 green onions, chopped
6 whole peppercorns
2 lemon wedges

Place fish along with remaining ingredients in a large skillet. Add two cups of water, cover, and simmer about 6–8 minutes. Remove fish filets, and put them on an ovenproof platter in a low oven to keep them warm. Strain, and reserve ½ cup of the poaching liquid (cooking water).

Sauce:

½ cup poaching liquid
¼ cup dry sherry
1 cup seedless green grapes, halved
1 teaspoon fresh tarragon, chopped
¼ teaspoon sea salt
1 teaspoon arrowroot, moistened in 1 tablespoon water

In a small saucepan combine poaching liquid and sherry, and bring to a boil. Add grapes, tarragon, and sea salt. Lower heat, and cook until thoroughly hot. Stir in arrowroot, and continue to cook until mixture thickens. Divide fish into 4 portions, and top each with a quarter of the sauce. Granish with extra grapes if desired. Serves 4.

OVEN-CRISPED PERCH

Per serving:
266 calories
36 g protein
2 g fat
24 g carb.

2 pounds perch filets
⅓ cup plain nonfat yogurt
10 unseasoned rye crackers, finely crushed
½ teaspoon dillseed
¼ teaspoon vegetable salt
¼ teaspoon freshly ground pepper

Spread fish lightly on both sides with yogurt. Mix crackers and seasonings together in a flat shallow dish. Dredge filets through crackers to coat both sides. Arrange filets on a rack in a baking pan, and allow them to dry ½ hour before baking. Bake uncovered in a preheated 400° oven for 8–10 minutes or until the crust has browned. Serves 4. If desired serve with Seafood Cucumber Sauce (page 82) on the side.

SEAFOOD CUCUMBER SAUCE

Per cup:
95 calories
6 g protein
3 g fat
11 g carb.

½ cup plain nonfat yogurt
½ cup cucumber, peeled, seeded, and finely chopped
2 tablespoons fresh dill, minced
2 tablespoons onions, finely minced
2 teaspoons prepared yellow mustard
1 teaspoon capers
¼ teaspoon sea salt
¼ teaspoon freshly ground pepper

Combine all ingredients together, and refrigerate. Makes about 1 cup. Serve with Oven-Crisped Perch (page 81).

STUFFED TROUT

Per serving:
638 calories
57 g protein
28 g fat
36 g carb.

Optional: If you prefer to use fresh corn off the cob, one medium ear per fish will be enough. Again there is no need to precook the corn. If you wish to cook your own lima beans, soak ½ cup of dried beans in 2 cups cold water 6–8 hours before cooking. Rinse, and drain, then simmer them covered for approximately 45–50 minutes in 2 cups of water. If you stir them, be careful not to break the skins. Rinse, and drain before adding to the recipe. Yields about 1½ cups.

4 whole fresh trout, dressed—heads, tails, and fins removed
Vegetable salt and freshly ground pepper
1 package (10 ounces) frozen corn (see below)
1 package (10 ounces) frozen lima beans
1 small white onion, chopped
1 red bell pepper, diced
1 tablespoon butter
1 teaspoon fresh thyme, minced
¼ teaspoon paprika
4 brown rice cakes, crushed (commercially seasoned optional)

Wash trout, and pat them dry. Season them with vegetable salt and freshly ground pepper if desired. Thaw out corn and lima beans. Remove from packages, rinse in a colander, and let them drain. There is no need to precook them; they will cook enough in the oven.

Meanwhile, in a medium-size nonstick skillet, sauté onion and red pepper in butter until semitender. Remove from heat, and toss in corn, lima beans, thyme, and paprika. Arrange trout in a large shallow baking dish. Into each fish, spoon one quarter of the stuffing. Sprinkle the top of each fish with 1 crushed rice cake. Bake uncovered for approximately 15 minutes in a 350° oven. Serves 4.

ISLAND BAKED MAHIMAHI

Per serving:
265 calories
37 g protein
8 g fat
11 g carb.

1 egg, beaten
½ cup unsweetened pineapple juice
1½ pounds mahimahi filets
1 cup puffed-brown-rice cereal, finely crushed
½ cup unsweetened coconut, shredded
¼ teaspoon curry powder
Sea salt

Mix egg and pineapple juice in a large bowl. Add mahimahi pieces, and turn them all around to coat well. Let them stand for 1 hour in the refrigerator, turning once. Mix rice cereal, coconut, curry powder, and salt to taste in a large shallow dish.

Dredge each piece of fish in the dry mixture, thoroughly coating it all around. Place the fish pieces on a rack in a shallow baking pan. Let them stand for ½ hour to dry. Bake uncovered in a 350° oven for 15 minutes or until coconut turns golden. Serves 4.

FILET OF SOLE WITH LEMON RICE

Per serving:
462 calories
54 g protein
7 g fat
42 g carb.

4 well-formed sole filets (about 1¼ pounds)
1 tablespoon butter
½ cup fresh mushrooms, thinly sliced
½ cup cooked brown rice (see section Main Grains, page 191, for cooking method)
1 tablespoon each fresh chives and parsley, chopped
1 teaspoon fresh thyme, chopped
2 tablespoons freshly squeezed lemon juice
½ teaspoon lemon rind, grated
Vegetable salt and freshly ground pepper to taste
2 sprigs fresh dill
2 lemon wedges

Wash filets of sole, and place them on paper towels to dry. In a medium nonstick skillet, melt butter, and lightly sauté mushrooms until they are semi-soft. Add remaining ingredients, and stir everything together well.

With a teacup form 2 mounds of rice in a shallow baking dish. Wrap 2 filets of sole (on each side) around each mound of rice, securing the overlap with wooden toothpicks. Place sprigs of dill and wedges of lemon in the baking dish.

Loosely cover with foil, and bake in a 350° oven for about 10 minutes. Remove the foil, and bake another couple of minutes, or until fish flakes easily with a fork. With a metal spatula, carefully remove stuffed sole to a serving plate, and remove toothpicks. Serve with Chenin Blanc Sauce (page 84) on the side. Makes 2 servings.

CHENIN BLANC SAUCE

Per serving:
34 calories
1 g protein
1 g fat
4 g carb.

¼ cup chenin blanc wine
¼ cup plain nonfat yogurt
1 teaspoon fresh dill, chopped
Pinch of freshly ground white pepper

Blend all ingredients together well, and serve in a small cruet. Makes enough for 2 servings of sole.

CELEBRATED MEALS

DINING WITH HEART AND SOUL

Crab-Stuffed Artichokes
with Seafood Sauce Louis
Vegetables Marinated in Basil Dressing
Filet of Sole with Lemon Rice
and Chenin Blanc Sauce
Heart Beet Cake
with Buttercream Frosting
Champagne

BUTTERFISH WITH HONEY MUSTARD SAUCE

Per serving:
442 calories
67 g protein
13 g fat
11 g carb.

1 pound butterfish filets
1 shallot, minced
1 tablespoon Dijon mustard
1 tablespoon low-sodium tamari
2 teaspoons raw honey
½ cup semidry white wine

Place fish filets in a large shallow baking dish. Bake uncovered in a 400° oven for 8–10 minutes. Meanwhile, blend remaining ingredients in a small saucepan, and simmer over a low heat for several minutes. Move butterfish to a serving dish, and pour sauce over the top. Serves 2.

BROILED SALMON WITH ROSÉ BASTE

Per serving:
385 calories
21 g protein
32 g fat
2 g carb.

2 tablespoons butter
1 clove fresh garlic, pressed
2 teaspoons freshly squeezed lemon juice
½ cup rosé wine
1 teaspoon dried rosemary, crushed
4 medium salmon steaks (approximately 1½ pounds)

Melt butter in a small saucepan over a low heat. Add remaining ingredients, and stir for 1 minute. Remove from heat. Place salmon steaks on a broiler rack. Spoon several tablespoons of the rosé baste over the top.

Broil 6 inches from the heat for about 4 minutes. Turn the salmon over, baste with a little more of the mixture, and broil 4 more minutes. Just before removing from the heat, pour remaining baste over the top. Serves 4.

CHILLED BONITO WITH WATERCRESS SAUCE

Per serving:
310 calories
50 g protein
9 g fat
4 g carb.

1½ pounds bonito or tuna steaks or chunks
1 lemon, halved
1 cup plain nonfat yogurt
2 tablespoons olive oil
2 cloves garlic, peeled
½ teaspoon capers
¼ teaspoon anchovy paste; or ½ of an anchovy filet
½ cup watercress leaves, packed
⅛ teaspoon freshly ground pepper

Place fish along with 1 of the lemon halves in a steam tray in a large pot or deep skillet. Pour 1 inch of water in the bottom of the pot. Cover tightly, bring to a boil, and steam for 3 or 4 minutes. Remove from heat, and let it stand covered for 5 more minutes.

Skin and bone fish, and chill it for at least 1 hour. Juice other half lemon, and add 1 tablespoon of the lemon juice to a blender along with remaining ingredients. Blend until creamy. Chill for 1 hour.

Arrange cold pieces of fish on a serving platter, and top with Watercress Sauce. Garnish with watercress sprigs. Serves 4.

SEA BASS BAKED WITH TANGERINE AND ONIONS

Per serving:
188 calories
36 g protein
2 g fat
8 g carb.

2 large tangerines
1 red onion, sliced into rings
1 tablespoon fresh thyme, chopped
1½ pounds thick sea bass filets
Freshly ground pepper to taste

Cut one tangerine in slices crosswise. Juice the other, and set aside. Arrange onion rings and sliced tangerine evenly in the bottom of a large shallow baking dish. Sprinkle with thyme.

Place fish filets over the top. Pour tangerine juice over the fish, and sprinkle with pepper. Bake in a 400° oven for 10 minutes. Move fish filets to a serving platter, and cover with baked tangerine and onions. Dribble pan juices over the top. Serves 4.

GRILLED SHARK WITH TAHINI SAUCE

Per serving:
367 calories
48 g protein
16 g fat
9 g carb.

4 medium shark steaks or filets (about 2 pounds total)
2 tablespoons low-sodium tamari
Juice of 1 lemon
⅓ cup tahini (sesame butter)
⅓ plain nonfat yogurt
1 clove fresh garlic, pressed
2 teaspoons sesame seeds

Brush shark steaks on both sides with a mixture of 1 tablespoon of the tamari and half the lemon juice. Grill or barbecue 6 inches from heat, about 5 minutes on each side.

Meanwhile, combine remaining 1 tablespoon tamari, half of the lemon juice, tahini, yogurt, and garlic in a small saucepan. Stir over a low heat until warm and well blended. Do not boil. Arrange shark steaks on a plate. Pour tahini sauce over the top and sprinkle with sesame seeds. Serves 4.

SWEET AND SOUR POACHED COD

Per serving:
312 calories
50 g protein
9 g fat
4 g carb.

1½ pounds thick cod filets
1 green pepper, julienned
1 cup Fumet (Fish Stock, page 101); or water
¾ cup rice vinegar
½ cup tomato sauce
2 tablespoons dry sherry
2 tablespoons freshly squeezed lemon juice
2 tablespoons raw honey
1 tablespoon low-sodium tamari

Arrange cod filets and green pepper in a large nonstick skillet. Combine Fumet or water and ½ cup of the rice vinegar, and pour into pan. Cover tightly. Bring to a boil, then immediately lower heat. Simmer for 3–4 minutes. Remove from heat, and let it stand covered for 5 minutes.

Meanwhile, put remaining ¼ cup of the rice vinegar, tomato sauce, sherry, lemon juice, honey, and tamari in a small saucepan. Heat until honey has dissolved. Carefully move fish and green peppers to a serving platter, and pour sweet and sour sauce over the top. Serves 4.

SHELLFISH WHIMS

Tidbit: To remove fish odors from ovens, cook or microwave 1 cup of water with lemon juice and cloves on high for 8–10 minutes.

Tidbit: Steam, never boil peeled shellfish (unless it is in a soup or stew), otherwise it will become tough and nutrients will be lost.

Shellfish are the genuine delicacies of the sea. When obtained fresh, they're truly sublime. Anyone who has ever strolled along the oceanfront knows that nothing can surpass the reminiscent smell of frying clams and salt air. It fondles the senses as it somehow tells you that this is what the sea is really about. In this collection of fun and flamboyant recipes, we've traded the deep-fried clams for some leaner but just as delightful versions of shellfish.

Cooking shellfish is a sea breeze. It only takes about 6 to 8 minutes in the oven or broiler, and it does extremely well on the grill or barbecue. One of the great things about shellfish is that it can be cooked in a microwave oven, in place of steaming or poaching it, without destroying its taste or texture. Arrange it flat in a covered baking dish, and microwave it about 4 minutes per ½ pound for large shellfish such as lobster and crab legs, and 3 minutes per ½ pound for smaller ones such as clams, mussels, oysters, shrimp, and scallops. Rearrange them halfway through cooking to assure even doneness. Let them stand five minutes after cooking. Split lobster and shrimp shells to avoid curling.

If you are micro-cooking frozen shellfish, rinse it first to separate it and add on 1 minute to the prescribed cooking time per ½ pound of fish. Check it frequently. To reheat shellfish in a microwave, about 30 seconds to 1 minute will do the trick.

LEMON SAUTÉED SCALLOPS

Per serving:
155 calories
19 g protein
6 g fat
7 g carb.

2 tablespoons butter
2 shallots, finely minced
1 pound scallops, fresh or frozen
1 teaspoon thyme, finely chopped
Juice of one lemon
Sea salt and freshly ground pepper

Melt butter in a medium nonstick skillet. Add shallots, and toss them over a medium low heat to sauté them lightly. Raise heat to medium, and add scallops. Cook them for about 1 minute. Stir in thyme, lemon juice, and salt and pepper to taste, and continue to sauté them another minute or two until scallops become opaque. Serves 4.

NUTTY BAKED SCALLOPS

Per serving:
180 calories
20 g protein
7 g fat
11 g carb.

1 pound fresh large scallops
½ cup unsweetened pineapple/coconut juice
½ cup dry-roasted unsalted macadamia nuts, finely crushed
Sea salt to taste

Rinse and dry scallops on a paper towel. Place them in a bowl with pineapple/coconut juice, and mix them until well coated. Drain them. Put crushed macadamia nuts in a plastic bag, and add sea salt to taste if desired. Shake several scallops at a time in the bag until covered with the nuts, and place them apart on a rack in a shallow baking pan.

Repeat this with all of the scallops. Let them dry for 30 minutes to 1 hour so that the nuts adhere while baking. Bake uncovered in a preheated 375° oven for 8 to 10 minutes or until the outside is slightly browned. Serves 4.

COLD LOBSTER WITH AVOCADO DRESSING

Per serving:
203 calories
23 g protein
10 g fat
5 g carb.

2 medium lobster tails (about 1¼ pounds, cooked and chilled)
8 leaves of Bibb or green-leaf lettuce
1 medium ripe avocado, pitted and peeled
2 medium ripe tomatoes, peeled, seeded, and chopped
1 clove garlic
1 tablespoon freshly squeezed lemon juice
Pinch of cayenne pepper
Sea salt to taste

1 hard-boiled egg, grated
Cilantro sprigs

Remove lobster tails from shells. Slice them thin crosswise, and fan them out on the lettuce leaves arranged on a serving platter. Whirl remaining ingredients, except for egg and cilantro, in a blender. Spoon dressing over the lobster, and sprinkle with grated egg. Garnish with sprigs of cilantro. Serves 4.

STEAMED CLAMS WITH BASIL CHABLIS SAUCE

Per serving:
139 calories
14 g protein
1 g fat
18 g carb.

3 dozen live hard-shell clams
¼ cup fresh basil leaves, finely chopped, plus extra whole leaves (optional)
2 shallots, finely minced, plus extra shallots, chopped
3 tablespoons sweet butter
⅔ cup Chablis wine
Sea salt and freshly ground pepper

Serving suggestion:
This sauce is also excellent for dipping jumbo shrimp.

Place clams in a steam tray in a large pot with one or two inches of water. If desired, put some extra whole basil leaves or chopped shallots in the water for flavor. Cover tightly, and cook 8 to 10 minutes over a medium heat until shells have opened. Discard any that do not.

Meanwhile, melt 1 tablespoon of the butter in a small saucepan. Briefly sauté minced shallots and chopped basil over a medium low heat. Add wine and remaining butter, and heat until butter melts. Salt and pepper to taste. Serve on the side for dipping clams. Makes enough for 4.

SEVICHE

Per serving:
91 calories
10 g protein
4 g fat
5 g carb.

½ pound each raw scallops and shelled crab legs, cut into ½-inch chunks
1 cup freshly squeezed lime juice
2 tablespoons olive oil
1 large tomato, peeled, seeded, and chopped
2 tablespoons red onion, finely diced
2 tablespoons seeded and chopped jalapeño chilies
2 tablespoons cilantro, finely chopped
½ teaspoon fresh oregano, minced
Sea salt to taste

In a large bowl marinate scallops and crab in lime juice, and refrigerate for 4 hours, or until shellfish becomes opaque. Add remaining ingredients, and toss well. Cover, and chill one hour more. Makes 8 appetizer servings.

CLAMS IN GARLIC CREAM SAUCE OVER SPINACH

Per serving:
98 calories
7 g protein
3 g fat
8 g carb.

1 cup plain nonfat yogurt
½ cup clam juice
⅓ cup Parmesan cheese, freshly grated
2 cloves fresh garlic, minced
Freshly ground pepper
12 ounces clams (fresh or frozen), chopped
1 bunch fresh spinach leaves, blanched and chopped;
 or 1 package (10 ounces) frozen, drained
1 tablespoon chives, finely minced

Over a double boiler combine yogurt, clam juice, Parmesan cheese, garlic, and pepper to taste. Bring to a simmer while stirring for several minutes, but do not boil. Add clams, and continue to simmer several more minutes, just until clams are cooked. Remove from heat. Arrange spinach in a bed on a serving platter. Pour clams in cream sauce over the top. Sprinkle with minced chives. Serves 4.

HERB-BROILED OYSTERS IN THE HALF SHELL

Per serving:
84 calories
8 g protein
4 g fat
3 g carb.

1 dozen live oysters
1 tablespoon each fresh marjoram, parsley, and thyme, chopped
¼ cup part-skim ricotta cheese
Half of 1 lemon
¼ cup provolone cheese, grated
Paprika to taste

Hold oyster in one hand with a dish towel or cloth. Insert a short ridged knife between the two shells in the hinge area. Slide the knife all the way around the rim, cutting through the hinge muscle. Force open the shell, and discard top half, leaving oysters in the half shell. If desired, save liquor in a bowl, and strain through cheesecloth or paper towel.

Place oysters, shell side down, in a broiler pan. Combine chopped herbs with ricotta cheese. Squeeze lemon juice over the top of the oysters. With a teaspoon, spread a thin amount of the ricotta mixture on each oyster. Sprinkle the tops with provolone cheese and paprika.

Place under a broiler, about 6 inches from the heat, and broil them about 6–7 minutes until cheese is crusty and golden. Makes 4 appetizer servings.

OYSTERS AND PEAS IN MILK

Per serving:
136 calories
10 g protein
6 g fat
12 g carb.

1 tablespoon butter
¼ cup onions, chopped
1½ cups low-fat milk
½ cup oyster liquor
1 dozen fresh oysters, shucked
½ cup fresh or frozen peas
Freshly ground pepper to taste
2 tablespoons fresh parsley, chopped

Melt butter in a large saucepan, and briefly sauté onions over a medium low heat. Add remaining ingredients, except for parsley, and simmer over a low heat for 10 minutes, but do not boil. Sprinkle with parsley just before serving. Serves 4.

SHRIMP AND BROCCOLI AU GRATIN

Per serving:
201 calories
23 g protein
9 g fat
11 g carb.

1 tablespoon butter
2 tablespoons onion, finely minced
1 cup nonfat milk
2 tablespoons whole wheat pastry flour
4 ounces aged cheddar cheese, grated
⅛ teaspoon freshly ground white pepper
3 cups broccoli florets, steamed
1 pound fresh medium-size shrimp, peeled and deveined
Juice of ½ lemon
2 tablespoons toasted wheat germ
Paprika to taste

Melt butter in a small saucepan over a low heat. Quickly sauté onions, then add ⅔ cup of the milk and stir until hot. Blend remaining ⅓ cup of milk with flour, and add to saucepan. Stir over a medium heat until mixture thickens. Add cheese and pepper, and continue to stir until cheese melts.

Arrange broccoli and shrimp in a 9 x 12-inch baking dish. Squeeze lemon juice over the top, then cover with cheese sauce. Sprinkle with wheat germ and paprika, and bake in a 350° oven for 20–25 minutes. Serves 6.

LOW-CAL CRAB AND MUSHROOM LASAGNA

Per serving:
221 calories
28 g protein
7 g fat
13 g carb.

1 pound zucchini, thinly sliced lengthwise
⅔ cup fresh mushrooms, sliced
2 cups Marinara Sauce (page 142)
1 pound shredded crabmeat, fresh or frozen
1½ cups low-fat cottage cheese
½ cup part-skim Mozzarella cheese, shredded
¼ cup Parmesan cheese, freshly grated

In a 9 x 12-inch baking dish, arrange half the zucchini to cover the bottom. Add sliced mushrooms. Spoon some Marinara Sauce over the top. Spread the crab over the vegetables and top with more sauce. Spread the cottage cheese over the crab. Sprinkle with half the Mozzarella and Parmesan cheese.

Add a layer of the remaining zucchini and pour the rest of the sauce over the top. Sprinkle with remaining Mozzarella and Parmesan cheese. Loosely cover with foil, and bake in a 350° oven for 45–50 minutes. If top needs browning, remove foil 10 minutes before baking is done. Serves 6.

ESCAPE FROM ALBACORE AND OTHER CANNED FISH

Fat Buster: Look for low-sodium canned tuna now being widely marketed. It has only half the salt of other tunas.

Do you know what the most popular bodybuilding chow is? Here's a hint: It comes in a small can that says "water packed," and it tastes slightly better than sawdust. That's it! Tuna in the can—chunk light and solid white albacore. The inescapable tuna is the main staple of the bodybuilder's diet and, we might add, a favorite topic of gym rap—just behind muscle size. Like sets and reps, a daily dose of this stuff has been part of bodybuilding tradition since Muscle Beach began.

But what happens when you get stuck in a tuna rut, and you can't get out? Some suggest "injectable tuna." We would rather you try these exciting new recipe ideas. Yes, it is possible to do something different with tuna that won't threaten the obliques. But don't worry about the difficulties. We know that, whether you're a big-time bodybuilder or still thinking about it, you don't have the time or the strength to labor over weighty concoctions, so we've made them easy, fast, and fun. What's more, they're thrifty on cost and calories as well.

Let's face it, if you want to make gains you have to make change. So the next time you're in the gym swapping tales of tuna, share a few of these new ways to embellish it. And just what will everyone say? Baby, that's progress!

Here's a word about tuna. There are several different kinds of canned tuna. Albacore, also known as the "chicken of the sea," is a solid filet of white meat tuna and is a little milder tasting than ordinary tuna. Tuna, usually labeled "chunk light," comes from various types of tuna fish (yes, there is more than one kind). Nutritionally, they're all excellent, with dark meat being slightly higher in vitamin A, B vitamins, and trace minerals. However, any kind you prefer—or that your budget will allow—will do well in these recipes. It is always recommended buying tuna packed in water instead of oil. It cuts the calories by over half, leaving virtually no fat. Another good suggestion is to rinse the tuna right in the can by running water over it for 10 or 15 seconds. Then squeeze the water out of it by pressing down on the lid while you drain it. This will remove excess salt too.

Now here's a word about other canned fish. They are equally nutritious as tuna, especially those with fine, edible bones. They include red or pink salmon, sardines, and other small variety fish filets. Again, rinse and drain off any of the packing oil. Remove the large bones from salmon if you want but leave the tinier bones. They break up quite easily and are an excellent source of calcium.

You may add extra tuna or canned fish to your recipes to boost the protein intake. One can of water-packed tuna provides about 190 calories, 42 grams of protein, 1 gram of fat, and less than 1 gram of carbohydrate.

TUNA MOUSSE

Per serving:
170 calories
36 g protein
2 g fat
3 g carb.

1 packet unflavored gelatin
¾ cup water
½ cup plain nonfat yogurt
1 cup low-fat cottage cheese
1 tablespoon onion, grated
2 tablespoons fresh dill, chopped
1 teaspoon prepared horseradish
½ teaspoon paprika
2 tablespoons dry white wine
1 tablespoon fresh squeezed lime juice
2 cans (6½ ounces each) albacore

Sprinkle gelatin into boiling water in a medium saucepan. Wait 1 minute, then stir over a low heat until gelatin is dissolved. Cream remaining ingredients together, except for tuna, in a blender. Stir into gelatin. Fold in flaked tuna, and pour into a 6-cup serving bowl or decorative mold. Chill overnight.

To unmold, dip bottom of container into hot water until the edges of the mousse loosen, then invert onto a serving platter. Garnish with fresh dill and thin slices of lime if desired. Serves 4.

TUNA RANCH CASSEROLE

With this South of the Border favorite, you can have your enchiladas and eat them too without the fussiness of frying and stuffing the tortillas. The luscious sauce and yogurt topping make it taste richer than it actually is.

Per serving:
467 calories
38 g protein
5 g fat
65 g carb.

Casserole:

6 corn tortillas, halved
½ cup Poultry Stock (page 70), warmed
1 can (10 ounces) enchilada sauce
1 can (6½ ounces) albacore
1 can (4 ounces) diced green chilies
1 medium tomato, seeded and chopped
2 ounces aged cheddar cheese, shredded

Dip the tortillas in warm poultry stock. In a small baking dish arrange 6 of the tortilla halves, and spoon on some of the enchilada sauce to cover them. Crumble the tuna over the tortillas. Then spread a layer of chilies and tomatoes on top. Sprinkle with half the shredded cheese, and drizzle in a little more sauce. Arrange the remaining tortilla halves evenly over the top.

Cover with a little more of the sauce, and sprinkle with the rest of the cheese. (If there should be some sauce left over, serve it warmed up on the side with the casserole, or blend it with the yogurt to pour over the top.) Bake in a preheated 350° oven uncovered for 18–20 minutes, or until cheese bubbles slightly. Serves 2.

Alternate note: If you wish to make Tuna Ranch Enchiladas with this recipe, dip uncut tortillas in warm Poultry Stock to soften them, then coat them with enchilada sauce. Spoon equal amounts of tuna, chopped chilies, tomatoes, and 1 ounce of the grated cheese across the center. Close them, overlapping the two sides. Place them in a baking dish, and secure the overlap with wooden toothpicks. Top with remaining enchilada sauce and cheese, and bake as you would the casserole. Serve with topping.

Topping:

½ cup plain nonfat yogurt
½ teaspoon Mexican seasoning
2 green onions, chopped

Blend yogurt and seasoning together. Spoon half on each serving of casserole, and sprinkle with green onions.

WHEAT AND TUNA CASSEROLE

Per serving:
302 calories
24 g protein
10 g fat
29 g carb.

1 cup uncooked cracked wheat
2 cups water
½ cup pecans, chopped
¼ cup ripe olives, sliced
2 green onions, chopped
2 tablespoons fresh parsley, chopped

½ teaspoon ground turmeric
½ cup Münster cheese, shredded
½ cup plain nonfat yogurt
⅔ cup nonfat milk
2 cans (6½ ounces each) tuna
1 cup chopped broccoli
Vegetable salt and freshly ground pepper to taste

In a large saucepan, bring cracked wheat with water to a boil for 5 minutes. Lower heat, cover, and simmer for about 25 minutes until dry and fluffy. Remove from heat. Add remaining ingredients, except for tuna and broccoli, and blend well. Stir in tuna and broccoli until just combined. Turn into a 2-quart glass casserole dish. Bake in a 300° oven for 45 minutes. Serves 6.

PUFFY TUNA PIE

Healthy and high in protein, this tuna trick is impressive to serve, but quite easy and economical to make.

Filling:

Per serving:
355 calories
48 g protein
14 g fat
10 g carb.

Cheesy suggestion:
When done, sprinkle the top of the crust with two ounces of grated Swiss cheese and bake for another couple of minutes.

½ cup low-fat cottage cheese
½ cup nonfat milk
2 teaspoons Dijon mustard
1 clove fresh garlic, pressed
¼ teaspoon freshly ground white pepper
1 package (10 ounces) frozen spinach, thawed and well drained
1 can (6½ ounces) tuna
4 mushrooms, sliced

Cream cottage cheese, milk, mustard, garlic, and pepper together in a blender. Add spinach, and stir well. Then mix in tuna and mushrooms, and turn into a 9-inch-square baking dish or pie tin. Set it aside, and preheat oven to 375°.

Crust:

4 eggs, separated
¼ teaspoon dry mustard
1 teaspoon lemon juice, freshly squeezed

In a small mixing bowl, beat yolks and dry mustard to a thick, light yellow foam. In a separate medium bowl, beat egg whites and lemon juice until soft, airy peaks form. Carefully fold the two together, and pour over the top of the tuna. Bake it at once in a 375° oven for 20–25 minutes or until a knife comes out clean. Makes 2 main dish servings.

BAKED TUNA CROQUETTES

These smoke-flavored croquettes are a takeoff on the all-around favorite salmon. The carrots add more consistency for fewer calories than bread crumbs alone. But for a few extra calories, make up for it with Tangy Barbecue Dipping Sauce (page 97). It's delicious!

Per serving:
186 calories
26 g protein
4 g fat
11 g carb.

1 can (6½ ounces) tuna
1 egg, beaten
¼ cup whole wheat bread crumbs
1 medium carrot, grated
¼ cup onion, finely chopped
⅛ teaspoon liquid smoke
Freshly ground pepper to taste

Combine all the ingredients together in a medium bowl. Form 2 patties, and place them on an aluminum baking sheet. Bake in a preheated 375° oven for 12–15 minutes, turning them once to brown them on both sides. Serves 2.

TURKEY BREAST WITH TUNA TOMATO SAUCE

Per serving:
462 calories
63 g protein
6 g fat
33 g carb.

Serving suggestion:
This is an excellent sauce to make in advance, and keep on hand in the refrigerator for a quick and interesting meal fix. Simply pour it over other bland meats, fish, pasta, brown rice, polenta, or cooked vegetables such as eggplant, squash, green beans, or potatoes for an all-in-one dish.

Here's a delicious, super-high protein way to eat otherwise dry tuna and tasteless turkey together in one dish.

2 cans (8 ounces each) tomato sauce
2 tomatoes, peeled, seeded, and chopped
1 small white onion, finely diced
1 sprig fresh parsley, chopped
1 clove fresh garlic, pressed
1 bay leaf
1 teaspoon dried basil
1 teaspoon raw honey
½ cup dry red wine
1 can (6½ ounces) tuna
8 ounces turkey breast, sliced

In a medium saucepan combine tomato sauce, tomatoes, onion, seasonings, and honey. Cover, and simmer for 20–25 minutes. Stir in wine and tuna, and simmer another 10–15 minutes. When ready to serve, remove bay leaf, and pour sauce over two 4-ounce servings of sliced turkey breast. Sprinkle with freshly grated Parmesan cheese if desired. Serves 2.

TANGY BARBECUE DIPPING SAUCE

Per serving:
29 calories
2 g protein
1 g fat
14 g carb.

¼ cup plain nonfat yogurt
¼ cup tomato sauce (or natural-style catsup)
1 tablespoon rice vinegar
1 teaspoon onion, grated
1 tablespoon low-sodium tamari
2–3 drops liquid smoke
Pinch of cayenne pepper

Blend all ingredients together well in a small serving bowl. Makes 2 servings.

TUNA TOSS WITH CHARDONNAY VINAIGRETTE

Light, elegant, and attractive, this tuna and veggie salad makes a complete main dish, or, in smaller portions, a wonderful antipasto salad. Serve with a good bottle of chardonnay, of course.

Salad:

Per serving:
244 calories
11 g protein
19 g fat
10 g carb.

1 large rib celery, thinly sliced
1 small red onion, diced
6 mushroom caps, sliced
1 green bell pepper, diced
1 small carrot, sliced into curls
4 radishes, sliced
1 can (6½ ounces) albacore
10 leaves romaine lettuce

Combine all ingredients together well, and serve in a bowl or platter lined with lettuce leaves.

Chardonnay Vinaigrette Dressing:

⅓ cup safflower oil
¼ cup chardonnay wine
2 tablespoons white wine vinegar
1 teaspoon raw honey
1 small clove fresh garlic, pressed
¼ teaspoon each dried basil, rosemary, tarragon, thyme, and dried mustard
⅛ teaspoon sea salt
Pinch of freshly ground white pepper

Blend all ingredients together. Pour over tuna salad, and toss well to coat. Cover, and chill several hours before serving. Serves 4.

SALMON EGGPLANT PIE

Per serving:
255 calories
28 g protein
9 g fat
17 g carb.

2 tablespoons olive oil
1 clove fresh garlic, pressed
2 scallions, chopped
1 green pepper, diced
1 can (8 ounces) tomato puree
1 can (8 ounces) tomato sauce
1 teaspoon dried thyme
½ teaspoon dried oregano
¼ teaspoon freshly ground pepper
Dash of Worcestershire sauce
1 can (1 pound) red salmon
1 large eggplant, thinly sliced crosswise
¼ cup raw bran
¼ cup Parmesan cheese, freshly grated
1 teaspoon sesame seeds

Heat oil in a medium saucepan. Over a medium low heat, quickly sauté garlic, scallions, and green pepper. Add tomato puree, tomato sauce, thyme, oregano, pepper, and Worcestershire sauce to taste. Simmer sauce over a low heat for 15 minutes. Add a little water if it becomes too thick.

Meanwhile rinse and drain salmon, and remove skin and large bones. Arrange half the eggplant slices on the bottom of a round or square 2-quart baking dish. Spoon a little sauce over them. Crumble salmon over the eggplant, and spoon some more of the sauce over the salmon. Arrange remaining eggplant to cover the top. Pour over remaining sauce.

Bake uncovered in a 350° oven for 30 minutes. Combine bran, Parmesan cheese, and sesame seeds, and sprinkle over the top of the pie. Bake another 15 minutes. Serves 4.

CURRIED SALMON LOAF

Per serving:
231 calories
27 g protein
11 g fat
7 g carb.

Serving suggestion: If desired, serve topped with ⅔ cup plain nonfat yogurt mixed with 1 teaspoon curry powder.

1 can (1 pound) pink salmon
⅔ cup puffed-brown-rice cereal or rice cakes, crushed
1 small white onion, finely chopped
2 tablespoons fresh parsley, chopped
1 teaspoon curry powder
⅓ cup nonfat milk
1 egg, beaten
1 tablespoon freshly squeezed lemon juice
⅓ cup green olives, sliced
Pinch of cayenne pepper

Drain salmon, remove skin and large bones, and set aside. In a large bowl combine crushed cereal or cakes, onion, parsley, and curry powder, and combine with salmon. Add milk, egg, lemon juice, green olives (save a few sliced olives to garnish the loaf), and cayenne pepper to taste. Mix everything together well.

Press into a 9 x 5-inch nonstick loaf pan. Bake loosely covered with foil in a 350° oven for 40 minutes. Remove foil during the last 10 minutes of baking to brown the top. Garnish with reserved olive slices. Makes 4 servings.

SARDINE CORNBREAD SURPRISE

Per serving:
313 calories
22 g protein
20 g fat
15 g carb.

½ cup stone-ground yellow cornmeal
¾ teaspoon baking soda
Pinch of sea salt
⅓ cup green onions, finely chopped
2 tablespoons pimientos, chopped
1 cup buttermilk
2 eggs, beaten
2 tablespoons corn or safflower oil
1 teaspoon raw honey
4 cans (3½ ounces each) sardines, rinsed and drained
2 tablespoons Dijon mustard
Paprika to taste

In a medium bowl combine cornmeal, baking soda, and salt. Toss in onions and pimientos. Combine buttermilk, eggs, oil, and honey, and add to cornmeal. Stir until just blended.

Pour half of the mixture into a nonstick 9 x 12-inch baking pan. Lay sardines evenly across the cornbread batter. Brush or spread mustard over the top of the sardines. Pour remaining batter over the sardines. Sprinkle with paprika and bake in a 425° oven for 20 minutes. Serves 4.

TUNA STUFFED TOMATOES

This simple tuna salad gets rave reviews.

Per serving:
342 calories
44 g protein
10 g fat
14 g carb.

2 cans (6½ ounces each) tuna
⅓ cup Low-Cal Mayonnaise II (page 67)
⅓ cup onion, finely chopped
1 teaspoon celery seeds
¼ teaspoon freshly ground pepper
2 large ripe tomatoes
2 sprigs parsley

In a medium bowl blend tuna, mayonnaise, onion, celery seeds, and pepper together well, and set aside. Starting from the stem end, slice each tomato into 8 sections, stopping ¼ inch from the bottom. Spread it apart, and fill the center with the tuna mixture. Garnish each one with a sprig of parsley. Serves 2.

SEVEN SEAFOOD STEWS

Expand your horizons but not your waistline with a pot of the Ultimate Bouillabaisse or an exotic Scallop Curry. Fish makes the leanest and tastiest of all the stews. If you're lucky enough to live near a seacoast, you may have a reasonably good selection of fresh fish and shellfish. If not, frozen will do. The real secret of a good fish stew or chowder anyway is in the fumet or stock.

Coming up is a divinely inspired collection of low-starch, low-fat recipes fueled by wintery days near a cozy fire and a vision of a body sculptured like Neptune. Cook them up and feel what it's like to be king of the sea.

FUMET
(Fish Stock)

Per cup:
60 calories
5 g protein
3 g fat
3 g carb.

1 pound fish trimmings (heads, tails, and bones from fish)
1 small onion, chopped
½ cup shallots, chopped
1 carrot, sliced
1 rib celery with leaves, sliced
2 tablespoons fresh parsley, chopped
½ bay leaf
¼ teaspoon dried marjoram and thyme
2 cloves
4 peppercorns
½ teaspoon lemon rind, grated
1 quart water
1 tablespoon butter
1 cup dry white wine

Place all ingredients in a large kettle or stockpot, except for wine. Bring to a boil, and simmer for 15 minutes. Skim off any scum that comes to the surface. Add wine, and continue simmering covered for another 15 minutes. Strain through a colander. Makes about 1 quart.

SCALLOP CURRY

Exotic and rich because it is made with coconut milk, this delicately mild curry dish is the answer for weight watchers who must stay off dairy products but love them anyway.

Per serving:
256 calories
38 g protein
5 g fat
11 g carb.

1 medium onion, chopped
1 tablespoon sesame oil
2 cups Poultry Stock (page 70)
1 tablespoon sesame seeds
2 teaspoons curry powder
1 bay leaf
1 cup Coconut Milk (page 102)
1¼ pounds scallops
Sea salt to taste

In a large saucepan, sauté onion in sesame oil until translucent. Add stock and spices, and simmer slowly for ½ hour. Remove bay leaf, add Coconut Milk, and cook over a high heat for about 5 minutes, stirring constantly. Add scallops, and simmer them briefly until they are opaque. Sprinkle with freshly grated coconut. Serves 4.

COCONUT MILK

Per cup:
86 calories
1 g protein
8 g fat
3 g carb.

1 cup hot water
1 cup freshly grated coconut; or dried unsweetened coconut

Pour hot water over grated coconut. Let it stand for 10 minutes, and press the liquid through a cheesecloth-lined sieve. Makes about 1 cup.

RATATOUILLE WITH "MUSCLES"

Enjoy the best of both worlds. Go for the high protein of cioppino and the flavor and heartiness of ratatouille in this nutritious, low-calorie Gallic stew.

Per serving:
187 calories
15 g protein
5 g fat
18 g carb.

3 dozen mussels
1 tablespoon olive oil
3 shallots, minced
1 clove fresh garlic, minced
1 small green pepper, diced
3 cups Fumet (page 101)
2 cups eggplant, peeled and cubed
2 medium zucchini, sliced
2 cups tomatoes, peeled, seeded, and chopped
2 tablespoons fresh parsley, chopped
½ teaspoon each dried marjoram, rosemary, and thyme
1¼ cups Marsala wine
Sea salt and freshly ground pepper to taste

Scrub and debeard mussels. Steam them in 3 cups water for about 5 minutes. When shells are opened, remove meat, and discard shells.

In a large stockpot or kettle, heat olive oil and sauté shallots, garlic, and green pepper for several minutes. Add Fumet, vegetables, and seasonings, and cook over a medium heat until vegetables are semitender. Add wine and mussels. Lower heat, and simmer for several more minutes. Serves 4.

MUSHROOM AND OYSTER BISQUE

Vive l'élégance (but not les calories) with this thick, egg-rich bisque fragrant of sherry. Just the name alone will stir the senses. Serve it with a good bottle of cabernet sauvignon, and the compliments will flow.

Per serving:
210 calories
19 g protein
10 g fat
16 g carb.

1 tablespoon butter
1 tablespoon onion, grated
1 clove fresh garlic, pressed
½ pound fresh mushrooms, sliced
1 pint oysters with liquor
2 cups low-fat milk
1 cup fresh parsley, chopped
3 tablespoons sherry
⅛ teaspoon paprika
Sea salt to taste
2 egg yolks

In a large saucepan, melt butter, and sauté onion, garlic, and mushrooms until semisoft. Add oysters, milk, parsley, sherry, and seasonings. Simmer over a medium heat for about 5 minutes or until oysters are plump. Mix a small quantity of the hot bisque with the egg yolks separately, then stir them into the bisque slowly, and simmer over a low heat for about 1 minute. Do not boil. Makes 4 servings.

COCKTAIL CLAM CHOWDER

Fast and fancy and lowest in calories of all the chowders, whip this snappy recipe up from scratch in a couple of minutes, and your guests will think you're a genius.

Per serving:
133 calories
9 g protein
3 g fat
20 g carb.

1 can (24 ounces) vegetable juice cocktail; or see recipe for
*   Vegetable Herb Cocktail (page 226)*
1 bottle (8 ounces) clam juice
2 cans (6 ounces each) chopped clams, not drained
1 package (10 ounces) frozen mixed vegetables
Dash of Worcestershire sauce
Freshly ground pepper to taste
8 Romano cheese cubes; or any sharp cheese
4 ribs celery

Combine vegetable and clam juices, clams, vegetables and Worcestershire sauce in a large saucepan. Stir over a high heat for several minutes or until vegetables are semitender. Pour into 4 large soup mugs. Drop 2 cheese cubes into each one and a celery stick to stir the cheese as it melts. Makes 4 servings.

SHRIMP AND CRAB GUMBO

Here is a reminder that old recipes never die. A lean and mean seafood gumbo is always a good Southern standby.

Per serving:
254 calories
39 g protein
5 g fat
10 g carb.

¼ cup onion, chopped
½ cup celery with leaves, chopped
1 tablespoon butter
3 cups Fumet (page 101)
1 cup tomatoes, peeled, seeded, and chopped
2 cups okra, thinly sliced
2 tablespoons fresh parsley, chopped
¼ teaspoon paprika
1 dozen fresh medium shrimp, peeled and deveined
1 pound fresh crabmeat, shelled
¾ teaspoon filé powder
Sea salt to taste

In a large stockpot or kettle, sauté onions and celery in butter until semisoft. Add Fumet, vegetables, parsley, and paprika, and simmer until okra is tender crisp. Add shrimp, crabmeat, and filé powder (moistened with a little of the stock), and continue simmering about 5 minutes more, or until shrimp and crabmeat are opaque. Serves 4.

SMOKED FISH CHOWDER

This is a tasty and versatile play on ordinary fish chowders. You can add just about any vegetable on hand. The smoked flavor will give them a new zing.

Per serving:
279 calories
34 g protein
10 g fat
16 g carb.

Note: If you can't get smoked fish, use fresh fish, and substitute a can of drained smoked clams or oysters for a portion of it.

¾ pound smoked fish filets (cod, haddock, swordfish, halibut, etc.)
2 cups Poultry Stock (page 70)
1 small onion, chopped
1 tablespoon butter
¼ pound fresh green beans, finely sliced
½ cup fresh or frozen corn
¼ cup celery leaves, chopped
2 cups low-fat milk
Sea salt and freshly ground pepper to taste

In a covered pan or skillet, simmer the fish filets in a small amount of Poultry Stock until they break easily into small chunks. In a separate large saucepan, briefly sauté onion in butter. Add stock and vegetables, and cook over a medium heat until vegetables are semitender. Add chunked fish. Lower heat, add milk, cover, and continue simmering for 15 minutes more to allow smoky flavor to enhance the chowder. Serves 4.

THE ULTIMATE BOUILLABAISSE

Light the candles! Bouillabaisse is a romantic favorite of seafood lovers, gourmet lovers, or—just lovers. Though it commonly includes lobster, clams, and chunks of fish, the more variety that is used in the making, the more exciting is it.

Per serving:
293 calories
37 g protein
8 g fat
9 carb.

2 tablespoons olive oil
3 leeks (bulbs only), julienned
2 cloves fresh garlic, minced
2 cups Fumet (page 101)
1 cup tomatoes, peeled, seeded, and chopped
1 cup carrots, diced
¼ teaspoon each fennel seeds and finely crumbled saffron
⅛ teaspoon celery seeds
2 tablespoons fresh parsley, chopped
1 bay leaf
1 cup dry white wine
1 pound assorted fish (perch, red snapper, yellowtail, whitefish, etc.)
1 dozen scallops (about ½ pound)
1 dozen live hardshell clams or mussels
2 lobster tails (about 8 ounces each) or 8 large crab legs, shelled
1 teaspoon orange rind, grated
Sea salt and freshly ground pepper to taste

In a large stockpot or kettle, heat olive oil, and briefly sauté leeks and garlic. Add remaining ingredients except for fish, shellfish, and orange rind. Simmer for about 15 minutes, until carrots are semitender. Meanwhile cut fish and lobster tail into ½-inch chunks. Scrub and clean shellfish. Then add fish, shellfish, orange rind and salt and pepper to taste. Cover, and cook over a medium heat for another 15 minutes until shellfish open and fish are opaque. Makes 6 servings.

7
EGGS

EGG MAGIC

Consider the egg. It's the only single item of protein other than meat, fish, or fowl that contains all the essential amino acids. One egg provides 7 grams of first-rate protein, making it an excellent muscle-building source of energy. It is high in vitamins A, B-2, D, E, niacin, biotin, and the minerals copper, iron, and phosphorus, as well as necessary unsaturated fats. It's also the richest known source of choline (an element found in lecithin) that keeps the cholesterol in the egg emulsified.

Now consider the versatility of the egg. It is economical, easily stored, readily available, and virtually limitless in its uses. It can be a main dish, a side dish, or whipped into a dessert. It can take on the character and flavor of any food, or it can be the main attraction all by itself. It can stretch a casserole, thicken soups, stews, and sauces, or it can be a stuffing for meats and vegetables. It can bake magic to make goodies turn out higher and fluffier and incredibly delicious. If you just want to "egg-it," it's quick to fix too. In minutes you can have your egg over easy, over medium, basted, scrambled, poached, soft boiled, hard boiled, and more. You can even throw in a raw egg to add punch to your juice or a protein drink.

And just think. You can have all this for only 75 fast-burning calories per egg! That's a lot of magic. What more can be said about the divine egg except more ways to fix it?

Fat Buster: If you're concerned about the cholesterol in eggs, relax. Eggs will not give you "high cholesterol" but do contain a natural cholesterol that is emulsified or "neutralized" by their high choline content. The cause of harmful serum cholesterol is consuming a diet too high in saturated fats (such as ice cream and fried foods) and leading a sedentary life-style. That causes a raised level of circulating triglycerides in the blood which in turn causes a buildup of the cholesterol that clogs the arteries. Although eggs do contain cholesterol, they do not cause or promote its effects in the body.

Also, the risk of "high cholesterol" is not necessarily determined by the total levels of cholesterol in the blood, but by the ratio of those cholesterols. A high level of HDL (high density lipoprotein or "good cholesterol") and a lower level of LDL (low density lipoprotein or "bad cholesterol") is the result of staying with a diet that is high in polyunsaturated fats and low in saturated fats. High HDL is apparently a crucial factor in the body's defense against heart disease.

Eggs are a healthful, natural food that should be eaten in balance with all of the other food groups. So before you go about eliminating natural foods from your diet, start with the junk foods.

PUMPING IRON SPECIAL

Easy to fix, this high protein scramble is made with iron-rich spinach. It's a great bodybuilding dish, because it's high in vitamins and minerals, and low in fats, carbohydrates, and calories.

Per serving:
355 calories
40 g protein
17 g fat
7 g carb.

½ pound lean ground sirloin
1 small onion, chopped
1 clove fresh garlic, pressed
4 eggs, beaten
1 bunch fresh spinach leaves, chopped
Vegetable salt and freshly ground pepper to taste

In a large nonstick skillet, brown sirloin along with onion and garlic over a medium heat. Drain off any excess fat. Stir in the eggs and scramble until firm. Spread spinach leaves over the top, cover, and remove from heat. Wait 3 minutes to allow spinach to wilt. Add salt and pepper, mix thoroughly, and serve. Makes 2 servings.

CARROT RAISIN CUSTARD

Naturally sweet with carrots and raisins, this versatile custard can be eaten as a side dish or a dessert.

Per serving:
111 calories
5 g protein
6 g fat
8 g carb.

1 pound carrots, steamed
1 tablespoon butter, melted
4 eggs
1 cup nonfat milk
1 teaspoon freshly ground nutmeg
Sea salt to taste
¼ cup seedless raisins, soaked in ½ cup water for 1 hour

Puree carrots in a food processor or blender. Add remaining ingredients, except for raisins, and blend for 15–20 seconds more. Stir in drained raisins and pour into a 1½-quart soufflé or baking dish.

Place it inside a larger baking pan containing enough water to go halfway up the sides of the dish. Bake in a preheated 375° oven for 45–50 minutes or until set. Makes 6 servings.

SWISS ALPINE SOUFFLÉ

Per serving:
266 calories
25 g protein
17 g fat
5 g carb.

Creamy option:
Blend ½ cup of plain nonfat yogurt and 1 teaspoon of chopped fresh dill together to pour over the top.

This light and puffy omelet made from mostly egg whites is both practical and fancy.

6 egg whites
3 egg yolks
½ cup plain nonfat yogurt
2 ounces aged Swiss cheese, grated
Vegetable salt and freshly ground pepper to taste

Let egg whites stand, until they reach room temperature, then beat until stiff. Blend egg yolks, yogurt, and all but 2 tablespoons of cheese. Fold into egg whites and turn mixture into a lightly oiled 9- or 10-inch soufflé dish. Bake on a high rack in a preheated 350° oven for 15 minutes. Sprinkle the top with the remaining cheese and bake 5 minutes more. Serves 2.

CELEBRATED MEALS

SPRING CUISINE

Swiss Alpine Soufflé
Turkey Patties Roquefort
Broiled Tomatoes
Cheese and Herb Popovers
Chantilly Fruit in Cantaloupes
Mocha au Lait

TOMATO CAULIFLOWER SOUFFLÉ

Impress a guest yourself with this healthy, easy-to-make gourmet egg dish made entirely with egg whites.

Per serving:
276 calories
25 g protein
3 g fat
35 g carb.

2 pounds fresh tomatoes
2 cups cauliflower florets
1 cup nonfat milk
1 tablespoon tomato paste
4 tablespoons Parmesan cheese, freshly grated
6 egg whites
½ teaspoon cream of tartar
4 tablespoons powdered nonfat milk

Wrap whole tomatoes in foil and steam, along with cauliflower, for 10–12 minutes. When cooled, press tomatoes through a strainer to remove skin and seeds. In a large nonstick saucepan over a low heat, blend milk, tomato paste, and Parmesan cheese, stirring constantly until cheese melts. Mix with tomato puree and cauliflower. Remove from heat and let it cool.

Meanwhile let egg whites stand to room temperature, then beat them with cream of tartar until stiff, but not dry. Fold in powdered milk. Gently blend everything together and turn into a lightly oiled 2-quart soufflé or deep baking dish. Bake in a preheated 350° oven for 30 minutes, or until golden. Makes 2 large servings.

STUFFED PEPPER OMELET

For ages Italians have been eating green peppers and eggs fried in lots of olive oil. Here's a novel, slimmer variation of an old tradition.

2 large green bell peppers
1 small potato, peeled and diced
½ clove fresh garlic, pressed
1 teaspoon olive oil
4 eggs, beaten
2 tablespoons fresh parsley, minced
Vegetable salt and freshly ground pepper to taste

Slice tops off peppers and clean out cavities, being sure not to cut through the bottoms. Parboil peppers in boiling water for 2 minutes, then let them stand in cold water. In a small nonstick skillet, sauté potato and garlic in olive oil over a medium heat until lightly brown and tender. Remove from heat.

In a medium bowl, mix together eggs, parsley, salt and pepper if desired, and add sautéed potato. Place green pepper shells snugly in a small baking dish with enough water to go halfway up the sides of the peppers.

Pour equal amounts of egg mixture into pepper shells. Cover loosely with foil and bake in a preheated 350° oven for approximately 45 minutes or until eggs are firm. Serves 2.

Per serving:
250 calories
16 g protein
15 g fat
16 g carb.

Delicious suggestion:
Sprinkle the tops with freshly grated Romano cheese if desired. Instead of potatoes you can use ¼ pound of Easy Turkey Sausage (page 121) precooked and crumbled into the egg mixture before it's baked.

HAM AND EGG ASPIC

Here's yet another high-protein, low-calorie surprise. It's the perfect solution when you're in a quandary about what to do with leftover ham and eggs.

1 meaty ham bone; or ½ pound lean ham
1 quart water
1 sprig fresh parsley, chopped
¼ pound fresh asparagus tips
1 packet unflavored gelatin, softened in ¼ cup cold water
2 hard-boiled eggs, sliced

Put ham bone in a medium kettle or stockpot with water and parsley. Simmer slowly for about 1½ hours to make a stock. Remove ham bone and meat, and strain stock. Put stock back into the pot with asparagus tips and simmer for approximately 10 minutes or until the asparagus is semitender.

Remove asparagus carefully with a slotted spoon and set aside. Add softened gelatin to hot stock and stir until completely dissolved. Pour half the gelatin mixture into a 1-quart mold. Chill until it begins to set.

Arrange asparagus tips, hard-boiled egg slices, and any diced leftover ham in the semiset gelatin. Cover with remaining gelatin mixture and chill until completely set. Unmold onto a serving platter. Makes 2 large servings.

Per serving:
371 calories
33 g protein
25 g fat
4 g carb.

More protein: If you wish, garnish the aspic with more sliced or grated hard-boiled eggs. You may also substitute beef or lamb bones for ham, and any other vegetables you prefer for asparagus.

SUPER-STUFFED OMELETS

There are two surefire ways to get into the best shape of your life: taking action-packed workouts and eating a well-balanced diet that's low in calories with lots of eggs for protein. You can't miss. But if dieting on eggs makes you slightly less than "egg-static," whip up these Super-Stuffed Omelets, filled with delicious, nutritious ingredients. At around 300 calories each, they're a dieter's dream, made with 4 egg whites and 2 egg yolks to keep protein high and calories low. Here's the shape of eggs to come, beginning with the perfect omelet.

OMELET EGG MIXTURE

4 egg whites
2 egg yolks
2 tablespoons water

Tidbit: If cooking refrigerator-cold eggs, start out with a low heat, then gradually increase the temperature to keep the eggs from getting tough. Before hard-boiling eggs, let them stand until they reach room temperature to avoid cracked shells and a rubbery result.

Gently whisk whites and yolks together with water in a medium bowl, until they're well blended and light yellow.

When preparing eggs for the omelet, let them stand to room temperature before cooking; otherwise cold eggs hitting a hot pan will cause the omelet to toughen. Use a nonstick pan and lightly oil it with safflower oil (wiping off the excess with a paper towel) to be sure the omelet doesn't stick. For this amount of egg, the pan should be 6 to 8 inches at the base so that the Omelet Egg Mixture is not more than ¼ inch deep while cooking.

Since omelet making is a very quick process, have your filling (and anybody you're going to feed) ready before you cook the eggs. Heat the pan over a medium heat until it's thoroughly hot. Pour in the egg mixture and cook over a medium (medium low if you're using an electric stove) heat.

As the eggs begin to set, run a spatula around the sides of the omelet, lifting it enough to allow the uncooked portion to flow underneath. Then allow it to cook a few moments undisturbed. When the eggs are set but shiny, spoon the filling in a row across the center.

Finish the omelet. With the spatula, carefully lift one side of the omelet over the filling and then the other side, forming an overlapping closure. Remove the pan from the heat. Lift the pan at an angle and gently slide the omelet, with the help of the spatula, to an inverted position on a hot serving plate. Each of these recipes makes one omelet.

Nutritonal information is given in individual recipes.

CRAB AND ARTICHOKE OMELET WITH CAPER SAUCE

Per serving:
307 calories
35 g protein
12 g fat
11 g carb.

Note: Fresh-cooked crab and artichoke heart are best, but ready cooked will do if need be. Rinse them to remove any salty or oily liquid.

¼ cup plain nonfat yogurt
2 tablespoons nonfat milk
½ teaspoon Dijon mustard
1 teaspoon capers
Vegetable salt and freshly ground pepper to taste
Omelet Egg Mixture (page 112)
2 ounces cooked crab, shredded (see below)
½ cooked artichoke heart, chopped

In a small saucepan, blend yogurt, milk, and mustard, and cook over a medium heat for 1 minute. Stir in capers and salt and pepper if desired. Set sauce aside.

Make the omelet. Combine crab and artichoke and lay them across the top of the cooking omelet. Top with caper sauce. Finish the omelet.

GARDEN SAUTÉ OMELET

Per serving:
299 calories
25 g protein
18 g fat
9 g carb.

1 teaspoon olive oil
½ small clove fresh garlic, pressed
1 green onion (bulb only), chopped (reserve leaves for topping)
¼ cup eggplant, peeled and diced
¼ cup zucchini, diced
¼ cup fresh mushrooms, sliced
½ tomato, seeded and chopped
1 teaspoon fresh parsley, minced
½ teaspoon fresh basil, minced
1 tablespoon Parmesan cheese, freshly grated
Omelet Egg Mixture (page 112)

Lightly sauté olive oil, garlic, and green onion in a medium nonstick pan. Add remaining ingredients, except for Parmesan cheese and eggs, and continue to sauté over a medium low heat until vegetables are semitender. Drain off any excess liquid and set aside.

Make the omelet, spoon in the vegetables, and sprinkle with Parmesan cheese. Finish the omelet. Garnish the top with reserved chopped chives.

CALIFORNIA OMELET

Per serving:
294 calories
38 g protein
14 g fat
3 g carb.

⅛ medium ripe avocado, peeled and mashed
1 teaspoon buttermilk
1 teaspoon freshly squeezed lime juice
1 teaspoon fresh dill, minced
½ small clove fresh garlic, pressed
Dash of Tabasco sauce
2 ounces water-packed tuna, rinsed and drained
Omelet Egg Mixture (page 112)
¼ cup alfalfa sprouts

In a small bowl combine until creamy avocado, buttermilk, lime juice, dill, garlic, and Tabasco. Lightly toss with the tuna (just like mayonnaise). Make the omelet.

Spoon in the tuna mixture, sprinkle with sprouts, and finish the omelet. Garnish with the reserved sprig of dill if desired.

ASPARAGUS OMELET WITH MALTAISE SAUCE

Per serving:
308 calories
26 g protein
20 g fat
6 g carb.

1 egg yolk
1 tablespoon plain nonfat yogurt
1 teaspoon butter
1 teaspoon freshly squeezed orange juice
⅛ teaspoon orange rind, grated
Pinch of nutmeg
Omelet Egg Mixture (page 112)
6 cooked asparagus spears, tough ends removed (see below)

Note: Fresh steamed asparagus is best, but frozen will do.

In the top of a double boiler (with 2 inches of very hot, but not boiling, water on the bottom), blend egg yolk and yogurt together by hand until smooth. Add butter and continue stirring until melted. Add orange juice, orange rind, and a pinch of nutmeg, and stir, but do not boil. Set the resulting Maltaise sauce aside.

Make the omelet. Lay asparagus spears across the center. Spoon half the Maltaise sauce over the asparagus. Finish the omelet, then spoon the remaining sauce over the top.

CHILI OMELET

Per serving:
300 calories
34 g protein
16 g fat
8 g carb.

2 ounces lean ground sirloin
1 tablespoon onion, chopped
½ clove fresh garlic, pressed
⅛ green bell pepper, diced
1 tablespoon fresh or frozen corn
1 tablespoon tomato paste, plus ¼ cup water
½ teaspoon chili powder
Vegetable salt and freshly ground pepper to taste
Omelet Egg Mixture (page 112)

In a medium nonstick pan, sauté ground beef, onion, and garlic until meat is brown. Add green pepper and corn, and continue to sauté over a medium heat until pepper and corn are semitender. Drain off any fat. Stir in tomato paste and water, chili powder, and salt and pepper if desired, and simmer for several minutes. The chili mixture should be thick but not dry. Remove from heat and set aside.

Make the omelet and spoon the mixture across the center. Finish the omelet. Sprinkle the top with chili powder and add a dollop of plain nonfat yogurt if desired.

BANANA OMELET

''Where's the banana?'' This delectably different dessert omelet has fruit in the center, but the banana is—surprise!—discreetly in the eggs.

Per serving:
282 calories
21 g protein
11 g fat
24 g carb.

¼ cup sliced fresh or frozen strawberries
½ medium ripe peach, peeled and cut into small chunks
1 tablespoon unsweetened applesauce
Pinch of cinnamon
½ medium ripe banana, mashed
¼ teaspoon vanilla extract
Omelet Egg Mixture (page 112)

In a small bowl combine strawberries, peaches, applesauce, and cinnamon and set aside. In another bowl, mash together banana and vanilla and blend in with the egg mixture. Be sure there are no large lumps of banana in the eggs, or they may get too brown while cooking.

Make the omelet and fill with the fruit. Finish the omelet and sprinkle the top with cinnamon. It's yummy!

REAL MEN EAT CRUSTLESS QUICHE

Legend has it that real men don't eat quiche. Well, they obviously didn't try crustless quiche, because if they did, they'd love it. In fact, they'll get plenty of power and protein from all the milk, eggs, cheese, fish, turkey, and spinach without that dainty, fattening crust. And since these quiches are crustless, they're much easier to make. Plain or fancy, either way, they're pure muscle and gourmet.

To begin with, use a 9-inch quiche or pie pan. A nonstick surface is preferable, but if you're using a glass or aluminum pan, prepare it by oiling it lightly with a little corn or safflower oil. To make a lovely free-standing quiche, use a 7-inch deep-dish torte pan with a lift-out bottom. (Most gourmet stores carry them.) When the quiche cools, separate the sides from the pan with a knife to free it for cutting. The ingredients in all these recipes are for a standard shallow 9-inch pan or a 7-inch deep-dish pan.

QUICHE EGG MIXTURE

Fat Buster: Eat eggs! They have "negative" calories. It takes almost as many calories to digest eggs as they supply.

Tidbit: To get a smoother textured quiche, place the quiche pan in a larger pan of water just as you would a custard when baking and allow about 15 minutes more cooking time.

4 eggs
1 cup low-fat milk

Beat eggs and milk together lightly with a fork and combine with the ingredients of the following individual recipes.

Pour the quiche mixture into the prepared pan and bake in a preheated 350° oven for 45 minutes to 1 hour, or until the tip of a knife comes out clean. (The baking time may vary a bit from recipe to recipe, since vegetables take a little longer.) Each quiche serves 4. Nutritional information is given in individual recipes.

CONTINENTAL QUICHE

Per serving:
259 calories
25 g protein
15 g fat
5 g carb.

Leftover ideas:
Precooked chicken
or meat make a
great substitute for
turkey.

Quiche Egg Mixture (page 116)
4 ounces turkey breast, diced
1 medium zucchini, diced
4 ounces aged Swiss cheese, grated
1 small clove fresh garlic, pressed
Pinch of dried oregano
Vegetable salt and freshly ground pepper to taste

Combine Quiche Egg Mixture with other ingredients. Pour into a prepared pan and bake in a preheated oven, 350°, for 45 minutes to 1 hour, or until the tip of a knife comes out clean. Serves 4.

MEXICAN QUICHE

Per serving:
254 calories
16 g protein
17 g fat
11 g carb.

Fresh idea: Garnish
with tomato wedges
and top with fresh
salsa or plain nonfat
yogurt.

Quiche Egg Mixture (page 116)
½ cup fresh or frozen corn
1 can (4 ounces) green chilies, diced
6 ripe olives, sliced
½ cup green onions, chopped
4 ounces aged cheddar cheese, grated
1 small clove fresh garlic, pressed
1 teaspoon ground cumin
Vegetable salt and freshly ground pepper to taste

Combine Quiche Egg Mixture with other ingredients. Pour into a prepared pan and bake in a preheated oven, 350°, for 45 minutes to 1 hour, or until the tip of a knife comes out clean. Serves 4.

SMOKY SALMON QUICHE

Per serving:
289 calories
25 g protein
18 g fat
5 g carb.

Tasty topping: Serve
with sliced avocado
and plain nonfat
yogurt.

Quiche Egg Mixture (page 116)
1 can (6½ ounces) pink salmon, drained, large bones removed
½ cup green onions, chopped
4 ounces aged cheddar cheese, grated
⅛ teaspoon liquid smoke
Vegetable salt and freshly ground pepper to taste

Combine Quiche Egg Mixture with other ingredients. Pour into a prepared pan and bake in a preheated oven, 350°, for 45 minutes to 1 hour, or until the top of a knife comes out clean. Serves 4.

QUICHE FLORENTINE

Per serving:
193 calories
15 g protein
11 g fat
6 g carb.

A must: Top with
Marinara Sauce
(page 142) and
sprinkle with a little
more Parmesan
cheese.

Quiche Egg Mixture (page 116)
½ bunch fresh spinach leaves, chopped, steamed, and drained; or ½ package
  (10 ounces) frozen, drained
½ cup fresh mushrooms, sliced
2 ounces part-skim ricotta cheese
2 ounces Provolone cheese, grated
2 tablespoons Parmesan cheese, freshly grated
¼ teaspoon dried basil
Vegetable salt and freshly ground pepper to taste

Combine Quiche Egg Mixture with other ingredients. Pour into a prepared pan and bake in a preheated oven, 350°, for 45 minutes to 1 hour, or until the tip of a knife comes out clean. Serves 4.

GARDEN QUICHE

Per serving:
230 calories
16 g protein
15 g fat
7 g carb.

Healthy suggestion:
Sprinkle the top
with sunflower seeds
or soy bacon bits.

Quiche Egg Mixture (page 116)
½ cup carrots, diced
½ cup each broccoli and cauliflower florets, broken into small pieces
4 ounces aged cheddar cheese, grated
1 small clove fresh garlic, pressed
1 teaspoon fresh dill, chopped
⅛ teaspoon celery seeds
Vegetable salt and freshly ground pepper to taste

Combine Quiche Egg Mixture with other ingredients. Pour into a prepared pan and bake in a preheated oven, 350°, for 45 minutes to 1 hour, or until the tip of a knife comes out clean. Serves 4.

HIGH PROTEIN QUICHE

Per serving:
229 calories
30 g protein
9 g fat
6 g carb.

Tasty option: Serve it
with a spicy low-fat
Nøkkelost cheese
melted over the top.

Quiche Egg Mixture (page 116)
1 can (6½ ounces) water-packed tuna, rinsed and drained
1 cup low-fat cottage cheese
½ cup green bell pepper, diced
2 tablespoons pimientos, chopped
2 tablespoons onion, finely chopped
1 tablespoon fresh parsley, chopped
Vegetable salt and paprika to taste

Combine Quiche Egg Mixture with other ingredients. Pour into a prepared pan and bake in a preheated oven, 350°, for 45 minutes to 1 hour, or until the tip of a knife comes out clean. Serves 4.

EGGS, PIZZA STYLE

Tidbit: Never rinse eggs in the shell unless you intend to use them immediately. This washes away a protective coating that can allow bacteria and contaminants to enter the egg. Of course you should never use raw eggs that come cracked. And watch out for eggs that are exceptionally watery or light colored; they may be old or nutritionally inferior.

Does the thought of another scrambled egg make you want to die rather than diet? Then try this unique and creative "egg pizza" and really live. Baked similar to a frittata (an Italian omelet with filling or seasoning cooked right in the egg mixture and served flat), the eggs are the top layer on a whole wheat pizza crust. The wholesome and delicious ingredients make each slice a complete meal. Whip up several or all of the toppings and present them buffet style in individual chafing dishes. Then everyone can make his own egg pizza the way he likes it.

With these versatile recipes you can have a traditional pizza by omitting the egg layer. Or if you prefer a truly low-calorie, high-protein egg dish without the crust, simply bake the eggs in a nonstick quiche pan for 10–12 minutes at 400°. Serve it in wedges on warm plates using the suggested sauce and toppings. It will taste so much like pizza that all you'll miss will be the calories.

But if you're a pizza lover, beware! Either way you try it, you'll find this new egg pizza irresistible. The rest is history. Ah, well. that's amore!

PIZZA DOUGH

Per serving:
122 calories
3 g protein
3 g fat
22 g carb.

1 packet active dry yeast
1 cup lukewarm water
1 teaspoon raw honey
2 tablespoons olive oil
3 cups whole wheat flour
½ teaspoon sea salt (optional)

In a small bowl dissolve yeast in water and honey, and stir in olive oil. In a large bowl, add flour, and mix in salt if desired. Then add the liquid to the flour and combine to make a soft dough. Turn out onto a floured surface and knead until smooth and elastic (about 7–8 minutes).

Cover the dough and let it rise for 10–15 minutes. Divide the dough into 2 balls. With a rolling pin, roll each one into a 15-inch circle.

Transfer the dough onto 2 lightly oiled pizza pans. Press dough up the sides of the pan and crimp the edges at least ¾ of an inch high. Prick crust all over with a fork and bake in a 425° oven for 15 minutes or until edges are golden.

Prepare the Pizza Egg Mixture (page 120) while crust bakes. When the crust is done, turn off the oven and open the oven door to let it cool down before adding Egg Mixture. Makes 2 pizzas, enough for 12 servings.

PIZZA EGG MIXTURE

Per serving:
86 calories
7 g protein
6 g fat
1 g carb.

12 eggs
½ cup nonfat milk
1 teaspoon dried basil
1 tablespoon fresh parsley, chopped
½ teaspoon vegetable salt (optional)

In a large bowl, whisk eggs with all the ingredients until well blended. Carefully pour half of the egg mixture onto one crust and half onto the other. Bake at 400° for another 10 minutes or until eggs are set.

Remove from the oven to cool and cut each pizza into 12 wedges. The smaller the wedges, the more people can try the different toppings. Makes enough filling for two pizzas, enough for 12 servings.

PIZZA SAUCE

Per serving:
30 calories
1 g protein
1 g fat
4 g carb.

1 tablespoon olive oil
3 cloves fresh garlic, pressed
2 cans (6 ounces each) tomato paste, plus 2 cans water
1½ cups Italian plum tomatoes, peeled, seeded, and diced
1 tablespoon dried basil
1 teaspoon dried oregano
Vegetable salt to taste

Heat oil in a medium saucepan and lightly sauté garlic. Stir in remaining ingredients, and simmer covered for 35–40 minutes until sauce is thick. If sauce is too thin, remove cover and simmer a little while longer. Makes enough for 2 pizzas or 12 servings.

CLAMS IN ALFREDO SAUCE

Per serving:
64 calories
7 g protein
2 g fat
2 g carb.

2 cups part-skim ricotta cheese
½ cup nonfat milk
2 tablespoons Parmesan cheese, freshly grated
2 cloves fresh garlic, pressed
Freshly ground pepper to taste
12 fresh shelled clams, minced; or 2 cans (6½ ounces) clams, chopped, rinsed, and drained

In a medium saucepan blend ricotta, milk, Parmesan cheese, garlic, and pepper. Cook over a low heat for 5 minutes, stirring constantly. When sauce is hot and smooth, stir in clams and heat through. Serves 12.

ROASTED PEPPERS

Per serving:
18 calories
0 g protein
1 g fat
2 g carb.

Bell peppers, 2 green, 2 red, and 2 yellow (depending on availability)
2 cloves fresh garlic, pressed
Vegetable salt and freshly ground pepper to taste

Roast the peppers by placing them on a wire rack under a preheated broiler, about 4–5 inches from the heat. Broil them for 20 minutes (or until they are semisoft and the skins are charred), turning them every 5 minutes or so.

When done, enclose the peppers in a plastic bag and let them steam until they are cool enough to handle. Then cut off the tops and peel them whole. Slice into thin strips and clean out the seeds and pulp. Place them in a chafing dish with remaining ingredients. Serves 12.

EASY TURKEY SAUSAGE

Per serving:
108 calories
18 g protein
3 g fat
1 g carb.

1½ pounds fresh ground turkey
2 tablespoons onion, finely minced
2 cloves fresh garlic, pressed
½ teaspoon dried sage
¼ teaspoon each dried marjoram and savory
1 rounded teaspoon fennel seeds
Vegetable salt and freshly ground pepper to taste

Combine all ingredients together well in a medium bowl and let them stand in the refrigerator for several hours, to allow seasonings to permeate the meat. In a large nonstick skillet, coarsely crumble in turkey mixture and cook over a medium heat approximately 10–12 minutes, tossing occasionally. Serves 12.

BROCCOLI PESTO

Per serving:
65 calories
4 g protein
4 g fat
2 g carb.

¼ cup pignolias (pine nuts)
3 cloves garlic, peeled
1 tablespoon extra virgin olive oil
1 cup part-skim ricotta cheese
2 tablespoons Parmesan cheese, freshly grated
½ cup fresh basil leaves, chopped
2 cups broccoli florets

In a blender or food processor process pine nuts, garlic, and olive oil. Add remaining ingredients and continue to process until pesto is speckled green. Place in an airtight container and chill overnight. Serve warm. Makes 12 servings.

HOT TUNA AND ZUCCHINI

Per serving:
83 calories
10 g protein
3 g fat
2 g carb.

1 tablespoon olive oil
2 cloves fresh garlic, pressed
¼ cup chives, chopped
1 cup zucchini, grated
½ teaspoon dried thyme
2 cans (6½ ounces each) water-packed tuna, rinsed and drained
Freshly ground pepper
⅔ cup Provolone cheese, grated

In a medium nonstick skillet, heat oil and sauté garlic and chives until they are semisoft. Add zucchini and thyme, and continue to sauté, tossing occasionally. Mix in tuna and pepper, and cook over a medium heat until hot. Turn off heat, add grated cheese, and mix thoroughly. Serves 12.

EGGPLANT RELISH

Per serving:
49 calories
1 g protein
3 g fat
5 g carb.

Option: Sprinkle
with freshly grated
Parmesan cheese.

2 tablespoons olive oil
1 medium eggplant, peeled and cut into ½-inch cubes
2 cloves fresh garlic, pressed
1 small onion, diced
4 medium tomatoes, chopped
1 cup fresh mushrooms, sliced
½ cup fresh parsley, chopped
½ teaspoon dried oregano
Vegetable salt and freshly ground pepper to taste

Heat oil in a large nonstick skillet, and sauté eggplant with garlic and onion until eggplant is semisoft. Add remaining ingredients, cover, and simmer about 5 minutes until vegetables are done. They should be soft, but not mushy. If liquid accumulates, remove the cover and simmer slowly for a minute or two until mixture has a relishlike consistency. Serves 12.

TOPPING SUGGESTIONS

The following toppings for Egg Pizza are all delicious, natural, and low calorie:

avocado chunks
raw sunflower seeds
artichoke hearts (rinsed and drained)
fresh pineapple chunks
sardines (rinsed and drained)
smoked oysters (rinsed and drained)
tiny shrimp
shredded chicken breast
small chunks of freshly steamed vegetables
shredded part-skim Mozzarella cheese
a shaker of your favorite dried herbs.

8
VEGETABLES

FESTIVE VEGETABLES

Tidbits: Buy an upright steaming rack for vegetables like broccoli and asparagus. It cooks them stalks down while leaving the tips tender.

Add a little freshly squeezed lemon juice or vinegar to the steaming water to help vegetables retain their color.

Add herbs or garlic to the steaming water to give vegetables a more distinctive flavor.

Fabulous healthy vegetables are undisputably one of nature's great food values. They offer fiber, vitamins, minerals, and other essential nutrients in a cornucopia of beautiful, colorful, flavorful shapes and sizes. Instead of considering them necessary side dishes or plate fillers, think of vegetables as a splashy complement to a main dish. Or double the recipe and make vegetables the main dish itself.

The virtue of fresh vegetables is undisputed. Caring for vegetables takes a little know-how. Most fresh vegetables, except leafy ones, store quite well in the refrigerator—a few days to a few weeks. The best method for storing vegetables is to wrap them in paper towels and seal them in airtight containers or plastic bags and place them in the bottom part of the refrigerator where it's least cold and not as likely to freeze.

Steaming, pressure cooking, baking, broiling, or stir-frying are the preferred methods of cooking vegetables. These are the methods that minimize damage to valuable fibers, enzymes, and nutrients. When done just right, vegetables should be tender but crunchy. Steaming requires a pot with a tight-fitting lid, a steam tray, and enough water, usually one inch on the bottom, so that it doesn't evaporate during the cooking time. Pressure cooking is a tricky business, but an excellent and rapid way to cook vegetables. It is best to cook vegetables 30 seconds to 1 minute less than the prescribed cooking time to compensate for the fact that you may be working with smaller sizes or cuts of vegetables. Be sure they're hot and tender-crisp all the way through. Undercooked vegetables are good for you, but overcooked vegetables in comparison are a nutritional waste. You can always pressure-cook them a little longer if necessary.

It's not a good practice to boil most vegetables. This includes broccoli, cauliflower, carrots, eggplant, most squash (especially summer squash), cabbage or brussels sprouts, snap beans and peas, and all greens. The cellulose structure is broken down too quickly, and nutrients are lost in the water. It is okay, however, to boil tuberous vegetables with inedible skins such as turnips, parsnips, and beets. Corn and potatoes are fine parboiled so that they're tender but firm. And always leave the skins on when boiling any of these vegetables (except corn) to protect the inside goodness.

Here's some good news on easy cooking. Microwave ovens do a marvelous job cooking vegetables and baking potatoes. If cooked correctly, vegetables always come out with a perfect texture and color. Arrange vegetables evenly in a microwave-proof dish with about ¼ inch of water on the bottom. Except for corn and asparagus, cook 1 pound of vegetables approximately 10 minutes. As a rule, add on 50 percent more cooking time for each additional pound of vegetable. Corn and asparagus take about half the cooking time of other vegetables. Rearrange vegetables halfway through cooking to assure even doneness. When done, let them stand 2 to 3 minutes with the cover on before serving.

If fresh vegetables are not available, substitute fresh frozen, never canned. Rinse and drain them first to get rid of any excess salt in the packaging process. Cook them in accordance to the time given on the package. It's normally less than the cooking time for fresh vegetables. Pressure-cooking usually takes 30 seconds or less. And many frozen vegetables, such as greens, peas, and corn, are excellent heated through but not overcooked.

Leftover vegetables should be eaten cold (try pouring a little dressing over them) or barely warmed. Heating them through a second time further destroys most of their food value. If you must have them hot, puree or finely chop them and add them to other dishes such as soufflés, omelets, or sauces where precooked vegetables are called for.

Even if you're not a vegetable lover, you'll find these appetizing vegetables, delicately cooked with herbs and spices and accompanying low calorie sauces, hard to pass up. Enjoy them in good health.

Fat Busters: Add a squeeze of fresh lemon juice with a dash of low-sodium tamari to cooked vegetables instead of butter or rich sauces.

Use plain nonfat yogurt with chopped chives on baked potatoes instead of sour cream. When dining out, ask for your baked potato ''au jus'' (with meat juice), instead of the usual fattening toppings.

BROCCOLI WITH CITRUS SHALLOT SAUCE

Per serving:
57 calories
4 g protein
1 g fat
10 g carb.

1½ pounds broccoli stalks
½ cup Poultry Stock (page 70)
1 shallot, finely minced
½ cup freshly squeezed orange juice
2 tablespoons freshly squeezed lemon juice
1 teaspoon each orange and lemon rind, grated
1 rounded teaspoon arrowroot, moistened with 2 tablespoons Poultry Stock
Pinch of vegetable salt

Steam broccoli 20–25 minutes until tender but crunchy (or pressure-cook it approximately 3 minutes). In a small saucepan bring stock to a boil. Lower heat, add the shallot, and simmer 1 minute. Stir in citrus juices and rinds, and simmer for another minute. Add moistened arrowroot to saucepan, and stir until it thickens. Salt to taste. Arrange broccoli in a serving dish, and pour sauce over the top. Serves 6.

KASHA AND CORN-BAKED ZUCCHINI

Per serving:
88 calories
4 g protein
3 g fat
12 g carb.

4 large well-formed zucchini
1 tablespoon corn oil
2 tablespoons onion, finely minced
¼ cup medium-ground uncooked kasha (buckwheat kernels)
½ cup Poultry Stock (page 70); or water
1 cup fresh or frozen corn
¼ cup Münster cheese, shredded
2 tablespoons fresh parsley, chopped
½ teaspoon dried oregano
Pinch of cayenne pepper
Vegetable salt to taste

Halve zucchini lengthwise. Scoop out center, leaving ¼ inch of shell. Chop pulp, and set aside. Heat oil in a large nonstick skillet. Add onion, zucchini pulp, and kasha, and sauté over a low heat for 1 minute. Add stock or water, and bring to a boil. Lower heat, cover, and simmer 10 minutes until kasha is tender.

Remove from heat, and stir in remaining ingredients until well combined. Arrange zucchini in a large shallow baking dish. Spoon equal parts of the corn mixture into zucchini shells. Lay a piece of foil loosely over the top of the zucchini, and bake in a preheated 350° oven for 45 minutes or until zucchini is tender-crisp. Serves 8.

CREOLE CABBAGE

Per serving:
53 calories
2 g protein
0 g fat
10 g carb.

1 can (6 ounces) tomato paste, plus 3 cans water
1 small yellow onion, sliced
1 green pepper, diced
1 rib celery, finely sliced
2 medium tomatoes, peeled, seeded, and chopped
1 small head white cabbage, shredded
2 tablespoons fresh parsley, chopped
1 clove fresh garlic, pressed
¼ teaspoon each dried thyme, marjoram, ground cloves, and cayenne pepper
Vegetable salt and freshly ground pepper to taste

Put all ingredients in a large saucepan. Bring to a boil, lower heat, and simmer covered for 15–20 minutes, or until cabbage is tender-crisp. Serves 8.

GREEN BEAN AND TOMATO STROGANOFF

Per serving:
99 calories
5 g protein
3 g fat
13 g carb.

2 cups fresh green beans, sliced
1 tablespoon butter
2 cloves fresh garlic, pressed
1 large white onion, sliced
1 cup fresh mushrooms, sliced
¼ cup vermouth
1½ cups plain nonfat yogurt
½ cup nonfat milk
2 tablespoons fresh dillweed, minced
2 tablespoons low-sodium tamari
½ teaspoon paprika
2 medium tomatoes, peeled, seeded, and cut into large chunks

Steam green beans in a steam tray for 20 minutes (or pressure-cook them for 2 minutes). Melt butter in large nonstick skillet. Add garlic, onions, and mushrooms, and sauté over a medium low heat until onions and mushrooms are semisoft. Pour in vermouth as needed for braising liquid. Add remaining ingredients, including green beans, and stir until heated through. Serves 6.

STRING BEANS DIJONNAISE

Per serving:
91 calories
5 g protein
6 g fat
6 g carb.

1 pound fresh green beans
1 egg yolk
½ cup Poultry Stock (page 70)
2 small cloves fresh garlic, pressed
1½ tablespoons Dijon mustard

1 teaspoon white wine vinegar
⅛ teaspoon freshly ground pepper
Vegetable salt to taste
¼ cup pignolias (pine nuts)

Rinse beans. Snap off ends, and place them in a steam tray. Steam them for 15–20 minutes until tender-crisp (or pressure-cook 1–2 minutes).

In a double boiler, heat egg yolk with 1 teaspoon of the stock. Pour in remaining stock and garlic, and stir until hot. Add mustard, vinegar, pepper and salt, and stir several minutes until mixture is heated through. Do not boil. Mix green beans and pignolias in a serving dish. Pour in Dijonnaise Sauce, and toss until beans are coated. Serves 4.

TOMATO PUDDING

This is a great little side dish or condiment to serve along with meats.

Per serving:
69 calories
2 g protein
2 g fat
12 g carb.

1 pound ripe tomatoes, peeled, seeded, and chopped
2 teaspoons fresh basil, chopped
3 tablespoons raw sugar
½ cup whole wheat bread crumbs
1 tablespoon butter

Puree tomatoes in a blender with basil and raw sugar. Combine bread crumbs and butter until well mixed. Add tomato puree to bread crumbs, and turn into a 1-quart soufflé or baking dish. Cover and bake in a 350° oven for 1¼ hours. Uncover and bake another 15 minutes. Serves 8.

SWEET AND SOUR CARROTS

Per serving:
88 calories
1 g protein
0 g fat
22 g carb.

¼ cup seedless raisins
½ cup apple cider
¼ cup red wine vinegar
1 tablespoon raw honey
1 tablespoon dry sherry
Pinch each ground cinnamon, cloves, and cardamom
1¼ pounds carrots, steamed and sliced
Vegetable salt and freshly ground pepper to taste

Rinse raisins, then soak them for 1 hour or more in apple cider to plump them up. In a small saucepan, stir vinegar, honey, sherry, and spices together quickly over a low heat until blended. Mix in raisins and cider. Place carrots in a serving dish, and pour sweet-and-sour mixture over the top. Serves 4.

TERIYAKI EGGPLANT

Per serving:
119 calories
2 g protein
9 g fat
7 g carb.

6 Japanese eggplants (about 1¼ pounds), cubed
2 tablespoons sesame oil
1 clove fresh garlic, pressed
⅓ cup sake or mirin (Japanese cooking wine)
3 tablespoons low-sodium tamari
2 tablespoons raw honey
2 teaspoons fresh ginger, finely grated
1 rounded teaspoon sesame seeds

Soak eggplant cubes in water for 10 minutes. Drain and let them dry. Heat oil in a large nonstick skillet or wok. Add garlic and eggplant, and sauté several minutes over a medium low heat until semitender.

Combine remaining ingredients except for sesame seeds and pour in with the eggplant. Continue sautéing until liquid is absorbed. Sprinkle the top with sesame seeds. Serves 4.

CREAMED PARSNIPS IN SAUTERNE

Per serving:
108 calories
3 g protein
5 g fat
13 g carb.

1 pound parsnips
2 tablespoons butter
1 scallion, minced
2 tablespoons fresh parsley, chopped
1 tablespoon fresh chervil, chopped
1 cup low-fat milk
⅓ cup sauterne
¼ teaspoon prepared horseradish
Vegetable salt and freshly ground pepper

Place parsnips in a medium pot with enough water to cover them. Bring to a boil and parboil for 10–15 minutes so that they are tender but still crunchy. Drain, peel, and cut them into 1-inch cubes.

Melt butter in a large nonstick skillet. Add scallion, parsley, and chervil, and quickly sauté over a medium low heat for 1 minute. Pour in milk, and stir until hot. Add parsnip cubes, cover skillet, and simmer for 5–10 minutes until parsnips are nearly tender. Add sauterne, horseradish, and salt and pepper to taste, and stir until hot. Serves 6.

MUSHROOMS AND POTATOES WITH MISO SAUCE

Per serving:
132 calories
4 g protein
3 g fat
24 g carb.

1 tablespoon corn or peanut oil
1 tablespoon whole wheat pastry flour
⅔ cup Meat Stock (page 43)
1 clove fresh garlic, pressed
1 tablespoon fresh parsley, minced
2 tablespoons fresh chives, minced
1 tablespoon light miso (fermented soy paste)
4 large new potatoes (white or rose), sliced ¼-inch thick
1 cup fresh mushrooms, sliced
Freshly grated Parmesan cheese (optional)

Heat oil in a small saucepan and stir in flour. Add stock, garlic, parsley, chives, and miso, and blend over a medium low heat until the resulting Miso Sauce is smooth.

Place potatoes and mushrooms in a small oblong baking dish. Pour in Miso Sauce, and toss them just enough to coat. Arrange them evenly in the baking dish, loosely cover with foil, and bake in a preheated 350° oven for 35 minutes until potatoes are tender crisp. Sprinkle with Parmesan cheese if desired. Serves 6.

SWISS CHARD ROMANO

Per serving:
81 calories
4 g protein
6 g fat
4 g carb.

2 medium bunches Swiss chard (about 1½ pounds)
2 cloves garlic, peeled
2 tablespoons olive oil
2 teaspoons balsamic vinegar
3 tablespoons Romano cheese, freshly grated
Vegetable salt and freshly ground pepper to taste

Rinse Swiss chard and remove thick stems. Arrange leaves in a steam tray. Place it in a large pot with about 1 inch of water and 2 whole cloves of garlic on the bottom. Steam about 10 minutes. Remove steam tray, and let Swiss chard drain well. Place in a serving bowl. Add remaining ingredients and toss until well combined. Serves 4.

ASPARAGUS WITH SAVORY HOLLANDAISE SAUCE

Per serving:
67 calories
3 g protein
5 g fat
4 g carb.

1 bunch asparagus (approximately 1 pound)
1 tablespoon butter
1 egg yolk
2 tablespoons plain nonfat yogurt
½ cup Poultry Stock (page 70)
1 scallion, finely minced
2 teaspoons fresh savory, chopped
⅛ teaspoon cayenne pepper
Vegetable salt to taste

Cut off woody ends of asparagus stalks. Steam them 10–15 minutes (or pressure-cook them 1 minute). Over a double boiler melt butter and stir in egg yolk and yogurt. Continue creaming until hot. Add remaining ingredients and stir until heated through for several minutes. Do not boil. Arrange asparagus on a serving platter and top with the hollandaise sauce. Serves 4.

VEGETABLE LATTICE PIE

Per serving:
124 calories
4 g protein
4 g fat
18 g carb.

3 tablespoons butter
2 carrots, sliced into ¼-inch rounds
1 cup broccoli florets
1 cup cauliflower florets
⅔ cup fresh or frozen lima beans
1 medium onion, coarsely chopped
½ teaspoon each dried basil and savory
1 bay leaf, crumbled
Vegetable salt and freshly ground pepper to taste
3 medium white or sweet potatoes, quartered
2 tablespoons nonfat milk
¼ teaspoon paprika

Melt butter in a large nonstick skillet. Sauté carrots, broccoli, cauliflower, lima beans, onions, and herbs in 2 tablespoons of the butter until vegetables are semitender. Use a little water as needed for braising, but there should be no liquid in the skillet when cooking is done. Season with salt and pepper. Arrange vegetables in a 12-inch square baking dish.

Meanwhile boil or steam potatoes for about 20 minutes. Let them cool, and peel them. In a medium bowl mash potatoes with remaining 1 tablespoon butter, milk, and paprika. Pipe the potatoes through a pastry bag with a large star tip, forming a lattice design over the vegetables. Bake in a 325° oven for about 15 minutes until vegetables are hot. Serves 8.

SPINACH STUFFED ONIONS

Per serving:
158 calories
11 g protein
9 g fat
11 g carb.

4 medium white onions
1 bunch spinach, washed, stems removed
1 egg
⅓ cup plain nonfat yogurt
¾ cup aged cheddar cheese, grated
¼ cup onion, finely chopped
Dash of Tabasco sauce
Vegetable salt and freshly ground pepper to taste

Peel onions and cut a thin slice off the root end of each to make the onion sit level. Then cut a slice off each top and hollow out the onions, leaving about ¼-inch shell. Finely chop ¼ cup of the leftover onion, and set aside.

Chop the spinach and place it in a colander in the sink. Boil a quart of water and pour it over the spinach to wilt it. Drain off any excess water by placing a paper towel over the spinach and pressing it down by hand. Set it aside.

In a small bowl beat the egg, then blend in the yogurt, ¼ cup of the grated cheese, onion, Tabasco, and salt and pepper. Stir in the chopped spinach. Spoon mixture into the onion shells.

Place the onions close together in a 9-inch-square baking dish. Add ½ inch of water in the bottom, cover, and bake in a 350° oven for approximately 1 hour or until onions are semisoft. Remove the cover the last 10 minutes of baking and sprinkle the remaining ¼ cup of the grated cheese over the top of the onion cups. Bake uncovered for the remainder of the time. Serves 4.

BROILED TOMATOES

Per serving:
102 calories
4 g protein
6 g fat
10 g carb.

4 medium ripe tomatoes
4 cloves garlic, peeled
2 tablespoons toasted wheat germ
2 tablespoons Parmesan cheese, freshly grated
1 tablespoon olive oil

Cut tomatoes in half decoratively and arrange them, cut side up, on a flat broiler pan. Cut each clove of garlic into 8 slivers, and stud each tomato half with equal numbers of slivers. In a small bowl toss together wheat germ, Parmesan cheese, and oilive oil. Sprinkle equal amounts of the mixture over the tomato halves and place them under the broiler for approximately 5 minutes or until the tops are toasted. Serves 4.

BAKED WHOLE CAULIFLOWER
WITH TEX-MEX CHEESE SAUCE

Per serving:
88 calories
6 g protein
4 g fat
9 g carb.

1 whole head of cauliflower
1 cup Poultry Stock (page 70)
2 tablespoons whole wheat pastry flour
½ cup nonfat milk
2 tablespoons green onion, finely minced
1 can (4 ounces) green chilies, diced
½ teaspoon ground cumin
Dash Tabasco sauce
½ cup Jarlsberg cheese, grated

Rinse and remove leaves from cauliflower. Cut out tough bottom core. Steam 25–30 minutes or bake covered in a 300° oven for 1 hour.

In a small saucepan, bring stock to a boil. Dissolve flour in milk and add to stock. Lower heat to medium, stirring constantly until mixture begins to thicken slightly. Add remaining ingredients, and stir until cheese has melted. Place cauliflower on a round serving platter. Pour Tex-Mex cheese sauce over the top. Serves 6.

ZUCCHINI TORTE

Per serving:
128 calories
10 g protein
7 g fat
4 g carb.

2 teaspoons butter
3 medium zucchini, thinly sliced
1 cup mushrooms, sliced
1 green onion, finely chopped
1 clove fresh garlic, pressed
Vegetable salt to taste
1 egg
1 cup part-skim ricotta cheese
1 sprig parsley, chopped
½ teaspoon dried marjoram
¼ teaspoon dried tarragon
3 ounces Fontina cheese, shredded

Melt butter in a medium nonstick skillet. Lightly sauté zucchini, mushrooms, onion, and garlic until vegetables are semitender. Use a little water if needed for liquid. Set aside.

In a small bowl beat egg and combine with ricotta, parsley, and herbs. In a lightly oiled torte pan, place half the zucchini and mushrooms evenly on the bottom. Spread the ricotta mixture over it, and top with remaining zucchini and mushrooms. Sprinkle with the shredded cheese, and bake in a preheated 400° oven for 20 minutes. Serves 6.

GARBANZO BEAN SALAD
WITH SUN-DRIED TOMATOES

Per serving:
218 calories
8 g protein
11 g fat
23 g carb.

1½ cups dry garbanzo beans
1 large cucumber, peeled, seeded, and chopped
1 green bell pepper, diced
1 cup sun-dried tomatoes
⅓ cup extra virgin olive oil
3 tablespoons balsamic vinegar
1 tablespoon dry red wine
1 clove fresh garlic, pressed
2 tablespoons fresh mint, snipped
1 tablespoon each fresh basil and parsley, snipped
Vegetable salt and freshly ground pepper to taste

Rinse and drain garbanzo beans. Soak them in enough water to cover overnight. In a medium kettle or stockpot, bring garbanzo beans to a boil for 5 minutes. Make sure there is enough water to cover them. Lower heat and simmer covered for 2 hours.

Drain and add them to a large serving container with cucumber, green pepper, and tomatoes. Combine remaining ingredients and add to the salad. Toss well, being careful not to break the skin of the beans. Cover and chill several hours before serving to marinate. Serves 8.

ZUCCHINI AND TOMATOES
WITH WINE AND HERBS

Per serving:
37 calories
1 g protein
0 g fat
6 g carb.

1 pound zucchini, sliced into ½-inch rounds
3 cloves garlic, peeled
¾ pound tomatoes, peeled, seeded, and quartered
¼ cup dry red wine
1 scallion, chopped
3 tablespoons fresh basil, minced
2 tablespoons fresh oregano, minced
Vegetable salt and freshly ground pepper to taste
4 large leaves green leaf lettuce

Steam zucchini in a steam tray with garlic cloves for approximately 10 minutes, until slices are slightly crunchy. In a medium nonstick saucepan, heat tomatoes with red wine, scallion, and herbs. Cook over a low heat for 1 or 2 minutes, but do not allow them to overcook and turn to pulp. When tomatoes are heated through but firm, combine the steamed zucchini. Serve hot or chilled over 4 individual beds of lettuce. Serves 4.

ACORN SQUASH FILLED WITH FESTIVE FRUITS

Per serving:
223 calories
3 g protein
4 g fat
46 g carb.

2 small acorn squash
1 tablespoon freshly squeezed orange juice
½ teaspoon orange peel, grated
1 orange, peeled and chopped
1 pear, peeled, cored, and diced
½ cup fresh cranberries, coarsely chopped
½ cup dates, pitted and chopped
8 cloves
⅛ teaspoon ground ginger
1 tablespoon butter, melted
1 tablespoon raw honey
Sprinkle of freshly ground nutmeg

Cut squash in half. Do not remove seeds. Place cut side down in a large flat baking dish. Add ½ cup of water, and bake at 350° for 45 minutes or until tender-crisp. Let the squash cool and scoop out the seeds.

In a medium bowl combine the remaining ingredients except for nutmeg. Place the squash, flesh side up, in the baking dish, and fill each cavity with one quarter of the fruit mixture. Sprinkle the top with nutmeg and bake loosely covered for another 30 minutes or until fruit is just tender.

Add a little more water to the bottom of the baking dish if drying occurs. During the last few minutes of baking, remove the cover, and broil until the tops are lightly browned. Serves 4.

BUTTERNUT SPROUTS

Per serving:
105 calories
5 g protein
7 g fat
8 g carb.

1 cup Poultry Stock (page 70)
2 pounds brussels sprouts, washed and trimmed
1 tablespoon butter
¼ cup onion, chopped
½ cup pecans, chopped
1 tablespoon low-sodium tamari

In a small saucepan bring stock to a boil. Add sprouts, cover, and simmer 6–8 minutes until tender-crisp. In a small nonstick sauté pan, melt butter, and sauté onions several minutes until translucent. Mix in pecans and tamari. Toss mixture with brussels sprouts in a serving dish. Makes 8 servings.

WILD RICE AND VEGETABLE DRESSING

Per serving:
171 calories
6 g protein
7 g fat
23 g carb.

Note: The rice may
be cooked in Poultry
Stock instead of
water. Since you are
preparing 3 cups of
each kind of rice,
remember to triple
the amounts of
water and rice
proportionally when
following the
recommended
cooking methods.

3 tablespoons butter
2 medium onions, chopped
4 cloves fresh garlic, pressed
3 cups fresh mushrooms, sliced
2 cups broccoli florets, separated into very small pieces
1½ cups carrots, diced
1 cup celery, chopped
¼ cup fresh parsley, chopped
1 cup pine nuts
3 cups cooked wild rice (see Cream of Turkey Soup, page 74, for cooking method)
3 cups cooked brown rice (see Pork-Stuffed Whole Cabbage, page 42 for cooking
    method)
1 tablespoon poultry seasoning (or to taste)
Vegetable salt and freshly ground pepper to taste
Poultry Stock (page 70)

Melt butter in a large nonstick skillet. Lightly sauté onions, garlic, mushrooms, broccoli, carrots, and celery until vegetables are semitender. Toss in
parsley and pine nuts, and combine everything along with wild and brown
rice in a very large bowl or roasting pan.

Add poultry seasoning and salt and pepper. Use stock as needed for
liquid. Toss until seasoning is well blended. Makes enough dressing for one
12–14-pound turkey or 16 servings.

CHILLED EGGPLANT WITH COTTAGE CHEESE PESTO

Per serving:
127 calories
12 g protein
5 g fat
9 g carb.

¼ cup pignolias (pine nuts) or walnuts
3 cloves garlic, peeled
1 cup low-fat cottage cheese
4 cups fresh basil leaves, packed
1 cup fresh parsley leaves, packed
1 green onion, chopped
Vegetable salt and freshly ground pepper to taste
1 large eggplant, peeled and quartered

In a blender or food processor finely chop nuts and garlic. Add remaining
ingredients except eggplant, and blend until leaves are tiny flecks. Cover
tightly and chill overnight. Place eggplant in a steam tray and steam approximately 12–15 minutes so that it is still firm. Cool and chill it.

To serve, slice eggplant lengthwise and arrange it on a platter. Spoon
Pesto over it, and garnish with extra parsley if desired. Makes 4 servings.

GLAZED PEAS AND CARROTS WITH MINT

Per serving:
55 calories
2 g protein
2 g fat
8 g carb.

1 cup fresh shelled peas
1 pound carrots, peeled and cut into ½ x 2-inch lengths
1 tablespoon butter
1 teaspoon raw honey
2 tablespoons fresh mint, minced
1 tablespoon fresh thyme, minced
Sea salt to taste

Steam peas and carrots in a steam tray for 10–15 minutes until they are tender-crisp. In a small sauté pan, melt butter with honey over a low heat, and add mint and thyme. Place peas and carrots in a serving dish, and toss with glaze. Makes 6 servings.

VEGETABLE MEDLEY WITH TANGY CHEESE SAUCE

Cheese Sauce:

Per serving:
121 calories
7 g protein
8 g fat
6 g carb.

2 tablespoons butter
1 cup nonfat milk
1 cup aged cheddar cheese, grated
1 egg yolk
1 teaspoon freshly squeezed lemon juice
1 teaspoon Dijon mustard
½ teaspoon freshly ground white pepper
Vegetable salt to taste

In a small saucepan melt butter over a medium heat. Add milk and cheese. When cheese has melted, stir in egg yolk. Do not boil. Continue stirring 3 minutes until thick. Add lemon juice, mustard, and seasonings, and stir for 1 minute more. Remove from heat, and let it stand for 10 minutes to allow it to thicken.

Vegetables:

1 large stalk broccoli (florets only)
½ head cauliflower (florets only)
½ pound brussels sprouts, washed and trimmed

Place vegetables in a steam tray in the bottom of a large pot or saucepan. Steam them for 10–15 minutes (or pressure-cook them approximately 1½–2 minutes) until tender-crisp. Arrange them in a shallow casserole dish and pour cheese sauce over the top. Serves 8.

CRAB-STUFFED ARTICHOKES

Per serving:
216 calories
16 g protein
12 g fat
14 g carb.

2 large globe artichokes
1 tablespoon olive oil
1 clove fresh garlic, pressed
¼ cup celery, finely chopped
1 tablespoon pimientos, chopped
3 tablespoons plain nonfat yogurt
½ teaspoon Dijon mustard
¼ cup aged Swiss cheese, shredded
3 ounces cooked crab (fresh or frozen), shredded
½ teaspoon paprika

Wash artichokes by dipping them vigorously in water. With a sharp knife, cut ¼ inch off the tops to remove the thorny tips. Cut the stalks off flush with the bottom. Press the artichokes hard upside down to force the leaves apart. Separate the outer leaves from the center but do not break them off. Hold artichoke in one hand with a dish towel. Then with a sharp rigid paring knife, cut out fuzzy choke. Peel off the tough bottom row of leaves.

Tie a string around each artichoke to hold it together. Steam them for 30–35 minutes (or pressure-cook them for 8–10 minutes). Turn them upside down to drain.

Meanwhile, heat olive oil in a nonstick sauté pan. Over a medium low heat, lightly sauté garlic with celery. Add pimientos, and toss until celery becomes tender-crisp. Remove from the heat, and stir in remaining ingredients.

Spoon crab filling into artichoke centers, and set them in a small baking dish with ½ inch of water on the bottom. If there is any filling left, spoon it in between the artichoke leaves. Loosely cover tops with foil and bake in a 350° oven for 15 minutes. Remove foil and bake another 10 minutes to brown tops. Serve with Creamy Louis Sauce (see below). Makes 2 servings.

CREAMY LOUIS SAUCE

Per serving:
147 calories
3 g protein
12 g fat
8 g carb.

Tasty note: This sauce is also excellent on seafood such as shrimp and lobster as well as other cooked vegetables.

½ cup plain nonfat yogurt
2 tablespoons safflower oil mayonnaise
2 tablespoons tomato sauce
1 teaspoon freshly squeezed lemon juice
1 tablespoon chives, minced
½ teaspoon prepared horseradish
1 teaspoon low-sodium tamari

Combine all ingredients together well and refrigerate in an airtight container. Serve on the side for dipping artichokes. Makes about 1 cup, enough for 2 servings.

MEATLESS CLASSICS

How do you handle a healthy appetite? By eating hearty, of course. But hearty doesn't always mean heavy, especially when long-term leanness is the goal. These meatless classics are low in calories, yet as satisfying and tasty as meatier versions, with seasonings as the key to flavor.

They're packed with power beause what they lack in meat, they make up for in protein from other sources. Some of the recipe ideas have been borrowed from ethnic cooking, which traditionally relies on staples other than meat for protein. Eggs, cheeses, grains, and legumes all add up to a high quality nutritious source of protein that many foreign countries have thrived on for centuries.

Economy-wise they can't be beat. Eliminating meat cuts down on cost. Serve these casseroles as a main dish accompanied by a green salad and some delicious whole grain bread, or as a side dish when meat is the focus. You can even *add* meat to any of these casseroles for extra protein and flavor, and stretch the servings to 6 or 8 to wow a crowd in one easy dish.

VEGETARIAN TAMALE PIE

Filling:

Per serving:
343 calories
11 g protein
17 g fat
42 g carb.

1 tablespoon safflower or olive oil
1 large onion, finely chopped
2 cloves fresh garlic, pressed
1 can (6 ounces) tomato paste, plus 2½ cans water
1 pound ripe tomatoes, peeled and coarsely chopped
2 green bell peppers, diced
1 package (10 ounces) frozen corn; or fresh corn from 2 large ears
1 can (4 ounces) sliced ripe olives, rinsed and drained
1 heaping tablespoon chili powder
½ teaspoon each dried thyme, oregano, and cumin seeds
1 teaspoon raw honey
Vegetable salt and freshly ground pepper to taste

Heat oil in a large saucepan over a medium heat, and sauté onion and garlic. Add tomato paste with water, and stir well. When sauce becomes hot, add tomatoes, peppers, corn, olives, seasonings and honey, and simmer until vegetables are semitender. The filling should be slightly thick, but add more water if it becomes too dry. Pour mixture into a roasting pan or a large ovenproof dish.

Topping:

> *²/₃ cup stone-ground yellow cornmeal*
> *2²/₃ cups water*
> *Pinch of sea salt*
> *½ cup aged cheddar cheese, grated*

In a large saucepan bring cornmeal, water, and salt to a boil. Boil 5 minutes, then lower heat to simmer, cover, and cook slowly for 25 minutes until cornmeal becomes a thick mush. Spoon cornmeal mush evenly over the tamale mixture, then sprinkle the top with grated cheese. Bake loosely covered with foil in a 350° oven for 50 minutes, or until the casserole is heated through. Uncover the last 10 minutes of baking to brown the cheese slightly. Serves 4.

ZUCCHINI PATTIES

Per patty:
101 calories
6 g protein
4 g fat
10 g carb.

> *½ cup toasted wheat germ*
> *2 tablespoons toasted bran*
> *¼ cup Romano cheese, freshly grated*
> *1½ cups zucchini, shredded*
> *½ cup white potato, boiled and mashed*
> *2 eggs, beaten*
> *1 teaspoon fresh oregano, minced*
> *Vegetable salt and freshly ground pepper to taste*

Shake wheat germ, bran, and Romano cheese to mix in a plastic bag. In a medium bowl combine zucchini, potato, eggs, oregano, and salt and pepper. Add wheat germ mixture to zucchini mixture, and combine well. Form 6 hamburger size patties, and arrange on a nonstick baking sheet. Bake in a preheated 425° oven for 12–15 minutes until patties are solid and golden brown. Makes 6 patties.

SPINACH LASAGNA

Per serving (including sauce):
374 calories
31 g protein
14 g fat
27 g carb.

4 ounces spinach lasagna noodles, cooked according to directions on package
1 pound part-skim ricotta cheese
2 eggs
1 bunch spinach leaves steamed; or 1 package (10 ounces) frozen
3 cups Marinara Sauce (below)
2 ounces part-skim Mozzarella cheese, thinly sliced
¼ cup Parmesan cheese, freshly grated

While lasagna noodles are boiling, mash ricotta with 1 egg in a small bowl and set aside. In another bowl, mix 1 egg and spinach together, and set aside.

In a 9-inch-square baking dish, spoon in a little of the sauce. Place half the lasagna noodles on the bottom, overlapping them a little. Spread half the ricotta mixture over the noodles, topping evenly with half the Mozzarella cheese. Spoon in half the spinach mixture, then half of the sauce. Repeat layering, ending with the remaining sauce.

Sprinkle the top with Parmesan cheese. Bake loosely covered in a preheated 350° oven for 40–45 minutes or until lasagna is heated through. Uncover, and let it stand in the oven for 15 minutes before serving. Serves 4.

MARINARA SAUCE

Per cup:
154 calories
4 g protein
6 g fat
24 g carb.

1 tablespoon olive oil
2 cloves fresh garlic, pressed
3 cans (8 ounces each) tomato puree
¼ cup dry red wine
½ teaspoon dried basil
¼ teaspoon dried oregano
1 bay leaf
1 sprig parsley, minced
1 teaspoon raw honey
Vegetable salt to taste

In a medium saucepan, heat oil, and lightly sauté garlic. Add remaining ingredients, cover, and simmer sauce for 35–40 minutes. Add a little water if sauce should become too dry. Makes about 3 cups.

ZIPPY VEGETABLE PILAF CASSEROLE

Per serving:
393 calories
21 g protein
14 g fat
42 g carb.

Quick-cooking note:
You may also use
quick-cooking
brown rice for this
recipe. Use the
appropriate quantity
and follow the
directions for
cooking on the
package.

2 cups summer squash, sliced
1 red bell pepper, diced
1 small onion, chopped
1 can (4 ounces) green chilies, chopped
1 sprig parsley, minced
1 clove fresh garlic, pressed
1 cup uncooked bulgur
2 cups water (or Poultry Stock, page 70)
Vegetable salt and freshly ground pepper to taste
4 eggs
1 cup nonfat milk
1 cup Monterey Jack cheese, shredded

Combine vegetables, parsley, garlic, bulgur, and water (or Poultry Stock) in a large saucepan. Bring to a boil, then reduce heat, and simmer for 15 minutes.

Meanwhile, in a separate bowl beat eggs with milk and combine with cheese. Stir into vegetable-bulgur mixture when done, and pour into a 9-inch-square nonstick baking pan. Bake uncovered in a 350° oven for 30 minutes or until set. Let it stand 15 minutes before serving. Serves 4.

LENTIL LOAF WITH FRESH TOMATO SAUCE

Per serving:
184 calories
7 g protein
8 g fat
23 g carb.

Lentil Loaf:

½ recipe for Lentil Soup (page 153)
⅓ cup uncooked quick-cooking oats

Mix soup and oats together. Turn into a nonstick loaf pan, and bake uncovered in a 350° oven for 45 minutes. Top with sauce.

Fresh Tomato Sauce:

2 peeled and seeded ripe tomatoes
6 basil leaves
1 tablespoon chopped onion
1 tablespoon olive oil
Vegetable salt and freshly ground pepper to taste

Whir ingredients together in a blender. This tasty uncooked version of tomato sauce is marvelous on other casserole dishes as well. Serves 4.

SOY—THE HIGH-PROTEIN ALTERNATIVE

Fat Buster: Try
this Egg-Free
Mayonnaise made
with tofu. In a
blender, combine
½ cup soft tofu with
1 teaspoon Dijon
mustard and a pinch
of cayenne pepper.
Blend while adding
1½ tablespoons
freshly squeezed
lemon juice and
¼ cup safflower oil.
May be kept
refrigerated for 2 or
3 days.

   Cut peanut
butter calories
nearly in half by
blending equal
portions of soft tofu
and peanut butter
together until
creamy. Use it as
you would regular
peanut butter.

Soybeans and soybean products are becoming an increasingly popular food on the culinary scene. Not long ago, before their popularity arose, they were (and still are) an obscure addition to countless commercial products calling for a high protein or vegetable base and in Asia a staple food for centuries. But now they are considered an excellent alternative to eating meat because of their exceptionally high protein content and nutty meatlike taste.

Although soybeans are not a complete protein and should be supplemented with other protein foods or additional amino acids, their protein content is the highest of all legumes. One cup of cooked soybeans contains 22 grams of protein. Concentrated forms, such as protein powders, contain that much protein in ¼ cup. Soybeans and their by-products provide 8 to 10 grams of protein for every hundred calories. Calorie for calorie, they offer more usable protein than sirloin steak, eggs, and whole milk.

Soybeans are also extremely high in B vitamin complex, calcium, phosphorus, potassium, magnesium, and iron. They contain large amounts of linoleic acid, and unsaturated fatty acid essential to the human body. Soy milk is recommended for people who are allergic to cow's milk; it is low in fat and carbohydrates, and high in iron, thiamine, and niacin. Soy oil contains lecithin and vitamin E. Sprouted soybeans contain increased amounts of vitamin C and B vitamins.

There are numerous by-products of the soybean (as well as the soybean itself) with which you can do many things:

Tofu or bean curd is the pulpy custardlike product derived from soy milk.

Tempeh is made by inoculating cooked soybeans with a special culture and incubating them for twenty-four hours. It is firm and chewy with a mild meatlike taste. It is similar to tofu in its uses. Both are good mixed with eggs, added to meat, vegetable, or cheese dishes, or eaten alone cooked in various ways.

Okara, or soy pulp, is the solid material left after soy milk has been prepared. It is used as a nutritive filler or extender for various dishes and as a base for soy protein powders.

Soy grits are coarsely ground, uncooked soybeans. They are added to wheat or rice pilaf or to baked goods as a nutritional booster.

Soy flakes are made from lightly toasted soybeans and are also used in baking, or sprinkled on top of dishes for a nutty flavor.

Soy flour is made from ground soybeans and is used in baking in conjunction with wheat flour.

Soy milk is the liquid compound of soybeans and water. Use it as you would regular milk.

Soy oil is the strong, aromatic cooking oil derived from soybeans. Unrefined, it is best mixed with other milder oils.

Soy sauce, shoyu, tamari, and miso are fermented, rich-flavored by-products made from soybeans. They are used as seasonings or condiments and are quite high in salt. They are good, but use them sparingly.

Whole cooked soybeans, of course, make high-protein bean dishes and take on the flavor of other seasonings as well. The uses for soybeans and soybean by-products are endless, as are their exceptional nutritional values. In this section are some recipes that offer you just a few ways to use soy products.

CARROT PIE

Crust:

Per serving:
307 calories
15 g protein
12 g fat
36 g carb.

3 tablespoons soy protein powder
1⅔ cups whole wheat pastry flour
¼ cup butter
6 tablespoons cold water

Sift protein powder and flour together in a medium bowl. Cut in butter with a fork or pastry blender. Add water, a little at a time, and bring dough together to form a smooth nonsticky ball. Chill 10 minutes. Roll out on wax paper to make a 12-inch circle. Invert crust into a 9-inch pie tin and gently press into pan. Trim and crimp edge. Prick bottom dough with a fork. (If you want, use dried beans or pie weights to keep bottom dough from rising.) Bake in a preheated 350° oven for 10 minutes. Let it cool.

Filling:

1 teaspoon butter
⅔ cup yellow onions, chopped
¼ cup whole wheat flour
1 cup freshly squeezed orange juice
1 tablespoon unsalted almond butter
¼ teaspoon freshly ground nutmeg
3 tablespoons soy protein powder, moistened with ¼ cup water
3 cups carrots, diced and steamed
2 tablespoons black olives, sliced
Sprigs of thyme

Melt butter in a medium nonstick sauté pan. Add onions, and sauté over a medium heat until they are translucent. Stir in flour, and brown. Add orange juice, almond butter, and nutmeg, and stir until mixture thickens. Stir in moistened protein powder. Add carrots, and mix well. Remove from heat, and turn into prepared crust. Garnish with black olives and sprigs of thyme. Bake in a 350° oven for 35 minutes. Serves 8.

TOFUBURGERS

Per burger (without bun):
109 calories
9 g protein
44 g fat
10 g carb.

2 eggs, beaten
½ cup soft tofu, drained
½ cup onion, finely chopped
½ teaspoon dried basil
¼ teaspoon dried oregano
⅛ teaspoon freshly ground pepper
2 tablespoons Parmesan cheese, freshly grated
½ cup cooked brown rice (see page 195 for cooking method)
½ cup whole grain bread crumbs
2 tablespoons soy protein powder
6 Seven-Grain Sprouted Wheat Buns (page 180)

Mash eggs and tofu together in a large bowl. Blend in onion and herbs. Add grated cheese, brown rice, bread crumbs, and protein powder, and mix well.

Form 6 patties, and arrange them on a lightly oiled aluminum baking sheet. Loosely cover tops of burgers with foil, and bake in a preheated 350° oven for 20–25 minutes. Lift off foil the last 5 minutes of baking to brown tops. Serve on Wheat Buns with appropriate hamburger garnishes and condiments. Makes 6 Tofuburgers.

Per serving:
302 calories
21 g protein
20 g fat
11 g carb.

Nutritional note:
This is a wheat-free casserole. If you also wish to eliminate milk, replace the cheese with ½ cup soft tofu. Add additional yeast to taste for a nutrition boost.

Note: You may cut the amounts of water and rice in half proportionally when following the recommended cooking method.

HIGH PRO MUSHROOM CASSEROLE

1 tablespoon each sesame and safflower oil
4 scallions, minced
1 pound fresh mushrooms, sliced
1 cup soy milk
2 tablespoons soy protein powder, plus 1 tablespoon nutritional yeast (optional)
3 eggs, beaten
¾ cup aged Swiss cheese, grated
½ cup cooked wild rice (see Cream of Turkey Soup, page 74, for cooking method)
1 teaspoon dried savory
¼ teaspoon ground turmeric and paprika
Vegetable salt to taste
1 tablespoon sesame seeds

Heat oil in a large nonstick skillet. Sauté scallions and mushrooms over a medium heat until soft. In a medium bowl blend soy milk and protein powder together until smooth. Stir in eggs. Add remaining ingredients, and mix everything in together, except sesame seeds. Combine with mushrooms and scallions, and turn into a lightly oiled, 1½-quart casserole dish. Bake for 25 minutes in a 375° oven. Sprinkle sesame seeds over the top the last 10 minutes of baking. Serves 4.

SOY PIZZA with the WORKS

Crust:

Per serving:
434 calories
24 g protein
14 g fat
63 g carb.

¾ cup warm water
1½ teaspoons raw honey
1 tablespoon active dry yeast
1½ tablespoon olive oil
2 cups whole wheat flour
⅔ cup soy flour

In a medium bowl combine water, honey, and yeast, and let it stand about 5 minutes to proof. Add oil and flours, and mix into a firm ball. Turn out onto a floured surface, and knead until smooth and elastic, adding additional wheat flour if needed.

Place dough in a lightly oiled bowl, cover with a damp cloth, and let it rise in a warm place until doubled in bulk, about 1 hour. Punch down dough, knead several times, cover, and let it rise again until doubled in bulk.

Starting with a ball, roll it into a circle with a rolling pin to fit a 16-inch-round pizza pan. Crimp or turn up about 1 inch around the edge. Allow dough to rise again for another 30 minutes on pan.

Filling:

2 teaspoons olive oil
1 clove fresh garlic, pressed
¼ cup dry red wine
3 tablespoons soy protein powder, moistened with ¼ cup water
⅔ cup tomato sauce
1 tablespoon tomato paste
½ teaspoon each dried marjoram and rosemary

In a small nonstick skillet, heat oil and briefly sauté garlic. Add wine and reduce to a glaze. Add moistened soy protein, tomato sauce, tomato paste, and herbs. Spread mixture over pizza dough.

Topping:

¾ cup each fresh mushrooms and onions, sliced
½ cup each diced tomatoes and green pepper
½ cup artichoke hearts, chopped
¼ cup black olives, sliced
Fresh basil, snipped, and freshly ground pepper to taste

Arrange ingredients over the top of the filling. Sprinkle with basil and pepper. Bake pizza in a preheated 400° oven for 20–25 minutes. Serves 4.

TOFU MOUSSAKA

Per serving:
290 calories
24 g protein
15 g fat
18 g carb.

1 tablespoon olive oil
1 medium onion, finely chopped
3 cloves fresh garlic, pressed
8 fresh mushrooms, sliced
1 sprig parsley, minced
1 teaspoon each dried mint and oregano
½ teaspoon red pepper flakes
8 ounces firm tofu
Vegetable salt to taste
1 cup low-fat cottage cheese
1 egg
½ cup Monterey Jack cheese, grated
⅛ teaspoon nutmeg
1 large eggplant, peeled and sliced ½ inch thick
4 large tomatoes, sliced
¼ cup raw sunflower seeds

In a large nonstick skillet, heat oil and sauté onion, garlic, mushrooms, parsley, mint, oregano, and pepper flakes. Add a little water if necessary for liquid. When onions and mushrooms are semisoft, stir in the tofu, breaking it up into small pieces. Set the mixture aside. In a medium bowl, combine cottage cheese, egg, cheese, and nutmeg, and set it aside.

In a 9 x 13-inch nonstick baking pan, lay half the eggplant slices flat on the bottom. Lay half the sliced tomatoes over the eggplant. Spoon in the entire tofu mixture, spreading it evenly over the layers. Repeat layering with the last half of the eggplant and tomatoes. Then spoon in the entire cottage cheese mixture, spreading it evenly over the top.

Loosely cover with foil and bake in a 350° oven for approximately 1 hour, or until a knife can easily penetrate the bottom layer of the casserole. Uncover the last 10 minutes of baking, sprinkle with sunflower seeds, and brown the top. Serves 4.

LAYERED VEGETABLE TOFU MOLD

Carrot Layer:

Per serving:
147 calories
12 g protein
8 g fat
6 g carb.

1 egg, beaten
¼ teaspoon curry powder
1 teaspoon low-sodium tamari
½ teaspoon freshly squeezed lemon juice
⅔ cup pureed raw carrots, drained

Combine all ingredients together and spoon into the bottom of a lightly oiled 1-quart decorative ring or mold, smoothing the surface evenly.

Spinach Layer:

2 bunches spinach leaves, chopped
2 eggs, beaten
¼ cup nonfat yogurt
1 teaspoon fresh basil, chopped
2 teaspoons low-sodium tamari

Wilt spinach by placing it in a colander and pouring boiling water over it. Drain thoroughly. Combine spinach with the remainder of ingredients. Spoon on top of carrot layer, smoothing the surface evenly.

Tofu Layer:

½ pound soft tofu, drained
1 egg, beaten
1 teaspoon onion, finely grated
1 small clove fresh garlic, pressed
2 teaspoons low-sodium tamari

Mash tofu and mix in remaining ingredients. Spoon on top of spinach layer, again smoothing the surface evenly. Loosely cover top with foil and place mold inside a larger pan with water in it halfway up the side of the mold. Bake in a preheated 350° oven for 1–1¼ hours, or until a knife comes out clean. Cool, and invert onto a serving platter lined with a bed of lettuce leaves if desired. Serve chilled. Makes 4 servings.

GARDEN SOUPS

Tidbit: Dice a yellow
onion, sprinkle with
a little low-sodium
seasoning salt,
spread it out on a
baking sheet or foil,
and bake it in a 450°
oven until bits are
dry and golden.
They're wonderful
for sprinkling over
soups, or even
meats, casseroles,
and salads.

The secret to a good soup, especially vegetable soup, is in the stock, proving once again that stock reigns supreme. It is recommended that you do use stock instead of water for your base, or your soup won't be quite tasty enough. A fat-free stock or broth has only 25 to 35 calories per cup—not bad for all that flavor.

All of these soups are rich in flavor and thickened with vegetables or potatoes, not flour. Of course, if you want a thicker stew, you may moisten a little whole wheat pastry flour with stock or water and add it to the soup.

A rich, savory vegetable soup, served with a wedge of sharp cheese or a dollop of yogurt and complemented with some crusty whole grain bread, is sure to make a peasant feel like a king. And it's an ideal meal for anyone who doesn't want to fuss. These thick hearty soups are economical and blender-quick, and make a wonderful potpourri for vegetable leftovers or other asides such as meat or grains.

CREAMY GARDEN BISQUE

Per serving:
58 calories
3 g protein
1 g fat
10 g carb.

2 cups Poultry Stock (page 70)
2 carrots, diced
1 cup wax beans, sliced
2 ribs celery with leaves, sliced
1 large potato, diced
1 large white onion, chopped
1 clove fresh garlic, pressed
1 tablespoon fresh dill, chopped
½ cup nonfat milk
½ cup plain nonfat yogurt
⅓ cup dry white wine
Vegetable salt and freshly ground pepper to taste

In a medium stockpot or kettle, bring stock, vegetables, and herbs to a boil. Lower heat, cover, and simmer for 45 minutes until vegetables are semitender. Mash a few pieces of potatoes in the soup base to thicken it. Add milk, yogurt, wine, and salt and pepper, and stir until hot. Serve hot. Serves 8.

CHEDDAR CHEESE AND CORN CHOWDER

Per serving:
137 calories
7 g protein
5 g fat
17 g carb.

2 cups Poultry Stock (page 70)
1 medium potato, peeled and shredded
¼ cup red bell pepper, finely chopped
1 cup fresh or frozen corn
½ cup aged cheddar cheese, shredded
⅛ teaspoon paprika
Vegetable salt to taste

In a medium saucepan, bring stock and shredded potato to a boil. Lower heat, cover, and simmer 8–10 minutes. Puree mixture in a food processor or blender, then pour mixture back into the saucepan. Add bell pepper and corn, and simmer 5 minutes. Remove from heat, and sprinkle in cheese, paprika, and vegetable salt while still hot. Stir for 1 minute. Serves 4.

COLD CARROT AND POTATO VICHY

Per serving:
81 calories
5 g protein
1 g fat
14 g carb.

3 cups Poultry Stock (page 70)
2 cups leeks, finely chopped
1 cup potatoes, peeled and diced
1 cup carrots, diced
1 cup plain nonfat yogurt
Vegetable salt and freshly ground pepper to taste
1 tablespoon each fresh dill and parsley, snipped

In a large saucepan bring stock, leeks, potatoes, and carrots to a boil. Lower heat, and simmer about 30 minutes until potatoes and carrots are tender. Puree mixture in a food processor or blender, and chill. Just before serving, stir in yogurt and salt and pepper to taste. Sprinkle top with snipped dill and parsley. Serves 6.

SUMMER SQUASH SOUP

Per serving:
72 calories
5 g protein
2 g fat
10 g carb.

2 cups Poultry Stock (page 70)
1 pound yellow summer squash, chopped
½ white onion, chopped
1 cup low-fat milk
¼ teaspoon freshly grated nutmeg
Sea salt and freshly ground white pepper to taste

In a medium saucepan, bring stock, squash, and onion to a boil. Lower heat, cover, and simmer for 10–12 minutes. Puree mixture in a food processor or blender. Pour it back into the saucepan, and add remaining ingredients. Stir over a medium low heat until hot and butter is melted. Sprinkle top with extra nutmeg if desired. Serves 4.

HERBED TOMATO SOUP

Per serving:
121 calories
7 g protein
4 g fat
17 g carb.

1 tablespoon olive oil
1 medium onion, chopped
2 cups Meat Stock (page 43)
1½ pounds ripe tomatoes, peeled, seeded, and chopped
1 teaspoon each fresh basil, oregano, savory, and thyme, chopped
1 tablespoon fresh parsley, chopped
½ cup low-fat milk
Vegetable salt and freshly ground pepper to taste
Freshly grated Parmesan cheese (optional)

Heat oil in a large saucepan. Sauté onion for 1 minute over a low heat. Add stock, half of the tomatoes, and all the herbs, and bring to a boil. Lower heat, cover, and simmer for about 5 minutes.

Puree mixture in a food processor or blender with the milk, then pour it back into the saucepan. Add remaining tomatoes, and simmer several minutes until soup is hot. Serve sprinkled with Parmesan cheese if desired. Makes 4 servings.

CREAM OF BROCCOLI SOUP

Per serving:
78 calories
4 g protein
5 g fat
6 g carb.

2 tablespoons butter
3 shallots, finely minced
3 cups Poultry Stock (page 70)
3 cups broccoli florets
1 tablespoon each fresh basil and marjoram, chopped
⅔ cup nonfat milk
1 tablespoon low-sodium tamari
Freshly ground pepper to taste

Melt butter in a medium saucepan. Add shallots, and sauté briefly over a low heat. Add stock, broccoli, and herbs, and bring to a boil. Lower heat, partially cover, and simmer for 12–15 minutes. With a slotted spoon, strain out about half of the broccoli chunks and puree the remainder in a blender or food processor with milk. Pour it back into the soup, add the tamari, and season it with pepper. Serves 6.

CREAMY GAZPACHO

Per serving:
90 calories
4 g protein
4 g fat
11 g carb.

Cool option: Just
before serving, whir
again in the blender
with 1 cup crushed
ice.

2 cups chopped tomatoes, peeled and seeded
2 medium cucumbers, peeled and seeded
½ cup kefir (fermented cow's milk); or buttermilk
1 tablespoon freshly squeezed lime juice
½ ripe avocado, cut into chunks
1 green onion, chopped
1 clove garlic, chopped
1 tablespoon fresh basil, chopped
Vegetable salt and freshly ground pepper to taste
Cilantro sprigs

Process everything, except for cilantro, in a food processor or blender until tomatoes are tiny flecks. Chill and serve garnished with sprigs of cilantro. Serves 4.

LENTIL SOUP

There are many lentil soup variations, but this one is number one.

Per serving:
141 calories
7 g protein
5 g fat
19 g carb.

1 cup dry lentils
4 cups water
2 cloves garlic, finely minced
1 medium onion, diced
2 small ribs celery with leaves, sliced
1 carrot, diced
1 bay leaf
2 tablespoons olive oil
Vegetable salt and freshly ground pepper

Presoaking is not required with lentils, but they will have more nutritional value if they're soaked in water 2 times their volume overnight, to sprout them before cooking. (If you do not soak them first, rinse and drain.)

Bring lentils, water, garlic, onion, celery, carrot, and bay leaf to a boil for 5 minutes. Lower heat, partially cover, and simmer 45–50 minutes, until lentils are tender and thick. Add a little water if the soup becomes too dry. When done, add olive oil and salt and pepper to taste. Makes 6 servings.

9
SALADS

INTERNATIONAL GOURMET SALADS

Tidbit: To get the grit out of spinach leaves, wash them in a sink or large bowl of water with a few tablespoons of vinegar added.

Among today's diet-conscious people, the common garden salad is considered a staple, able to pinch-hit for a hearty meal yet satisfy a hungry appetite with fewer calories. It stands to reason that hardly a day goes by without a salad on the menu.

It also brings up a question of garden variety—how to make the common garden salad new and interesting without piling on the calories. The answer is to start with a few exotic greens (something other than head lettuce), add a pinch of herbs and spices and a few trimmings unique to your favorite foreign cuisine, and you'll find yourself on an international adventure in healthy gourmet dining.

These gourmet salads are guaranteed to be unique. In one attractively arranged dish, combining fresh vegetables, meats, and cheeses, they are ideal as an antipasto salad or an exciting solo meal. So treat yourself to a trip and discover the world for just a few calories.

GERMAN PORK AND POTATO SALAD

Salad:

Per serving:
309 calories
17 g protein
15 g fat
27 g carb.

4 ounces lean roast pork, sliced
2 small red-skinned potatoes, steamed and quartered with skin intact
1 small white onion, sliced into rings
½ medium cucumber, sliced into rounds
1 hard-boiled egg, halved
4 cherry tomatoes
¼ head red cabbage, shredded

In a bowl or serving platter, decoratively arrange all the ingredients over a bed of shredded cabbage.

GERMAN PORK AND POTATO SALAD *(continued)*

Dressing:

> *½ cup plain nonfat yogurt*
> *1 teaspoon cider vinegar*
> *1 teaspoon prepared horseradish*
> *1 small clove fresh garlic, pressed*
> *⅛ teaspoon dillseed*
> *Dash of Worcestershire sauce*

Blend all ingredients by hand with a whisk or fork in a small bowl. (Add buttermilk or skim milk to thin it if necessary.) Pour it over the top of the salad. Serves 2.

SALMON SALADE NIÇOISE

Per serving:
342 calories
27 g protein
18 g fat
18 g carb.

> *6–8 leaves Belgian endive*
> *2 small tomatoes, quartered*
> *½ cup string beans, sliced and steamed*
> *1 artichoke heart, cooked and quartered*
> *2 wedges (1 ounce each) soft ripened cheese (Brie or Camembert)*
> *6 green olives*
> *1 can (6½ ounces) red salmon, drained, large bones removed*
> *1 teaspoon Dijon mustard*
> *1 teaspoon capers*
> *1 sprig each fresh chervil and dill, snipped*
> *1 tablespoon walnut oil*
> *1 teaspoon tarragon vinegar*
> *Vegetable salt and freshly ground pepper to taste*
> *Lemon wedges*

Arrange the endive in a large bowl or platter. Decorate with remaining vegetables and cheese and olives, leaving the quartered tomato intact as a center cup.

Toss salmon, mustard, and capers together in a small bowl, then spoon into the center of the tomato. Top the salad with snipped herbs. Add oil, vinegar, and salt and pepper if desired. Garnish with wedges of lemon. Serves 2.

PICO DE GALLO WITH SHRIMP

Salad:

> *6 medium raw shrimp*
> *2 whole peppercorns*
> *4 leaves fresh Mexican sage*
> *2 limes, 1 halved crosswise, the other quartered*
> *8 leaves Boston or Bibb lettuce*
> *¼ medium avocado, sliced*
> *1 medium orange, peeled and sliced crosswise*
> *½ small red onion, sliced into thin rings*
> *1 medium jícama (a tropical tuber), peeled and sliced*
> *1 sprig cilantro, snipped*

Per serving:
242 calories
17 g protein
11 g fat
19 g carb.

Put the shrimp in a sauté pan with peppercorns, sage, and 1 of the lime halves with just enough water to cover. Bring to a boil and simmer for 1 minute. Rinse the shrimp under cool water to peel and devein them. Discard the cooking liquid and chill the shrimp.

Line large serving platter with the lettuce leaves. Arrange shrimp, fruit, and vegetables decoratively over the top. Sprinkle with snipped cilantro and garnish with 4 lime quarters.

Dressing:

> *1 tablespoon safflower oil*
> *1 teaspoon raspberry vinegar*
> *Juice of remaining half lime (2 teaspoons)*
> *1 teaspoon raw honey*
> *⅛ teaspoon chili powder*
> *Dash of vegetable salt*

Per serving:
273 calories
22 g protein
6 g fat
34 g carb.

In a cup, whisk dressing ingredients together until blended. Drizzle over the top of the salad.

Note: To cook beans, soak ¼ cup dry beans in a small pot with 1 cup water for 8 hours, or refrigerate overnight. Add more water if needed to cover the beans, and simmer covered for about 45–50 minutes until tender. Drain and chill. Makes about ⅔ cup cooked beans.

TURKEY TABOULI SALAD

> *½ cup cooked bulgur (see Lamb and Bulgur-Stuffed Eggplant, page 37, for cooking method)*
> *⅓ cup cooked navy beans (see below for cooking method)*
> *1 small ripe tomato, chopped*
> *⅓ cup cucumber, coarsely chopped*
> *1 tablespoon scallions, minced*
> *2 tablespoons fresh mint, chopped*
> *1 tablespoon fresh parsley, chopped*
> *1 teaspoon fresh tarragon, chopped*

TURKEY TABOULI SALAD *(continued)*

1 tablespoon freshly squeezed lemon juice
2 teaspoons safflower oil
Vegetable salt and freshly ground pepper to taste
10 large spinach leaves
4 ounces cooked turkey breast, sliced

Mix all ingredients, except spinach and turkey, in a large bowl. Line a bowl or platter with spinach leaves. Heap salad in the center and arrange with sliced turkey. Serves 2.

ITALIAN ANTIPASTO SALAD

Per serving:
340 calories
40 g protein
18 g fat
11 g carb.

Note: For convenience you may use store-bought red bell peppers that are already roasted and peeled.

2 red bell peppers, roasted
4 leaves each romaine lettuce and radicchio
6 ounces rare roast beef, thinly sliced
2 ounces part-skim Mozzarella cheese, thinly sliced
1 medium zucchini, lightly steamed, sliced, and chilled
8 mushroom caps
1 sprig fresh parsley, snipped
1 teaspoon fresh basil and thyme, snipped
1 tablespoon extra virgin olive oil
1 teaspoon white wine vinegar
Vegetable salt and freshly ground pepper to taste

To roast peppers, place them under a broiler whole for 4–5 minutes on each side until charred. While they're still hot, seal them tightly in a large plastic container or aluminum foil to allow the steam to separate skin from the pepper. Peel, and rinse them to remove the charred coating. Cut them in quarters, and remove the seeds.

Arrange romaine and radicchio on a platter. Roll the roast beef and cheese, and place them around the top. Decorate with red peppers, zucchini, and mushrooms. Top with snipped herbs, and dribble with blended olive oil and vinegar. Sprinkle with salt and pepper. Serves 2.

MEDITERRANEAN LAMB SALAD

Lamb:

Per serving:
344 calories
17 g protein
28 g fat
9 g carb.

1 teaspoon extra virgin olive oil
2 tablespoons red wine vinegar
1 small clove fresh garlic, pressed
½ teaspoon fresh rosemary, finely minced
1 lean boneless lamb chop (about 4 ounces)

Mix oil, vinegar, garlic, and rosemary in a shallow bowl. Add lamb chop, and marinate for 1½–2 hours, turning it several times in the liquid. If more liquid is needed, add a splash of red wine. After several hours, cook the lamb chop under the broiler 2–3 minutes on each side until done. Do not overcook. A pink center is better. Chill the lamb, and cut it into julienne strips.

Salad:

>   *12 spinach leaves*
>   *½ cup eggplant, cubed and steamed with a clove of garlic*
>   *1 medium tomato, sliced*
>   *2 ounces feta cheese*
>   *6 Greek olives*
>   *1 shallot, thinly sliced*
>   *1 sprig fresh parsley, snipped*
>   *1 teaspoon fresh oregano, snipped*
>   *1 tablespoon extra virgin olive oil*
>   *1 teaspoon sherry or red wine vinegar*
>   *Vegetable salt and freshly ground pepper to taste*

Arrange the spinach leaves in a large bowl or serving platter. Place the julienned lamb, eggplant, and tomato on the bed of spinach. Crumble the feta cheese over the top.

Decorate with olives and sliced shallots, and sprinkle with snipped herbs. Dribble with mixed olive oil, vinegar, and salt and pepper to taste. Serves 2.

Per serving:
316 calories
33 g protein
10 g fat
27 g carb.

Note: The Chinese noodles are made from rice flour and have a clear, gelatinous consistency when cooked. They are quite low in calories and make an unusual and pretty addition to the salad. You may find the noodles and the straw mushrooms in either the ethnic or specialty section of your supermarket.

CHINESE CHICKEN SALAD

Salad:

>   *6 leaves Chinese celery cabbage (also called napa)*
>   *½ cup boiled Chinese rice noodles, cooked according to directions on package (see below)*
>   *1 medium carrot, shredded*
>   *1 large chicken breast, cooked, skinned, and diced*
>   *8 snow peas*
>   *½ cup raw broccoli florets*
>   *6 straw mushrooms*
>   *4 green onions (bulbs only)*

Place cabbage leaves on a serving platter. Arrange noodles and shredded carrot on top to form a decorative bed for the chicken. Place the diced chicken over the bed with the snow peas, broccoli, and mushrooms all around it. Garnish with green onions.

CHINESE CHICKEN SALAD *(continued)*

Dressing:

> 1 tablespoon sesame oil
> 1 teaspoon rice vinegar
> 1 teaspoon low-sodium tamari
> ½ small clove fresh garlic, pressed
> 1 teaspoon fresh ginger, minced
> ½ teaspoon sesame seeds

Whisk all ingredients by hand in a cup. Drizzle over the top of the salad. Serves 2.

HAWAIIAN CHICKEN PLATTER WITH PUPULE DRESSING

Per serving:
329 calories
26 g protein
1 g fat
57 g carb.

Dressing:

> 1 small ripe papaya
> 1 lime
> ¼ cup dates, chopped; or seedless raisins

Cut the papaya in half to seed and peel it. Chunk one half into a blender container. Slice the other half and set it aside. Halve the lime. Squeeze in 1 tablespoon of lime juice, and reserve the other half for garnish. Add dates and blend everything together for about 30 seconds until dressing is creamy.

Salad:

> 1 bunch watercress, washed and thick stems removed
> 1 large chicken breast, cooked, skinned, and sliced
> ½ cup fresh pineapple slices
> 1 small ripe mango, peeled, pitted, and sliced
> 1 kiwi fruit, peeled and sliced
> 4 fresh strawberries

Spread watercress leaves in a bed on a platter. Arrange chicken slices, pineapple, mango, kiwi fruit, strawberries, and reserved papaya slices over the watercress. Pour dressing over the top. Garnish with wedges of reserved lime. Serves 2.

GREENS AND VEGGIES

There's nothing better than grazing over a fresh green salad with your favorite dressing. You can't improve too much on that. But instead of the usual lettuce and tomatoes, try some interesting combinations of mixed salads or crunchy vegetables topped with these tantalizing low-calorie dressings. It goes unchallenged that eating raw vegetables is far superior to cooking them. All fiber, enzymes, and nutrients are left intact the way nature intended. (Tuberous vegetables such as beets and potatoes are more palatable, of course, when they're cooked tender-crisp, but don't overcook them.) And do try to use fresh or home-dried herbs over commercially dried ones whenever possible. It makes a world of difference in the flavor.

Don't be put off by all the slicing and chopping required for the preparation of salads. A food processor is a big help here. You can prepare a week's worth of salad ingredients at a time, then store them as follows.

No vegetables, especially leafy ones, should ever be left directly in plastic bags or unwrapped. Immediately after you buy them, rinse them in water, wrap them thoroughly in paper towels, and put them in airtight plastic bags or containers, being careful not to let the plastic touch the vegetables. Then store them in the lower part of the refrigerator, where the temperature is cool.

If you follow this procedure, fresh uncut vegetables should keep for several weeks, and leafy ones up to a week. Then you'll always have crisp, ready-to-eat greens and veggies on hand.

Once you get used to eating all your vegetables fresh, you'll stage regular garden raids, and if you haven't already, you may even start a garden of your own.

Tidbits: Have freshly squeezed lemon or lime juice ready for dressings by freezing the juice ahead of time in ice-cube trays. Each cube makes about 1 tablespoon when melted.

Scoring the outside of peeled cucumbers with a fork helps remove bitterness and makes them look pretty when sliced.

FINGER SALAD
WITH OIL-FREE POPPY SEED DRESSING

Salad:

Per serving:
110 calories
5 g protein
1 g fat
23 g carb.

Health note:
Dextrose or sugar-free fruit pectin can be found in a health food store.

12 leaves Bibb lettuce
2 red bell peppers (julienned)
12 fresh baby carrots (trimmed, with 1 inch of green top left intact)
8 green onions (trimmed)
1 stalk broccoli florets (separated)
12 cherry tomatoes
¼ pound snow peas
4 hearts of celery

Line a salad platter with lettuce leaves, and arrange with finger vegetables. Chill. To prepare celery hearts, cut each whole heart in half lengthwise and cut out the root. Trim leaves (leaving a few tiny ones) and the nubby outer sheath. Cut into ½-inch pieces for the salad.

Dressing:

1 packet fruit pectin (without dextrose)
⅔ cup tomato juice

FINGER SALAD WITH OIL-FREE POPPY SEED DRESSING, DRESSING *(continued)*

> 3 tablespoons apple cider vinegar
> 2 teaspoons raw honey
> 1 shallot (minced)
> ½ teaspoon dried tarragon
> ⅛ teaspoon dry mustard
> 2 teaspoons poppy seeds

Whir all ingredients (except for poppy seeds) in a blender for 10 seconds. Stir in poppy seeds, and chill for several hours. Drizzle over salad, or serve it on the side for dipping. Serves 4.

GREEN SALAD WITH SLIMMING BLUE CHEESE DRESSING

Salad:

Per serving:
83 calories
7 g protein
2 g fat
11 g carb.

> 1 medium head red leaf, green leaf, or butter lettuce
> 2 medium ripe tomatoes, cut into wedges
> 1 medium cucumber, peeled, scored, and sliced
> 3 green onions, sliced
> 6 large mushroom caps, sliced
> 6 radishes, sliced

Tear lettuce leaves into bite-size pieces. Rinse and drain them in a colander. Toss all ingredients in a large salad bowl. Cover with wet paper towels and chill.

Dressing:

> ½ cup part-skim ricotta cheese
> ¼ cup nonfat milk
> 1 tablespoon freshly squeezed lemon juice
> 1 clove fresh garlic, pressed
> ⅛ teaspoon prepared horseradish
> Dash of vegetable salt and freshly ground pepper
> ¼ cup crumbled blue cheese

Blend or process all but the blue cheese until creamy. Stir in the blue cheese until well combined. Pour over the salad and toss. Serves 4.

PRIMAVERA PLATTER SALAD WITH CREAMY FLORENTINE DRESSING

Salad:

Per serving:
272 calories
12 g protein
20 g fat
12 g carb.

> 3 medium zucchini, sliced diagonally
> 2 medium ripe tomatoes, sliced crosswise

8 large mushroom caps, sliced
4 ounces part-skim Mozzarella cheese, thinly sliced
8 black olives
1 bunch spinach (leaves only)

Arrange other ingredients on a serving platter lined with 10 of the larger spinach leaves and chill. Reserve the remaining spinach leaves for the dressing.

Florentine Dressing:

½ bunch reserved spinach leaves, chopped
½ cup Low Cal Mayonnaise II (page 67)
¼ cup buttermilk
1 tablespoon white wine vinegar
½ teaspoon raw honey
1 clove fresh garlic, pressed
Vegetable salt and freshly ground pepper to taste

Place spinach leaves in a colander and pour boiling water over them to wilt. Press out excess water. Process remaining ingredients in a blender for 10 seconds. Add spinach and process once more until tiny green flecks remain. Chill. Pour Creamy Florentine Dressing over vegetables just before serving. Serves 4.

VEGETABLES MARINATED IN BASIL DRESSING

Vegetables:

Per serving:
168 calories
2 g protein
14 g fat
8 g carb.

2 large ripe tomatoes, cut into wedges
2 ribs celery, sliced diagonally
1 cucumber, peeled, scored, and sliced
1 green bell pepper, diced
1 red onion, diced
6 mushroom caps, sliced
2 sprigs fresh parsley, snipped

Delicious discovery:
This is the best basic Italian-style dressing ever invented. Make it in quantities, because once you taste it, you won't want to pay prices for bottled dressings again.

Combine all ingredients in a large container with an airtight cover.

Dressing:

¼ cup extra virgin olive oil
3 tablespoons balsamic vinegar
1 clove gresh garlic, pressed
1 teaspoon dried basil
⅛ teaspoon each vegetable salt and freshly ground pepper

VEGETABLES MARINATED IN BASIL DRESSING *(continued)*

Shake all ingredients together vigorously in a jar, and pour into vegetable salad. Toss until well combined. Cover tightly, and chill for at least 6 hours. Serves 4.

GINGERED BEETS, ONIONS, AND APPLES

Per serving:
63 calories
2 g protein
0 g fat
15 g carb.

1 pound fresh beets
½ cup rice vinegar
2 whole cloves
2 whole peppercorns
1 small red onion, thinly sliced
1 small tart green apple, cored and thinly sliced
2 teaspoons raw honey
½ teaspoon fresh ginger, minced

Scrub beets and place them in a medium saucepan with enough water to cover them. Add 2 tablespoons of the rice vinegar, cloves, and peppercorns. Bring them to a boil, cover tightly, then simmer for 35–40 minutes until beets are tender-crisp.

Drain and reserve liquid. Cut off ends, peel beets, and slice them thin into a large covered serving container. Add onions and apples. Mix remaining rice vinegar with honey, ginger, and ½ cup of the reserved beet liquid. Pour over beets, onions, and apples, and toss well. Cover tightly, and chill overnight. Serves 4.

CARROT RAISIN SLAW

Per serving:
127 calories
3 g protein
5 g fat
21 g carb.

½ medium head green cabbage, chopped
2 medium carrots, shredded
½ cup seedless raisins
½ cup Low Cal Mayonnaise II (page 67)
2 tablespoons raw honey
2 tablespoons cider vinegar

Toss all ingredients together well in a large serving bowl. Chill 1 hour before serving. Serves 6.

POTATO ONION SALAD

Per serving:
172 calories
3 g protein
9 g fat
20 g carb.

6 medium size red or white rose potatoes
1 large sweet red or white onion, sliced
1 cup Low Cal Mayonnaise II (page 67)
1 tablespoon each safflower oil and white wine vinegar
¼ cup fresh parsley, snipped
2 teaspoons celery seeds
½ teaspoon freshly ground black pepper
Vegetable salt to taste

Tasty temptation:
Toss in rinsed and drained canned salmon, tuna, or shrimp for a truly wonderful main dish salad.

Wash potatoes. Steam them whole with the skins on for 30–40 minutes (or pressure-cook them 5–10 minutes, testing them after 5 minutes). You may also cook them in a microwave oven for 20–25 minutes.

When cooked properly, potatoes should be tender on the outside but a little more firm toward the center. Since these 2 varieties of potatoes are rather thin-skinned, it's better not to boil them.

When done, let the potatoes cool, remove the skins, and cut them into large chunks. Combine all ingredients well in a large serving bowl. Cover and chill overnight for maximum flavor. Serves 8.

CUCUMBER AND EGG SALAD

Per serving:
187 calories
10 g protein
14 g fat
4 g carb.

2 medium cucumbers
2 ribs celery, thinly sliced
2 green onions, chopped
2 tablespoons fresh parsley, snipped (reserve 1 tablespoon)
1 tablespoon fresh dill, snipped
2 tablespoons safflower oil mayonnaise
2 tablespoons buttermilk
⅛ teaspoon freshly ground pepper
Vegetable salt to taste
6 hard-boiled eggs, cut into bite-sized chunks

Peel cucumbers and score the outside with a fork. Cut the cucmbers in half lengthwise, scoop out the seeds, then slice them ¼-inch thick. Set some slices aside for garnish. Combine everything in a medium serving bowl. Add the egg chunks last, tossing them carefully to keep them intact. Garnish the top with reserved cucumber slices and parsley. Serve chilled. Makes 4 servings.

Tidbits: If you have too many bananas all ripe at the same time, freeze some in their skins, and store in the freezer until you are ready to use them. Then, hold them under warm running water to peel them, and slice semifrozen. Or wait for them to thaw.

Instead of lemon or lime, dribble fresh pineapple juice over fruits to keep them from turning brown. It's sweeter and tastier.

Per serving:
104 calories
3 g protein
1 g fat
22 g carb.

Note: If they are not available fresh in your part of the country, frozen strawberries and peaches are suitable to use if they are packaged without sugar. Approximately 6 ounces equals 1 peach, and 10 ounces equals 1 pint of strawberries. If the other fruits are not available fresh, substitute fruits that are.

FABULOUS FRUIT SALADS

Man cannot live on whole wheat bread alone, but fruit is another story. Luscious ripe fruit is one of nature's greatest delights. High in fiber and abundant with vitamins and minerals, it can be a source of sustenance, a healthy snack, or the most delectable dessert. There's nothing like thirst-quenching fruit to cleanse the system and revitalize the body. You can even diet solely, safely, and successfully on fruit for up to a week.

To let a day go by without taking full advantage of the succulent seasonal fruits would be a sin, so indulge yourself without guilt. Whip up these fabulous fruit creations (or create your own with the fruits of your desire) and discover more new and exciting ways to get healthy and stay in shape.

FRUIT SALAD PARFAIT

Here is the ultimate in elegance, a fruit salad layered with a subtle orange-yogurt dressing. It makes a lovely centerpiece for alfresco dining.

2 cups plain nonfat yogurt
½ cup freshly squeezed orange juice
2 tablespoons raw orange blossom honey (or to taste)
¼ teaspoon almond extract
3 pears, peeled, cored, and sliced
2 pints fresh strawberries, hulled and halved (see below); reserve some for garnish
3 peaches, peeled, pitted, and sliced (see below)
6 plums, pitted and sliced with skins on
2 cups seedless green grapes, halved

Combine yogurt, orange juice, honey, and almond extract in a blender, and process until smooth. In a large clear trifle or parfait bowl, layer the fruits in the order given, alternating each layer with one fifth of the orange yogurt dressing, ending with the dressing.

Add the layers of dressing in dollops so that there are pretty areas of fruit showing through the bowl. Garnish the top with reserved strawberries and sprigs of mint if desired. Keep salad chilled until ready to serve. Makes 12 servings.

MANDARIN KIWI COLESLAW

This exotic fruit and cabbage salad is the perfect complement to a barbecue or summer meal. You get a glorious blend of sweet fruit and crunchy vegetables in one dish.

Per serving:
83 calories
2 g protein
4 g fat
9 g carb.

1 cup plain nonfat yogurt
¼ cup safflower oil mayonnaise
⅓ cup rice vinegar
1 medium head cabbage, shredded (remove 6 or 7 of the outer leaves and set aside)
8 kiwi fruit, peeled and sliced
4 tangelos or tangerines, peeled, seeded, and cut into 1-inch sections
2 cups fresh pineapple cubes

Blend yogurt, mayonnaise, and vinegar for the dressing. Combine cabbage and fruits in a bowl. Add dressing and mix in well. Line a large decorative bowl with reserved cabbage leaves and spoon in coleslaw. Makes enough for 12 people.

TROPICAL AMBROSIA WITH PEACHES AND CREAM

Fruit:

Per serving:
235 calories
4 g protein
5 g fat
44 g carb.

2 bananas, sliced
1 papaya, peeled, seeded, and cut into small chunks
1 cup fresh pineapple chunks
1 pint fresh strawberries, hulled and halved
1 cup seedless green grapes, halved
⅔ cup unsweetened coconut, shredded
Spinach leaves (or ti leaves if you can get them)

Carefully combine all of the fruits in a decorative bowl lined with spinach leaves and chill. Serve with Peaches and Cream Dressing.

Peaches and Cream Dressing:

2 large ripe peaches, peeled, pitted, and sliced
½ cup plain nonfat yogurt
1 tablespoon raw honey
1 teaspoon freshly squeezed lemon juice
1 teaspoon vanilla extract
¼ teaspoon ground ginger

Whir all ingredients in a blender until smooth. Chill. Mix in with the fruit just before serving. Serves 4.

BANANA BOAT WITH COCONUT CREAM TOPPING

If you like banana splits, this tropical fruit salad will sail you away to a "dessert" island. It takes some fussing, but eating it is paradise.

Fruit:

Per serving:
251 calories
8 g protein
3 g fat
51 g carb.

2 whole pineapples, with tops
2 mangoes
1 papaya
1 teaspoon fresh ginger, minced
4 large bananas

Tropical treat:
Sprinkle the top
with dry roasted
macadamia nut
pieces.

Cut pineapples in half lengthwise, leaving the tops on. With a sharp knife, carefully make cuts lengthwise from end to end 1 inch apart, then crosswise from side to side 1 inch apart. Do not cut through the skin.

With a sharp curved grapefruit knife, make a running cut around the inside of the rim, just as you would a grapefruit. Keep running the knife along in this fashion until the chunks of pineapple are free from the rind. Remove the center core, cut the pineapple in even pieces and put them in a bowl. Repeat this with each pineapple half. (This is actually an easier, more precise way to cut up pineapple than carving the rind away from it.) Set the 4 shells aside.

Halve each mango, peel with a knife, and cut small chunks away from the pit into a bowl. Halve the papaya, remove the seeds, and scoop out small bite-size chunks with a spoon or melon scooper into the bowl. Add the ginger, and mix the fruits together.

Peel and slice bananas lengthwise, and arrange 2 banana halves in each pineapple shell. Spoon 4 equal portions of the fruit into each boat and top with Coconut Cream Topping.

Topping:

²/₃ cup Coconut Milk (page 102)
2 tablespoons raw honey
¹/₂ teaspoon vanilla extract
1 rounded teaspoon arrowroot
6 egg whites, warmed to room temperature
¹/₂ teaspoon cream of tartar

In a small saucepan, bring the Coconut Milk to a boil. Lower the heat, and add honey, vanilla, and arrowroot, and stir until mixture is smooth. Remove from heat and let cool to thicken.

In a medium-size bowl beat egg whites with an electric mixer until foamy. Add cream of tartar and continue to beat until stiff peaks form. With a rubber scraper, gently stir coconut mixture into meringue, folding until just blended. Top each banana boat with ¼ of the Coconut Cream Topping and serve at once. Serves 4.

MELON MÉLANGE WITH HONEY LIME DRESSING

Try this nectary and refreshing melon salad with—surprise!—cucumbers in it. Serve it in a disposable watermelon shell to take along for that perfect picnic.

Fruit:

Per serving:
133 calories
2 g protein
3 g fat
28 g carb.

½ small watermelon
1 casaba melon
1 Cranshaw melon
1 large cucumber
1 large head red or green leaf lettuce

Scoop out balls of watermelon with a melon scooper, removing seeds, and put balls in a large bowl. Set the watermelon shell aside. Cut the casaba and Cranshaw melons in half, seed them, and scoop melon balls out of all halves into the bowl. Be sure to use only the sweet meat and not scrape too close to the rinds.

Peel the cucumber, and slice lengthwise to seed it. Score the outside with a fork. Thinly slice cucumber, and add to the melons, then carefully toss everything together.

Next, line the watermelon shell with large outer leaves of lettuce, leaving the ruffled tops showing past the rim. Secure them with half toothpicks if necessary, without piercing the rind. Pour the Melon Mélange into the lined watermelon shell. Serve with honey lime dressing.

Dressing:

⅔ cup freshly squeezed lime juice
½ cup raw honey
2 tablespoons safflower oil
1 teaspoon poppy seeds

Whir in a blender lime juice, honey, and safflower oil until blended. Stir in poppy seeds and drizzle over the top of the fruit.

MAGNIFICENT MOLDED SALADS

Fat Buster: If you like a sour cream topping but not the calories, blend equal parts of plain nonfat yogurt or buttermilk and low-fat cottage cheese with a squeeze of fresh lemon juice in a blender until smooth. This makes a great mock sour cream.

Remember the joys of Jell-O? Those little shimmering blobs brought us such pleasure as children. These grown-up, fanciful molds won't disappoint you, except now they're nutrition packed—without all the sugar.

Gelatin alone is a fair source of protein, but when it's combined with fish, meats, and cheese, it makes an extremely nourishing high-protein dish. It's also a catchy and pretty way to preserve perishable fruits and vegetables in one healthy salad. It will keep in the refrigerator for 3 or 4 days.

There is nothing catchy, however, about making a molded salad, and here are a few tips to help you. Use a packet (1 tablespoon) of unflavored gelatin to 2 cups of liquid. Always dissolve gelatin completely in very hot or boiling liquid before chilling. Use 25 percent less gelatin for a gelatinous base such as fish, meat, or poultry stocks.

When adding chopped ingredients to the mold, chill the gelatin to a consistency of raw egg whites before stirring them in, or they will sink to the bottom. If you want the ingredients to show through the top of the molded salad, however, drop them in while the gelatin is still very liquid.

To unmold the salad, place the mold pan in a sink or pan of hot water, or run the mold pan under hot tap water for about 30 seconds. Then run a very thin knife along the rim and shake the mold gently upside down until it drops onto a serving platter. If you place it directly on the platter, wet the platter first so that you can move the mold around easily into position. Chill it another 10–15 minutes to firm the top if necessary.

Never use any fresh fruit or juice from pineapples, papayas, kiwi fruit, or figs, as they contain an enzyme that interferes with the jelling property of gelatin. Unfortunately, they must be cooked first.

So go ahead and give these marvelous molded masterpieces a shake, and you'll discover that life is still a bowl of Jell-O in disguise.

CHEESE AND FRUIT IN WINE GELATIN

Per serving:
95 calories
3 g protein
1 g fat
16 g carb.

Serving suggestion:
Garnish with extra
cheese and fruit or
rye crackers. Serve
with white wine
spritzers.

2 cups unsweetened filtered white grape or pear juice
2 packets unflavored gelatin
2 cups fruity white wine
6 ounces Havarti cheese, cubed
1 cup seedless green grapes
1 large firm pear, peeled, cored, and chunked
1 tablespoon fresh mint, snipped

In a medium saucepan bring 1 cup of the juice to a boil. Sprinkle in gelatin and stir over a medium heat until dissolved. Remove from heat and stir in remaining juice and wine. Pour into a mold and chill. When mixture is the consistency of runny egg whites, fold in cheese, fruits, and mint until well distributed. Chill until firm. Unmold onto a serving platter. Makes 8 servings.

GARDEN VEGETABLES IN TOMATO ASPIC

Per serving:
68 calories
4 g protein
0 g fat
14 g carb.

2 packets unflavored gelatin
4 cups tomato juice
1 rib celery with leaves
1 shallot, chopped
1 tablespoon grated orange rind
¼ cup freshly squeezed orange juice
1 tablespoon low-sodium tamari
1 teaspoon raw honey
1 tablespoon white wine vinegar
Dash of cayenne pepper
2 packages (10 ounces each) frozen mixed vegetables, thawed and drained
Sprigs of watercress

Soften gelatin in 1 cup of tomato juice. In a medium saucepan bring 3 cups of tomato juice with celery, shallot, and orange rind to a boil. Lower heat and simmer 10–15 minutes. Strain mixture. Stir softened gelatin into hot tomato mixture along with orange juice, tamari, honey, vinegar, and cayenne pepper.

Let it stand about 5 minutes until gelatin has completely dissolved. Cool slightly and pour into a mold and refrigerate. When aspic chills to a jellylike consistency, fold in mixed vegetables until well combined. Chill until firm. Unmold onto a serving platter and arrange with watercress sprigs. Serves 8.

CHANTILLY FRUIT IN CANTALOUPES

Per serving:
222 calories
8 g protein
1 g fat
44 g carb.

Dessert idea: This recipe makes a wonderful snack, light lunch, or dessert, but the filling creates an excellent molded salad all by itself. Simply double the ingredients and chill in a 1-quart mold or the equivalent in dessert cups.

2 large cantaloupes, halved and seeded
1 packet unflavored gelatin, plus ⅓ cup boiling water
1 cup freshly squeezed orange juice
½ cup part-skim ricotta cheese
¼ cup plain nonfat yogurt
1½ tablespoons raw orange blossom honey
1 medium banana, sliced
½ cup fresh strawberries, sliced, plus 4 whole strawberries for garnish

Halve and seed cantaloupes. Level the bottoms slightly by cutting them with a knife so that they sit flat. Stuff them with paper towels to dry out any liquid.

In a medium bowl, completely dissolve gelatin in boiling water, then stir in orange juice. Cream ricotta, yogurt, and honey together with an electric mixer or wire whisk. Fold into orange juice mixture. Chill about 10 minutes, then gently stir in fruit. Remove paper towels, then spoon mixture into cantaloupe halves and chill until set. Garnish with whole strawberries. Serves 4.

FIESTA AVOCADO MOLD

Per serving:
180 calories
7 g protein
14 g fat
6 g carb.

1 packet unflavored gelatin
½ cup water
1 large ripe avocado, diced
½ cup Low Cal Mayonnaise II (page 67)
½ cup low-fat cottage cheese
2 tablespoons freshly squeezed lime juice
1 tablespoon onion, grated
1 can (4 ounces) green chilies, diced
1 tablespoon pimientos, chopped
¼ teaspoon chili powder
Dash of Tabasco sauce
Vegetable salt to taste
Cilantro sprigs

Sprinkle gelatin into ¼ cup of water to soften. Boil remaining water, and stir into gelatin mixture until completely dissolved. In a blender, process avocado, Low Cal Mayonnaise, cottage cheese, lime juice, and onion until smooth. Stir in chilies, pimientos, and seasonings. Pour into a 1-quart mold and chill until firm. Unmold onto a serving platter and garnish with cilantro. Serves 4.

CELEBRATED MEALS

CONTINENTAL DELIGHT

Seviche
Primavera Platter with Creamy Florentine Dressing
Cajun-Style Chicken Cutlets
Fiesta Avocado Mold
Cheddar Cheese Corn Muffins
Tropical Ambrosia with Peaches and Cream
Boysenberry Wine Julep

CRANBERRY GELATIN SALAD

Per serving:
164 calories
3 g protein
6 g fat
25 g carb.

1 cup unsweetened boysenberry juice
1 packet unflavored gelatin
1 tablespoon freshly squeezed lemon juice
1 cup granulated fructose
1 can (20 ounces) unsweetened crushed pineapple, drained (reserve liquid)
1 cup celery, chopped
1 whole orange, unpeeled and quartered
1 cup fresh cranberries
1 cup chopped walnuts

Heat boysenberry juice in a small saucepan. Add gelatin and stir until dissolved. Blend in lemon juice, fructose, and reserved pineapple juice. Partially chill. In a food processor or blender, coarsely chop celery, orange, and cranberries together. Add to gelatin mixture, and fold in crushed pineapple and walnuts. Chill in a decorative 1-quart mold or bowl until set. Makes 12 side dish servings.

10
BREADS AND GRAINS

Note: Each loaf of bread makes about 16 slices. Nutritional calculations are for one slice.

Fat Buster: To save a few calories in bread making, you may substitute water, liquid nonfat milk, or apple or orange juice mixed with an equal amount of water, for the amount of milk given in the recipes. This will lend, in varying degrees, a dry, crustier texture to breads.

You can increase the protein and calcium value of bread without increasing calories by substituting powdered nonfat milk for some of the flour. For one quarter of the flour used in the recipe, substitute an equal amount of powdered nonfat milk.

BREADS WITH BODY

Fresh homemade bread is a warm reminder of hearth and home and always a welcome treat. The aroma of baking bread has a way of making time stand still, and it it worth every second of effort that goes into it.

One of the wonderful things about homemade bread is the many whole grain flours you can use. All are high in vitamins, minerals, protein, and fiber, and each has its own unique taste. Some add nuttiness, some add maltiness, some are sweet, some are sour, and some are sprouted and very nutritious, but all of the flours are excellent in any combination. Pleasant-tasting whole wheat, however, is the most widely used and should make up about ½ to ¾ of the flour in bread making for the right texture.

Health food stores usually carry a full selection of whole grain flours, but if you want really superior flours, and you don't mind being a little industrious, you can buy the whole grains and grind your own with a grain mill. All flours should be kept refrigerated in airtight containers and may be stored this way for 3 or 4 months or more.

Bread making takes a little patience, but it's not at all difficult. Bake several loaves at a time and freeze them, because whether you make one or a dozen, the rising time is the same. These recipes call for making bread by hand, but a food processor with the proper attachment will mix and knead the dough and save you some muscle action. Otherwise, proceed with the directions given here.

Before you begin, here are a few tips to remember. The wheat flour amounts given in the recipe, although fairly accurate, are approximate. You may need a little less or a little more, depending on the dough. Hold back a little flour and add the remainder as you go. It's always better to start with less and add more. The dough should be firm and elastic after kneading, so that it doesn't stick to your hands or the work surface.

Use a standard 9 x 5-inch loaf pan with a nonstick surface if possible. If not, lightly oil a regular loaf pan and wipe off the excess with a paper towel. Then dust it lightly with flour.

Bread that is done baking should have a hollow sound when tapped. Remove loaves from the loaf pan and place them on a wire rack to cool. Salt is not included in these recipes, but if you prefer the taste of it, add ½ to 1 teaspoon of sea salt per loaf of bread in your dough making.

Making bread can be a simple process, or it can be extensive, depending on how enterprising you care to be. This small, exclusive selection of recipes is just a fraction of what you can do, but nonetheless guaranteed to turn the crustiest barbarian into a homebody at the first whiff.

PUMPERNICKEL RAISIN BREAD

Per slice:
108 calories
3 g protein
2 g fat
20 g carb.

1 cup low-fat milk
¾ cup water
¼ cup butter
¼ cup powdered carob, sifted
¼ cup blackstrap molasses
1 tablespoon active dry yeast
2 eggs
1 cup seedless raisins
3¼ cups whole wheat flour
2 cups rye flour

In a medium saucepan, heat milk, water, butter, and carob until butter has melted. Stir in molasses and cool to lukewarm. Stir yeast into mixture and allow it to proof (bubble slightly). Separate 1 egg, saving the white. Beat in 1 whole egg plus yolk. Stir in raisins and flours until well mixed.

Turn out onto a floured surface and knead for about 10 minutes, until dough is firm and elastic. Place dough in a lightly oiled mixing bowl, cover with plastic wrap, and allow it to rise in a warm place for about 30 minutes.

Punch down dough, and divide into 2 loaves. Place them on a nonstick or lightly oiled baking sheet. Cover and let them rise again, about another 30 minutes. Brush reserved egg white over the tops. Bake them in a preheated 350° oven for about 30 minutes or until loaves test done. Makes 2 loaves.

SESAME EGG BREAD

Per slice:
144 calories
4 g protein
6 g fat
20 g carb.

2 teaspoons active dry yeast
2½ cups whole wheat pastry flour
⅔ cup low-fat milk
¼ cup butter
1 tablespoon sesame oil
2 tablespoons raw honey
3 eggs

½ cup brown rice flour
¼ cup ground millet
2 teaspoons sesame seeds

In a large bowl combine the yeast with half the wheat flour. In small saucepan heat milk, butter, oil, and honey until just melted. Stir into flour and yeast, and beat for 2 minutes with an electric mixer. Add 2 eggs with remaining wheat flour, and beat again for 2 minutes. Stir in remaining flours, and mix to make a stiff dough.

Turn out onto a floured surface, and knead until smooth and elastic, about 8–10 minutes. Place dough in a lightly oiled bowl. Cover with plastic wrap, and let it rise in a warm place for about 1 hour or until doubled in bulk. Punch down dough, and turn into a prepared loaf pan. Cover, and allow it to rise again for about 30 minutes or until doubled in bulk.

Beat remaining egg, and brush it over the top. Sprinkle with sesame seeds. Bake in a 350° oven for 40–45 minutes until loaf tests done. Makes 1 loaf.

HERB BREAD

Per slice:
110 calories
4 g protein
2 g fat
17 g carb.

1 tablespoon active dry yeast
¼ cup warm water
1 tablespoon raw honey
¼ cup low-fat milk
2 tablespoons olive oil
1 cup part-skim ricotta cheese
1 egg
3 cups whole wheat flour
1 teaspoon each dried basil, sage, and thyme
½ teaspoon lemon rind, grated
1 tablespoon tomato paste, plus 2 tablespoons water

In a large bowl, dissolve yeast in warm water. Stir in 1 teaspoon of the honey and allow it to proof. In a small saucepan mix honey and milk, and heat until honey melts. Remove from heat, and stir in olive oil, ricotta, and egg. Stir into yeast. Add half the flour, and beat with an electric mixer for 2 minutes. Stir in remaining flour to make a stiff dough. Turn out onto a floured surface. Add herbs and lemon rind, and knead until dough does not stick, and herbs are mixed in well.

Place dough in a lightly oiled bowl, cover with plastic wrap, and allow it to rise for 1 hour. Punch down dough, and turn into a prepared loaf pan. Cover and allow it to rise another 45 minutes. Mix tomato paste with water, and spread over the top of the loaf. Bake in a preheated 350° oven for 35–40 minutes until it tests done. Makes 1 loaf.

POTATO ONION BREAD

Per slice:
115 calories
4 g protein
3 g fat
18 g carb.

1 small potato
1 teaspoon honey
2 cups rye flour plus 1 teaspoon
2 tablespoons active dry yeast
1 egg
3 tablespoons safflower oil
⅓ cup buttermilk, warmed
1 cup whole wheat flour
6 green onions, chopped
Freshly cracked pepper

Boil potato in enough water to cover. Drain water, reserving ⅓ cup of the warm cooking liquid. Peel and mash the potato. Add half of it to the reserved potato water along with honey and the 1 teaspoon of rye flour. Stir in yeast, and set aside to proof (bubble). In a large bowl, beat egg, and combine with oil and buttermilk. Add to yeast mixture along with rye flour. Stir well, cover with plastic wrap, and let it sit in a warm place to rise for about 1 hour.

Stir down dough, and add wheat flour and chopped onions. Knead until smooth and elastic. Shape into a prepared loaf pan, cover, and let it rise again for another 30 minutes. Brush the top with water and sprinkle with freshly cracked pepper. Bake in a preheated 375° oven for 30–35 minutes until it tests done. Makes 1 loaf.

WHOLE WHEAT BAGELS

This is a variation on the previous recipe, with some ingredient substitution.

1 small potato
1 teaspoon honey
2 cups rye flour plus 1 teaspoon
2 tablespoons active dry yeast
1 egg plus 1 yolk
3 tablespoons safflower oil
1⅓ cups water
1 cup whole wheat flour
Poppy seeds (optional)

Per bagel:
153 calories
5 g protein
4 g fat
24 g carb.

Boil potato in enough water to cover. Drain water, reserving ⅓ cup of the warm cooking liquid. Peel and mash the potato. Add half of it to the reserved potato water along with honey and the 1 teaspoon of rye flour. Stir in yeast, and set aside to proof (bubble). In a large bowl, beat whole egg, and combine with oil and water. Add to yeast mixture along with 2 cups rye flour. Stir well, cover with plastic wrap, and let it sit in a warm place to rise for about 1 hour.

Stir down dough, and add wheat flour. Knead until smooth and elastic. Cut the dough in 12 equal pieces, and with hands roll each piece into a rope about 7 inches long and ¾ inch thick. Form into a ring, moistening the ends with water to make them stick together when pressed.

Space them apart on a nonstick baking sheet, and let them rise again for 10 minutes. Boil 3 quarts of water in a large kettle. Drop the bagels into the pot, being careful not to crowd them. Boil about 2 minutes on each side. Remove with a slotted spoon, and arrange them back onto the baking sheet.

Mix 1 teaspoon water with extra egg yolk, and brush mixture over the tops. Sprinkle with poppy seeds if desired. Bake the bagels in a 425° oven for 20–25 minutes, or until golden. Move them to a wire rack to cool. Makes 1 dozen bagels.

Sour note: To make a traditional sourdough starter, put 1 cup of low-fat acidophilus milk in a small container. Cover with cheesecloth, and leave at room temperature for 24 hours. Then stir in 1 cup of whole wheat flour and ½ teaspoon of raw honey. Cover container with cheesecloth again and store in a warm place to allow mixture to activate. The starter will be ready to use when it becomes bubbly and begins to expand in size after 2 or 3 days.

A slightly faster method is to combine 1½ teaspoons of dry yeast with 1 cup each of warm water and whole wheat flour in a glass container. Cover with cheesecloth, and let it stand at room temperature for 48 hours. When mixture begins to bubble, stir down several times during the process, and just before using. The starter should be stored in the refrigerator, but used at room temperature.

SOURDOUGH WHOLE WHEAT BREAD

Good sourdough whole wheat bread is a rarity, and this recipe from the Happy Bake Shop in northern California, is a find. It makes 4 loaves, but after you've tasted them, you'll wish you had made more.

Per slice:
102 calories
3 g protein
0 g fat
21 g carb.

14 cups whole wheat flour
1½ cups whole wheat gluten
1½ teaspoons malt
⅛ ounce compressed yeast
1¾ cups sourdough starter (see note)
1½ tablespoons sea salt (optional)
3½ cups water

In a very large bowl combine all the ingredients together (except water) until blended. Add water, and mix until smooth, about 6–8 minutes. Cover dough with plastic wrap, and let it stand at room temperature for about 1–1½ hours.

Remove from bowl, and divide dough into quarters. Shape them into loaves, and place them in prepared loaf pans or on a large baking sheet. Cover, and let them rise for 5–6 hours. Slit the tops with a sharp knife, and bake in a 400° oven for 45–55 minutes or until they test done. Makes 4 loaves.

7-GRAIN SPROUTED WHEAT BREAD

Per slice:
114 calories
4 g protein
2 g fat
21 g carb.

2 tablespoons active dry yeast
2½ cups warm water
4 tablespoons blackstrap molasses
1 egg
¼ cup corn or sunflower oil
4 cups whole wheat flour
1 cups triticale flour
½ cup amaranth flour
½ cup brown rice flour
½ cup barley flour
½ cup millet flour
½ cup uncooked rolled oats
2 cups wheat sprouts, chopped

In a large bowl dissolve yeast in 1 cup of the warm water with 1 tablespoon of the molasses. Let it proof (bubble). Stir in remaining water with molasses, egg, oil, 1 cup of the wheat flour plus the triticale, amaranth, brown rice, barley, and millet flours, and the oats. Gradually beat in remaining wheat flour to make a stiff dough.

Turn out onto a floured surface, and knead dough for about 8–10 minutes until it's smooth and elastic. Place in a lightly oiled bowl. Cover with plastic wrap, and let it rise in a warm place for 1–1½ hours, until doubled in bulk.

Turn dough back onto a floured surface and knead in the wheat sprouts for several more minutes. Divide dough in half and shape into 2 prepared loaf pans. Cover, and let rise again for 1 more hour. Bake in a preheated 350° oven for 50 minutes or until loaves test done. Makes 2 loaves.

7-GRAIN SPROUTED WHEAT BUNS

This is a variation of the previous recipe. Try these buns with our Muscle Burgers for a nutritious cookout.

Per bun:
228 calories
8 g protein
4 g fat
42 g carb.

1 tablespoon active dry yeast
1¼ cups warm water
2 tablespoons blackstrap molasses
1 egg
⅛ cup corn or sunflower oil
2 cups whole wheat flour
½ cup triticale flour (see below)
¼ cup amaranth flour (see below)
¼ cup brown rice flour

¼ cup barley flour
¼ cup millet flour
¼ cup uncooked rolled oats
1 cup wheat sprouts, chopped

Note: Some of these nutritious flours may not be available in the summer months. When you can obtain them, wrap them airtight and stock them in your freezer. They will keep up to a year. You may also substitute wheat flour for any of the other flours in this recipe.

In a large bowl, dissolve yeast in ½ cup of the warm water with ½ tablespoon of the molasses. Let it proof (bubble). Stir in remaining water with molasses, egg, oil, ½ cup of the wheat flour plus the triticale, amaranth, brown rice, barley, and millet flours, and the oats. Gradually beat in remaining wheat flour to make a stiff dough.

Turn out onto a floured surface, and knead dough for about 8–10 minutes until it's smooth and elastic. Place in a lightly oiled bowl. Cover with plastic wrap, and let it rise in a warm place for 1–1½ hours until doubled in bulk.

Turn dough back onto a floured surface, and knead in the wheat sprouts. Divide dough into 8 parts, roll each part into a ball, and without squashing it, press it down with your hand. Or roll it out flat with a rolling pin to the diameter you want. Repeat with other parts. Place them on a lightly oiled baking sheet, cover them, and let them rise a second time, 30 minutes to 1 hour.

Bake them on the top rack in a preheated oven, 400°, for about 20 minutes, or until tops are brown. To keep them from drying out, place a pan of water in the oven while they bake. If they seem to be browning too quickly, put a baking sheet on the bottom rack underneath the buns to deflect some of the heat.

Place the baked buns on a wire rack to cool. Cut them in half horizontally to make sandwich buns. Makes 8 buns.

Tidbit: Make step-saving Fresh Berry Puree to serve on breads and biscuits by simply pureeing fresh (not cooked) ripe berries with a squeeze of fresh lemon juice and your favorite natural sweetener to taste. This may be refrigerated in an airtight jar for several days, so make only as much as you will need at one time.

SNACK BREADS AND BISCUITS

Coffee, tea, or . . . Perrier? With our busy life-styles today, afternoon tea (or any of the three) is a lost art, but a good practice. It is said to have originated with a certain duchess, who suffered fainting spells between lunch and dinner. She summoned her servants every afternoon to bring tea and cakes. Soon a circle of friends joined her, hence a wise tradition was born.

Taking a little time out each day for your favorite refreshment, complemented with a biscuit or a slice of tea bread, calms, rejuvenates and energizes your mind as well as your body. It elevates your blood sugar and enables you to finish your day with aplomb instead of feeling as if you're on the last leg of a marathon. Make these scrumptious quick breads ahead of time and freeze them. Keep them on hand for company or just such occasions as that late afternoon break for relaxation. Such a time-tested and gracious tradition can't be all wrong.

BASIC CORNBREAD

Per piece:
92 calories
3 g protein
1 g fat
16 g carb.

1¼ cups stone-ground yellow cornmeal
¾ cup whole wheat flour
2 teaspoons baking powder
1 teaspoon sea salt (optional)
1 egg, beaten
2 tablespoons butter, melted
1 tablespoon raw honey
1 cup nonfat milk

In a medium bowl, sift together cornmeal, wheat flour, baking powder, and salt if desired. In a small bowl, blend remaining ingredients together. Add to cornmeal mixture, and stir until just combined. Do not overstir. Pour into an 8-inch or 9-inch square nonstick baking pan. Bake in a preheated 425° oven for 20–25 minutes. Remove from oven and loosely cover with foil to cool. Makes 12 pieces.

Cornbread exclusive: Make Blueberry Cornbread by adding an extra tablespoon of raw honey and 1 cup of fresh or frozen blueberries (lightly dusted with whole wheat flour) to the cornbread batter before baking.

Whip up Cheddar Cheese Corn Muffins by adding 4 ounces of shredded aged Cheddar cheese to the cornbread batter before baking. Serve them warm with Apple Butter (page 183).

LEMON PECAN TEA BREAD

Per slice:
233 calories
4 g protein
10 g fat
34 g carb.

1 cup whole wheat pastry flour
½ cup brown rice flour
1 teaspoon baking powder
¼ cup butter, softened
⅔ cup raw honey
2 eggs, beaten
¼ cup nonfat milk
Juice of 1 orange
Grated peel of 1 lemon
½ cup pecans, finely chopped

Blend flours and baking powder in a medium bowl. Cream butter, honey, eggs, milk, and orange juice in another bowl. Stir in lemon peel and pecans. Add to flour mixture and blend well.

Turn batter into a nonstick 9 x 5-inch loaf pan. Bake in a preheated 350° oven for 50 minutes to 1 hour, until the loaf is spongy to the touch. Remove loaf from pan, and let it cool on a wire rack. Makes 10 slices.

APPLE BUTTER

Per cup:
150 calories
1 g protein
1 g fat
38 g carb.

1 pound sweet apples, cored and quartered
½ cup apple cider
½ teaspoon lemon rind, grated
⅛ teaspoon ground cloves
¼ teaspoon cinnamon
Pinch of allspice
Raw honey to taste

Cook apples slowly in apple cider, along with lemon rind and clove, until mixture becomes thick. When done, press mixture through a sieve or fine strainer, then spice with cinnamon, allspice, and raw honey. Keep it refrigerated in an airtight container for up to a week. Makes about 2 cups.

RAISIN FILLED COFFEE CAKE

Per piece:
207 calories
4 g protein
5 g fat
38 g carb.

1½ cups oat flour plus 2 tablespoons
1 teaspoon baking soda
¼ cup butter
½ cup raw honey plus 3 tablespoons
2 eggs
1 cup plain nonfat yogurt
1½ teaspoons vanilla extract
2 tablespoons oat flour
1½ teaspoons cinnamon
¾ cup seedless raisins
1 tablespoon raw honey
¼ teaspoon cinnamon

In a medium bowl, mix 1½ cups of the oat flour and baking soda. In another bowl cream butter, ½ cup honey, eggs, yogurt, and 1 teaspoon of the vanilla. Blend with flour mixture and set batter aside.

Make the filling by combining 3 tablespoons honey, oat flour, cinnamon, raisins, and the remaining vanilla in a small bowl. Pour half the cake batter into a 9-inch square nonstick baking pan. Spoon the filling over the top, then cover with the rest of the batter.

Bake for 30 minutes in a preheated 350° oven. Remove and dribble 1 tablespoon of honey to make a glaze over the top and sprinkle with cinnamon. Bake for another 15 minutes or until a wooden toothpick inserted in center comes out clean. Makes 12 pieces.

ORANGE BLUEBERRY BRAN MUFFINS

Per muffin:
153 calories
3 g protein
5 g fat
26 g carb.

1 cup whole wheat pastry flour
1 cup raw bran
2 teaspoons baking powder
1 teaspoon baking soda
1 cup fresh or frozen blueberries
1 egg, beaten
¼ cup butter, melted
½ cup raw honey
1 cup freshly squeezed orange juice
1 teaspoon grated orange rind
1 teaspoon vanilla extract

In a large bowl mix flour, bran, baking powder, and baking soda together. Rinse and drain blueberries, then stir them into the dry ingredients to coat them.

In another bowl blend remaining ingredients together, and carefully mix with flour and blueberries just enough to blend with flour mixture. Do not overstir. Drop equal spoonfuls of the batter into a nonstick 12-muffin tin. Bake in a preheated 375° oven for 25–30 minutes or until a wooden toothpick inserted in the center comes out clean. Makes 12 muffins.

STRAWBERRY BREAKFAST BREAD

Per slice:
206 calories
4 g protein
8 g fat
27 g carb.

1⅓ cups whole wheat pastry flour
⅓ cup soy flour
½ teaspoon baking soda
1 teaspoon cinnamon
2 eggs
¼ cup safflower oil
½ cup raw honey
½ teaspoon almond extract
1 pint fresh strawberries, hulled and sliced; or 1 package (10 ounces)
*   unsweetened frozen*
2 tablespoons sliced almonds

Sift flours, baking soda, and cinnamon together in a large bowl. In a medium bowl, beat eggs with an electric mixer until fluffy. Blend in oil, honey, almond extract, and strawberries. Stir in with flour mixture until just combined.

Turn into a 9 x 5-inch nonstick loaf pan. Sprinkle top evenly with sliced almonds. Bake in a preheated 350° oven for 1 hour, or until a wooden toothpick inserted in the center comes out clean. Remove loaf from pan and place on a wire rack to cool. Serve with No Cook Strawberry Jam (page 185). Makes 10 slices.

NO-COOK STRAWBERRY JAM

Per cup:
260 calories
1 g protein
1 g fat
70 g carb.

1½ cups granulated fructose (approximate)
1 pint fresh strawberries, hulled and crushed
1 tablespoon freshly squeezed lemon juice
¼ bottle liquid natural fruit pectin (without dextrose)

Mix fructose and strawberries in a large bowl, and let them stand 10 minutes. Mix lemon juice with pectin, and stir into strawberries. Continue to stir for 3 minutes. Pour at once into clean jars, and seal with airtight lids. Let them stand 24 hours at room temperature, then refrigerate. Jam may be kept up to 3 weeks. Makes about 3 cups.

CHEESE AND HERB POPOVERS

Per popover:
92 calories
6 g protein
4 g fat
8 g carb.

1 cup whole wheat pastry flour
½ teaspoon each dried basil and rosemary
1 cup low-fat milk
3 eggs, beaten
1 tablespoon safflower oil
½ cup aged Swiss cheese, shredded

Note: Bake plain dessert popovers by omitting herbs and Swiss cheese and adding 2 tablespoons raw honey to the batter.

Mix flour and herbs together in a medium bowl. Stir in milk, eggs, and oil. Beat with an electric mixer until batter is smooth. Stir in cheese. Fill 1 dozen lightly oiled popover or muffin cups (preferably with a nonstick surface) ½ full. Bake in a preheated 450° oven for 35–40 minutes until brown and puffed. Do not open the oven door until baking is done. Makes 12 popovers.

WHOLE WHEAT CHEESE ROUNDS

Per round:
23 calories
1 g protein
1 g fat
2 g carb.

1 cup whole wheat flour
1 teaspoon baking powder
1 cup aged sharp cheddar cheese, shredded
½ cup plain nonfat yogurt
2 tablespoons butter, softened
1 teaspoon Dijon mustard
⅛ teaspoon cayenne pepper

Mix flour and baking powder in a medium bowl. In another bowl combine remaining ingredients. Add to flour mixture, and blend well. Roll into a log about 1¼ inches in diameter, and chill for several hours. Cut into thin slices, and arrange on an ungreased aluminum baking sheet. Bake in a preheated 350° oven for 10 minutes or until lightly browned. Makes about 4 dozen.

GARLIC CHEESE BISCUITS

Per biscuit:
58 calories
3 g protein
2 g fat
8 g carb.

1½ cups whole wheat flour
1½ teaspoons baking powder
1 tablespoon butter
1 egg, beaten
½ cup low-fat cottage cheese
¼ cup buttermilk
2 tablespoons Parmesan cheese, freshly grated
2 tablespoons fresh parsley, minced
2 cloves fresh garlic, pressed

In a medium bowl combine flour and baking powder. Cut in butter with a fork or pastry blender. In a smaller bowl, cream egg, cottage cheese, and buttermilk until smooth. Stir in Parmesan cheese, parsley, and garlic. Fold mixture into flour, and mix lightly. Drop dough by tablespoons onto a lightly oiled or nonstick baking sheet. Bake in a preheated 375° oven for 12–15 minutes, or until golden brown. Makes about 16 biscuits.

BISCOTTI (Italian Nut Biscuits)

Per biscuit:
54 calories
1 g protein
2 g fat
7 g carb.

Suggestion: For a tempting taste variation, add 2 tablespoons of anise liqueur to dough, and decorate with star anise seeds before baking.

½ cup hazelnuts, roasted and crushed
¼ cup butter, softened
3 tablespoons raw honey
1 egg plus 1 egg white
¾ cup whole wheat pastry flour
1 teaspoon baking powder

Finely grind half the hazelnuts, leaving the other half crushed. In a small bowl, cream butter, honey, and whole egg together. In a medium bowl beat egg white with an electric mixer until stiff but not dry. Add butter mixture, and continue to beat at a high speed until entire mixture is light and fluffy. Blend flour, baking powder, and ground and crushed hazelnuts. Stir into egg mixture until just blended.

Spoon dough into 4 strips, 2 inches wide, on a lightly oiled or nonstick baking sheet. Bake in a preheated 350° oven for 12–15 minutes. When brown, remove from oven and cut crosswise into ½-inch-thick slices. Arrange them on a broiler or baking rack and bake for another 10 minutes to toast them on all sides. Makes about 2 dozen Biscotti.

BREAKFAST GRAINS AND GOODIES

No matter what you eat, breakfast is the most important meal of the day. You can live without it (and lots of people do), but you'll function better with it. Some insist protein is the only way to start the day, and some stick with carbohydrates.

There are two schools of thought on this. The first says that stick-to-your-ribs protein wards off hunger and sees you through the day. The other says that carbohydrates give you energy to perform the day's tasks. Both are true, but both depend on variables such as what you ate the night before, when and what you eat for lunch, whether your breakfast carbohydrates are simple or complex (complex are better), the kind of work you do, etc.

What people tend to forget is that breakfast foods made with whole grains contain complex carbohydrates and have a fairly high amount of protein too. They also provide satisfying bulk as well as many essential vitamins and minerals. If you want to supplement your breakfast with eggs or meat, that's fine, but you can't go wrong with whole grains to start your day. Here are some high-energy, high-protein breakfast grains to get your morning off to a supercharged start.

BRANOLA

Per cup:
292 calories
10 g protein
9 g fat
47 g carb.

Serving suggestion:
Eat Branola alone,
with milk, or top
with Apple and
Spice Yogurt. Make
this by mixing plain
nonfat yogurt with
apple juice
concentrate, vanilla,
and cinnamon to
taste.

3 cups uncooked rolled oats
½ cup raw wheat germ
½ cup raw bran
½ teaspoon cinnamon
½ cup dried apricots, apples, or pineapple, chopped
¼ cup walnuts, chopped
¼ cup unsweetened apple juice concentrate
2 tablespoons raw orange blossom honey
1 tablespoon corn or safflower oil
½ teaspoon vanilla extract

In a large bowl, combine oats, wheat germ, bran, cinnamon, dried fruits, and nuts. Mix apple juice concentrate, honey, oil, and vanilla, and toss with oat mixture to coat thoroughly. If desired, spread Branola on a large lightly oiled baking sheet, and bake in a preheated 300° oven for 5–10 minutes to toast it. Makes about 5 cups.

ORANGE FRENCH TOAST

Per slice:
221 calories
9 g protein
9 g fat
30 g carb.

2 eggs, beaten
⅓ cup buttermilk
⅓ cup orange juice concentrate
4 slices Sesame Egg Bread (page 176)

Mix eggs, buttermilk, and orange juice concentrate in a flat shallow bowl. Briefly soak slices of bread on each side in egg mixture. Do not allow them to become soggy. Cook them on both sides on a medium hot, lightly oiled griddle or large nonstick skillet until golden brown. Makes 4 slices. Serve topped with Sugarless Pineapple Marmalade (below).

SUGARLESS PINEAPPLE MARMALADE

Per tablespoon:
10 calories
0 g protein
0 g fat
2 g carb.

1 can (20 ounces) crushed pineapple, packed in its own juice
1 packet unflavored gelatin
1 orange
1 can (6 ounces) orange juice concentrate (not thawed)
NutraSweet to taste

Drain pineapple juice into a saucepan, and sprinkle with gelatin. Allow it to soften. Heat slightly until melted and set aside. Peel and dice orange. Process orange in a food processor or blender with half the peel. Add crushed pineapple and frozen orange juice concentrate and process again.

Add gelatin mixture and process until just blended. Add NutraSweet to desired sweetness. Spoon into jars with airtight lids. Refrigerate several hours before using. Makes about 3½ cups.

COCONUT SYRUP

Per tablespoon:
28 calories
0 g protein
1 g fat
5 g carb.

⅔ cup shredded unsweetened coconut, firmly packed
1 cup warm water
¼ cup raw honey
½ teaspoon vanilla extract

In a blender, puree coconut with ½ cup of water. Add remaining ½ cup water with honey and vanilla and process again. Strain mixture through a sieve. Makes about 1½ cups of syrup.

MACADAMIA NUT WAFFLES

Per waffle:
355 calories
13 g protein
14 g fat
36 g carb.

1 cup whole wheat flour
¼ cup raw wheat germ
1 teaspoon baking powder
½ teaspoon baking soda
1 tablespoon safflower oil
1 tablespoon raw honey
1½ cups low-fat acidophilus milk
1 egg, separated
½ cup dry roasted, unsalted macadamia nuts, crushed.

Mix dry ingredients together in a medium bowl. Combine oil, honey, milk, and egg yolk in a smaller bowl, and add macadamia nuts. Blend mixture with dry ingredients but do not overstir. Beat egg white with an electric mixer until fluffy. Fold into batter. Pour into a lightly oiled waffle iron, and cook until waffles are crisp. Top with Coconut Syrup. Makes 4 waffles.

BANANA PANCAKES

Per pancake:
80 calories
3 g protein
2 g fat
14 g carb.

¾ cup triticale flour
¾ cup buckwheat flour
2 teaspoons baking powder
2 eggs
1½ cups buttermilk
1 tablespoon raw honey
2 medium ripe bananas, mashed
1 tablespoon safflower oil
¼ teaspoon cinnamon

Mix dry ingredients together in a large bowl. In a medium bowl beat eggs with buttermilk. Blend with dry ingredients. Stir in honey, bananas, oil, and cinnamon until just blended. Heat a lightly oiled griddle to medium high. Pour desired amount of batter on the griddle and cook the pancakes until golden brown on both sides. Serve with Apricot Syrup (page 190). Makes about 16 pancakes.

PURE PROTEIN PANCAKES

Here's a special bodybuilding recipe for pancakes made with soy protein powder.

Per pancake:
48 calories
10 g protein
1 g fat
0 g carb.

½ cup soy protein powder (use flavored if desired)
1¼ cups water (or more if it's too thick to pour)
1 egg (beaten)
¼ teaspoon cinnamon

In a medium bowl, blend protein powder and water together with a whisk or fork. Stir in egg. Heat a lightly oiled griddle or skillet to medium high. Pour or spoon on batter. Cook until golden brown, about 2 minutes on each side. Serve with Lite Orange Mapled Syrup (below). Makes about 6 pancakes.

LITE ORANGE MAPLED SYRUP

Try this delicious, low-calorie imitation syrup made with all natural ingredients.

Per tablespoon:
3 calories
0 g protein
0 g fat
1 g carb.

1 packet fruit pectin (without dextrose)
¾ cup hot water
⅓ cup freshly squeezed orange juice
½ teaspoon each maple and vanilla extract
Pinch of sea salt
NutraSweet to taste (optional)

Combine pectin and water in a small pouring container. Stir until pectin thickens. Add orange juice, flavorings, and salt, and stir well. Serve warm over pancakes. Makes about 1¼ cups, enough for 6 pancakes.

APRICOT SYRUP

Per tablespoon:
31 calories
0 g protein
0 g fat
8 g carb.

1 cup pure light maple syrup
½ cup raw honey
1½ cups fresh apricots, finely chopped

Puree all ingredients in a blender to a slightly chunky consistency. Serve warm. Makes about 3 cups of syrup.

BREAKFAST BISCUITS

These nifty biscuits are great for a nutritious all-in-one breakfast on the go.

Per biscuit:
155 calories
13 g protein
6 g fat
13 g carb.

¾ cup soy flour
¾ cup oat flour
½ cup raw wheat germ
2 tablespoons powdered nonfat milk
2 teaspoons baking powder
2 eggs
2 tablespoons corn or safflower oil
½ cup low-fat acidophilus milk
⅔ cup unsweetened applesauce
½ pound Easy Turkey Sausage (page 121), cooked and crumbled; or ready-made natural-style turkey sausage, cooked
2 tablespoons raw bran or nutritional yeast plus 2 tablespoons low-fat acidophilus milk (optional)

In a large bowl combine flours, wheat germ, dry milk, and baking powder. In another bowl lightly beat eggs and mix in oil, milk, and applesauce. Combine well with flour mixture, and stir in cooked Turkey Sausage. (At this point add 2 tablespoons of bran or nutritional yeast with 2 tablespoons of milk to the biscuit batter if you wish.)

Drop batter by spoonfuls onto a nonstick or lightly oiled aluminum baking sheet. Bake in a preheated 400° oven for 15–18 minutes or until a wooden toothpick inserted in the center comes out clean. Makes 1 dozen large biscuits.

MAIN GRAINS

Tidbit: A nifty trick to stop eyes from watering when chopping onions is to place a full, unused book of matches near the cutting surface. The sulfur helps to absorb the fumes.

Grains are the staff of life and the foundation of good nutrition. They're best when they have had as little processing as possible, either stone ground or left whole. The whole grain contains the germ, the endosperm, and the hull (or bran), and is higher nutritionally than grains that have been degermed or dehulled in the process of milling. Whole grains are especially high in B vitamins, vitamin E, protein, unsaturated fat, minerals (especially iron), and fiber. Processed grains are primarily carbohydrate with only traces of vitamins, minerals, and protein left.

Grains are best for you when eaten slightly chewy, not overcooked. The cooking time depends on the grain. Wholly natural grains such as whole wheat, buckwheat, or rye berries require presoaking before cooking. Minimally processed grains such as rice, cornmeal, oats, pearl barley, and cracked and bulgur wheat, do not. Presoaking whenever possible, however, is a nutritional step saver. It cuts down the cooking time thus retaining more of the valuable nutrients and fiber of the grain.

On the following pages are some recipes and ideas that will turn plain grains into ''main grains.'' If you don't want to fuss with lots of ingredients, simply boil them in seasoned stock and add your favorite herbs and seasonings to the boiling water. Some suggestions for substitutions are kasha for bulgur, cracked wheat for wild rice, pearl barley for brown rice, and vice versa.

SPICED ORANGE RICE

Per serving:
292 calories
7 g protein
5 g fat
58 g carb.

1 cup water
1 cup freshly squeezed orange juice
1 cup uncooked long-grain brown rice
2 teaspoons orange peel, grated
½ cup onion, chopped
¼ cup seedless raisins
¾ teaspoon curry powder and pumpkin spice
2 tablespoons almonds, sliced
1 tablespoon fresh parsley, snipped
Vegetable salt and freshly ground pepper

Combine all ingredients except for almonds, parsley, and seasonings in a large saucepan. Bring to a boil for several minutes. Reduce heat, cover tightly and simmer about 35–40 minutes, until rice is tender and fluffy. Before serving, stir in almonds, parsley, and salt and pepper to taste. Serves 4.

HERB RISOTTO

Per serving:
207 calories
6 g protein
1 g fat
43 g carb.

3 cups Poultry Stock (page 70)
1 cup uncooked Italian rice (risotto)
2 green onions, minced
2 tablespoons each fresh marjoram, parsley, and sage, minced
1 bay leaf, crushed
Pinch of saffron
Vegetable salt and freshly ground pepper to taste

In a large saucepan, bring stock to a boil. Add rice and green onions, lower heat, and simmer covered. Just before all liquid is absorbed (about 30 minutes), add remaining herbs and saffron, and continue to simmer covered until risotto is fluffy. Add salt and pepper to taste. Makes 4 servings.

MUSHROOM KASHA (Ground Buckwheat Groats)

2 tablespoons butter
1 clove fresh garlic, pressed
½ pound mushrooms, chopped
⅔ cup uncooked fine-ground kasha
¼ teaspoon turmeric
Vegetable salt and freshly ground pepper to taste
¼ cup Meat Stock (page 43); or water
1 tablespoon each fresh chives and parsley, snipped

In a large nonstick skillet melt butter and lightly sauté garlic. Stir in mushrooms, cover, and cook over a very low heat for about 5 minutes. Uncover and cook about 10 minutes until moisture evaporates.

Stir in kasha, turmeric, and salt and pepper, and brown for several minutes. Add stock and bring to a boil. Immediately lower heat, cover, and simmer for 15–20 minutes, until tender. Remove from heat. Add chives and parsley, cover, and let it stand about 5–10 minutes more. Serves 4.

SAFFRON RICE

2 tablespoons butter
1 cup uncooked short-grain brown rice
¼ teaspoon saffron, finely chopped
⅛ teaspoon cardamom seeds, finely crushed
2 whole cloves
Pinch of cinnamon
2 cups Poultry Stock (page 70)
¼ cup almonds, sliced
¼ cup fresh parsley, chopped
Pinch of paprika

Melt butter in a large saucepan, add rice, and stir to coat. Lower heat, add seasonings, and toss until blended well. Pour in stock. Raise heat, and bring to a boil for 5 minutes. Cover tightly and lower heat. Simmer rice for about 40 minutes, until tender and fluffy. Stir in almonds, parsley, and paprika. Serve in the center of Crown Roast of Lamb (page 25). Serves 4.

PISTACHIO PILAF

Per serving:
247 calories
9 g protein
8 g fat
36 g carb.

½ cup onion, chopped
1 tablespoon almond or walnut oil
1½ cups Poultry Stock (page 70)
¾ cup uncooked cracked wheat
2 teaspoons freshly squeezed lemon juice
2 tablespoons low-sodium tamari
½ cup tomatoes, chopped
⅓ cup unsalted shelled pistachios, chopped
2 tablespoons fresh parsley, snipped
Freshly ground pepper

In a large saucepan, quickly sauté onion in oil. Add stock and cracked wheat and bring to a boil for 5 minutes. Add lemon juice and tamari. Lower heat, cover, and simmer for about 25 minutes, or until wheat is dry and fluffy. Stir in tomatoes, pistachios, parsley, and pepper to taste. Cover and simmer several more minutes just to soften tomatoes, Serves 4.

CORNBREAD DRESSING

This is a delicious and attractive variation of the usual bread dressing. It's light, fluffy, and wholesome, because it's made with homemade cornbread.

Per serving:
151 calories
4 g protein
6 g fat
18 g carb.

¼ cup butter
1 cup celery, chopped
¾ cup onion, finely chopped
1 tablespoon fresh parsley, minced
Turkey giblets, finely chopped (optional)
1 recipe Basic Cornbread (page 182), crumbled
1 teaspoon poultry seasoning
¾ cup pecans, chopped
Vegetable salt and freshly ground pepper
Turkey drippings or Poultry Stock (page 70)

In a large nonstick skillet, melt butter and sauté celery, onion, and parsley over a medium heat until they are semitender. (If you are using turkey giblets, sauté them along with celery and onion, about 5 minutes.) Mix in crumbled cornbread. Add poultry seasoning, pecans, and salt and pepper to taste, and toss until well blended. If dressing seems too dry, add enough drippings (mixed with a little water) or stock to achieve desired moistness. Makes enough for 12 servings.

BROWN AND WILD RICE SALAD

Per serving:
250 calories
5 g protein
8 g fat
39 g carb.

⅔ cup uncooked long-grain brown rice
⅓ cup uncooked wild rice
2 cups water
2 tablespoons extra virgin olive oil
1 tablespoon tarragon wine vinegar
8 green olives, sliced
1 tablespoon each fresh parsley and scallions, minced
Vegetable salt and freshly ground pepper

In a large saucepan, bring brown and wild rice and water to a boil for 5 minutes. Lower heat, cover, and simmer 45–50 minutes, until rice is dry and fluffy. Let it cool. In a small bowl whisk together oil and vinegar. Stir into rice and add olives, parsley, scallions, and salt and pepper if desired. Chill overnight in a covered container, but serve at room temperature. Makes 4 servings.

11
DESSERTS

HEAVENLY CAKES
AND COOKIES

Tidbit: Split a vanilla
bean and put it in an
airtight jar of
granulated fructose
to give it a vanilla
headiness.

Heavenly desserts await you in this chapter, and even heaven can't wait when
it's for these superdelicious, ultranutritious cakes and cookies. They're actually healthy because they're made with whole grain flours, fresh eggs, fruits,
low-fat milk products, and the natural sweeteners of raw honey, maple syrup,
and fruit sugars, so every calorie is good for you. And don't forget to try the
low-calorie icings created without any kind of cream or powdered sugar. All
of this adds up to a highly superior, lower-calorie dessert, something your
body will thank you for and your tastebuds will beg for more of.

Fat Buster: Eat raw unsalted nuts for a healthy dessert or snack. Cashews and
pistachios are among the lowest in calories. Whenever possible, get nuts in
the shell and crack them as you go, to keep you from eating too many.
Struggling with a nutcracker helps burn calories too!

UNSWEETENED BANANA OATMEAL COOKIES

Per cookie:
77 calories
1 g protein
4 g fat
10 g carb.

3 medium ripe bananas, mashed
¼ cup safflower oil
1½ cups uncooked rolled oats
½ cup whole wheat flour
½ cup dates, chopped
½ cup walnuts, chopped
1 teaspoon vanilla extract

Combine all ingredients in a large bowl. Drop batter by the tablespoon onto a nonstick baking sheet. Bake in a 350° oven for 20–25 minutes. Remove them from the oven and space them out on a wire rack to cool. Makes about 2 dozen large cookies.

CHUNKY PEANUT BUTTER AND BANANA MUFFINS

Per muffin:
222 calories
6 g protein
8 g fat
35 g carb.

Note: If you're using a regular muffin pan, use cupcake liners to prevent them from sticking.

1½ cups whole wheat flour
½ cup toasted wheat germ
1 teaspoon baking soda
4 medium ripe bananas, mashed
⅓ cup natural-style chunky peanut butter
3 tablespoons butter, softened
2 eggs, beaten
⅔ cup pure maple syrup

In a medium bowl mix flour, wheat germ, and baking soda. Mash remaining ingredients together in a separate bowl. Combine with flour mixture, and stir just enough to blend. Drop equal amounts of mixture in a nonstick 12-muffin tin. Bake in a 350° oven for 30 minutes or until a wooden toothpick inserted into a muffin comes out clean. Serve warm. Makes 1 dozen muffins.

SPICED ICING

Per serving:
38 calories
1 g protein
0 g fat
9 g carb.

3 egg whites
½ cup raw honey
¼ teaspoon each vanilla and almond extracts
⅛ teaspoon each ground cinnamon, nutmeg, and ginger

Warm egg whites to room temperature, then beat until frothy. Drizzle in honey, beating continuously. Add vanilla and spices, and beat another 10 minutes until stiff peaks form. Ice cake immediately. Makes enough for one Apple Dump Cake (page 199), or 15 servings.

APPLE DUMP CAKE

Per serving:
268 calories
4 g protein
9 g fat
46 g carb.

2 cups whole wheat flour
2 teaspoons baking soda
2 teaspoons cinnamon
¾ teaspoon nutmeg
2 eggs
1 cup buttermilk
½ cup safflower oil
⅔ cup raw honey
4 cups fresh apples, chopped
1 cup seedless raisins
4 whole apples, cored and sliced thin
Dash of cinnamon and nutmeg

Sift flour, baking soda, cinnamon, and nutmeg together in a large bowl. In a separate bowl, beat eggs and buttermilk together. Stir in oil and honey, then combine with flour mixture. Add apples and raisins and mix well.

Arrange apple slices on the bottom of a 12-inch square nonstick cake or baking pan. Sprinkle them with cinnamon and nutmeg, then pour in the cake batter. Bake in a preheated 350° oven for 45–50 minutes or until a wooden toothpick comes out clean. Top with Spiced Icing (page 198). Makes 15 servings.

HEART BEET CAKE

Per slice:
226 calories
4 g protein
12 g fat
25 g carb.

1 cup whole wheat pastry flour
1 teaspoon baking powder
¾ teaspoon baking soda
½ teaspoon cinnamon
2 eggs, beaten
¼ cup nonfat milk
¾ cup granulated fructose
⅓ cup safflower oil
1 teaspoon vanilla extract
1½ cups fresh beets, shredded
½ cup walnuts, chopped

In a large bowl sift flour, baking powder, baking soda, and cinnamon together. In another bowl cream eggs, milk, fructose, oil, and vanilla. Combine with flour mixture, and stir just enough to blend. Fold in beets and walnuts.

Turn into a lightly oiled and floured heart-shaped cake pan (approximately 9–10 inches wide). Bake in a 350° oven for 40 minutes or until a wooden toothpick inserted in the cake comes out clean. Let it cool, move cake to a plate, and top with Buttercream Frosting (page 200). Makes 10 slices.

BUTTERCREAM FROSTING

Per serving:
52 calories
1 g protein
3 g fat
5 g carb.

2 eggs, separated
2 tablespoons butter, softened
¼ cup granulated fructose
2 teaspoons vanilla extract

In a small bowl beat egg yolks until light yellow. Cream in butter, fructose, and vanilla, and set aside. Let egg whites warm to room temperature, then beat them until soft peaks form. Gently fold in egg yolk mixture, and continue to beat until peaks are stiff. Frost cake and serve immediately. Makes enough for one Heart Beet Cake (page 199), or 10 servings.

PINEAPPLE SQUASH CAKE

Here's an unusual upside-down cake made with yellow summer squash that's prettier than carrot cake and better than zucchini cake.

Per slice:
183 calories
4 g protein
4 g fat
32 g carb.

1½ cups whole wheat pastry flour
¾ teaspoon baking powder
¾ teaspoon baking soda
2 eggs
¾ cup plain nonfat yogurt
¾ cup raw sugar
1 teaspoon vanilla extract
1 teaspoon orange rind, grated
¼ pound yellow summer squash, grated
⅓ cup dried apricots, chopped
1 can (20 ounces) crushed pineapple, packed in its own juice, drained
½ cup unsweetened shredded coconut

Mix dry ingredients together in a large bowl and set aside. In another bowl, whisk eggs, then blend in yogurt, raw sugar, vanilla, and orange peel, and stir until raw sugar is dissolved. Mix in squash and apricots, then combine with flour mixture. Stir just enough to blend.

Mix pineapple and coconut together, and spread evenly over the bottom of a 10-inch round nonstick cake pan. Pour in batter, then bake in a preheated 350° oven for 40–45 minutes or until a wooden toothpick inserted in the cake comes out clean. Remove from oven, and immediately invert onto a cake plate. Makes 10 slices.

BANANA PUDDING BREAD

Heavy and moist, this bread is similar to the one I ate in Hawaii as a child.

Per slice:
187 calories
5 g protein
6 g fat
30 g carb.

5 medium ripe bananas, mashed
1 tablespoon raw honey
1 egg, beaten
1 tablespoon safflower oil
½ teaspoon each almond and vanilla extracts
1 cup whole wheat flour
1 teaspoon baking soda
1 teaspoon baking powder
½ cup walnuts, chopped

Combine bananas, honey, egg, oil, and almond and vanilla extracts in a large bowl. Sift all dry ingredients together, and stir into banana mixture. Mix in nuts, and turn into a 9 x 5-inch nonstick loaf pan. Bake in 350° oven for 45 minutes or until a wooden toothpick inserted in the loaf comes out clean. Serve warm. Makes 8 slices.

NO-BAKE CAROB COOKIES

Not for kids only. This recipe is perfect for the adulterated adult with an urgent sweet tooth.

Per cookie:
57 calories
1 g protein
3 g fat
8 g carb.

1½ cups uncooked quick-cooking rolled oats
½ cup unsweetened shredded coconut
¼ cup walnuts, chopped
⅓ cup nonfat milk
2 tablespoons butter
¾ cup date sugar
3 tablespoons carob powder, sifted

In a small bowl combine oats, coconut, and walnuts, and set aside. In a small saucepan add milk, butter, date sugar, and carob powder, and stir over a low heat until blended. Combine with oat mixture. Quickly drop teaspoonfuls of the cookie mixture onto a baking sheet lined with waxed paper. Refrigerate. Makes about 2 dozen cookies.

FRESH FRUIT DESSERTS

Tidbit: Marinate fresh fruits in wines or liqueurs for an easy, elegant dessert. Here are some spirited suggestions: Bing cherries in brandy, peaches in zinfandel, strawberries in Amaretto, pears in cassis, grapes in Galliano, bananas in Kahlúa, plums in port, oranges in anisette, raspberrie: in sweet riesling, honeydew in Benedictine, pineapple in rum, casaba in peppermint schnapps, and blueberries in crear sherry.

Per serving:
196 calories
4 g protein
6 g fat
36 g carb.

Tidbit: Freeze chunks of fresh fru soaked in liqueurs put on top of froze yogurt, ice cream, and ice milk.

Part of the art of living well is eating right. Knowing what foods to buy and how to cook them, or not cook them, is an art in itself. Take these fresh fruit desserts. The most tantalizing desserts can be healthy if you stick with the naturals—fresh fruits and juices, raw nuts, even dried fruits such as dates, raisins, and coconut. But instead of cooking these vital ingredients, a process that destroys or alters texture, fiber, and nutrients, try not cooking or not overcooking them. When you can, bake crusts or toppings before you add the fruits and fillings. Coming up are some mouth-watering recipes that show you how.

Master the art of eating raw. Raw fresh foods are energy economical, easier to prepare, better looking, better tasting, and better for you.

PINEAPPLE APRICOT COBBLER

Pineapple added to the filling with an oat-baked topping makes this an interesting takeoff on traditional cobbler.

Filling:

1 pound fresh apricots, pitted and quartered
1 cup fresh pineapple chunks
1/3 cup raw honey
1/4 teaspoon almond extract

Arrange fruit in a 13 x 9-inch baking dish or pan. Combine honey and almond extract, and drizzle evenly over the fruit.

Topping:

3/4 cup oat flour
3/4 cup uncooked rolled oats
2 teaspoons baking powder
1 teaspoon baking soda
2 tablespoons date sugar
3/4 teaspoon cinnamon
1/4 cup butter
1 cup nonfat mik

In a medium bowl, mix all dry ingredients together. With a fork or pastry blender, cut in butter until flour is crumbly. Add milk and blend well, but no more than 30 seconds. Spread batter over the top of the fruit. Sprinkle with a little more cinnamon, and bake in a 375° oven for 45 minutes. Serves 8.

RICOTTA CHERRY TORTE

If you can't bake a cherry pie, or even if you can, try this simple recipe that's half the work, but twice as good.

Crust:

Per slice:
149 calories
5 g protein
5 g fat
19 g carb.

½ cup part-skim ricotta cheese
¼ cup butter
1¼ cups whole wheat pastry flour

In a medium bowl blend ricotta, butter, and flour together with a fork or pastry blender and form a ball. Chill. When ready to use, flatten dough and press it into the bottom and up the sides of a 10-inch torte pan. Preheat oven to 425° and bake for about 12 minutes. Immediately remove from the oven, and let it cool.

Baking suggestion:
You may also use a torte pan with a lift-up bottom. Place the torte on a large serving dish, then cut the slices.

Filling:

1 cup part-skim ricotta cheese
⅓ cup filtered, unsweetened pear or white grape juice concentrate
¼ teaspoon mace

In a medium bowl, blend ingredients together, and spread evenly over the cooled crust.

Topping:

1½ cups fresh dark, sweet cherries, pitted
1 cup seedless green grapes
½ cup unsweetened pear or white grape juice concentrate,
   blended with ½ cup water
1 tablespoon freshly squeezed lemon juice
2 teaspoons arrowroot

Arrange cherries and grapes decoratively over the torte filling. In a medium saucepan combine ¾ cup of the juice concentrate mixture and lemon juice. Bring to a slow boil. Dissolve arrowroot in remaining ¼ cup of the juice concentrate mixture, and pour into saucepan. Lower heat to simmer, and stir until mixture thickens slightly. Remove from heat immediately, and spoon glaze over the fruit. Makes 12 slices of torte.

TROPICAL FRUIT PIE WITH YOGURT PIECRUST

Piecrust:

Per slice:
180 calories
5 g protein
9 g fat
21 g carb.

⅓ cup butter
1¼ cups whole wheat pastry flour
⅓ cup plain nonfat yogurt

In a medium bowl cut butter into pastry flour with a fork or pastry blender until mixture is crumbly. Blend in the yogurt, small spoonfuls at a time. Form a ball, and chill. When ready to use, carefully roll out dough, and line a lightly oiled 9-inch pie pan. Preheat oven to 450°, and bake for 12–15 minutes or until crust is golden. Let it cool.

Suggestion: If you have pie left over, squeeze a little juice from the fresh pineapple slice over the rest of the fruit to keep it from turning brown, and cover tightly with plastic wrap. Keep refrigerated.

Filling:

1 packet unflavored gelatin
1½ cups boiling water
2 tablespoons freshly squeezed lemon juice
2 egg whites
½ cup raw honey
1 cup plain nonfat yogurt
1 teaspoon fresh ginger, grated
1 teaspoon vanilla extract
3 large ripe peaches, peeled, pitted, and finely chopped

In a medium bowl combine gelatin and boiling water. Add lemon juice and stir until dissolved. Chill until partially set.

Meanwhile warm egg whites to room temperature, and beat until frothy. Slowly dribble in honey, and continue to beat rapidly until egg whites are stiff but not dry. Blend yogurt with ginger and vanilla. Then fold yogurt into egg whites along with 1 cup partially set gelatin. Stir fruit into remaining gelatin, and mix into egg white mixture. Pour filling into piecrust and chill.

Topping:

1 ripe payaya, peeled, seeded, and sliced
1 cup fresh pineapple chunks
½ cup unsweetened shredded coconut

Just before serving, arrange fresh fruit decoratively around the top. Sprinkle with coconut. Makes 10 slices.

BANANA BERRY SHORTCAKE

Strawberry shortcake is always a dream, but with bananas it's heaven.

Biscuits:

Per shortcake:
294 calories
9 g protein
8 g fat
49 g carb.

1 cup whole wheat pastry flour
1½ teaspoons baking powder
½ teaspoon baking soda
Dash of cinnamon
¼ cup butter, melted
¾ cup nonfat milk
1 large ripe banana, mashed

In a medium bowl sift together flour, baking powder, baking soda, and cinnamon, and set aside. In a separate bowl, blend butter, milk, and banana. Add to the flour mixture, and blend well. Drop by tablespoonfuls onto a nonstick baking sheet. Bake in a preheated 450° oven for 10–15 minutes or until golden. Remove from oven. When warm enough to handle, cut biscuits in half before spooning on the fruit. Makes 6 biscuits.

Fruit:

2 pints fresh strawberries, hulled and sliced
2 large bananas, sliced
2 tablespoons raw honey
2 tablespoons freshly squeezed lemon juice
½ cup warm water

Mix fruit together, then stir in remaining ingredients until syrupy. Add more liquid if needed. Spoon 6 equal portions over the halved warm biscuits.

Topping:

4 egg whites
½ cup powdered nonfat milk
2 tablespoons granulated fructose
½ teaspoon freshly squeezed lemon juice
¾ teaspoon vanilla
Cinnamon and nutmeg (optional)

Warm egg whites to room temperature. Beat them until frothy. Sprinkle in powdered milk and fructose, while continuing to beat them. Add remaining ingredients, and finish beating until stiff peaks form. Use immediately. Makes enough topping for 6 Banana Berry Shortcakes.

LATTICE BERRY PIE

Here it is, an authentic flaky, two-crust pie. The fresh unsweetened berries are only cooked long enough to bake the lattice crust.

Bottom Piecrust:

1½ cups whole wheat pastry flour
1½ cups brown rice flour
½ cup butter
3 tablespoons safflower oil
3 tablespoons ice water

Mix flours in a large bowl. Cut in butter with a fork or pastry blender. Add oil, a little at a time, working it in as you go. Mix in ice water and knead dough briefly. Form two balls, one twice as big as the other. Set small ball aside.

Roll the large ball out into a circle between two pieces of lightly floured wax paper. Remove top sheet, place a 9-inch pie tin upside down on the dough, and invert it. Remove other sheet of wax paper, and press dough evenly into the tin. Prick down well with a fork, and bake in a preheated 400° oven for 10–12 minutes. Remove from oven and let it cool.

Filling:

2 pints fresh boysenberries or blackberries
1 can (6 ounces) unsweetened berry or white grape juice concentrate, plus 1 can water
2 tablespoons arrowroot

Rinse berries and let them drain. Arrange them in the baked shell. In a small saucepan combine juice concentrate, water, and arrowroot. Slowly bring it to a boil, stirring constantly until it thickens. Remove it from the heat and let it cool down for several minutes, then spoon it over the berries. Set pie aside.

Lattice Top:

Roll out small ball of dough on lightly floured wax paper into an oblong shape. Cut into strips ½ inch wide. Lay one layer of strips 1 inch apart across the top of the pie filling, then the other layer of strips over that to form a diamond pattern. Run a continuous strip along the edge to cover the ends. Bake in a preheated 400° oven for 10 minutes or until crust is golden. Remove from oven and let the pie cool to room temperature before cutting. Makes 10 slices.

PERFECT BLUEBERRY CRISP

Topping:

Per serving:
175 calories
4 g protein
7 g fat
26 g carb.

1 cup rolled oats
¼ cup wheat germ
1 teaspoon cinnamon
3 tablespoons butter
2 tablespoons raw sugar

Note: You may also
substitute peaches,
other kinds of
berries, or nectary
fruit for the
blueberries. This
topping is great to
use with fresh fruit
pies instead of a
doughy crust.

Mix rolled oats, wheat germ, and cinnamon together in a medium bowl. In a large bowl, cream butter and sugar together. Add oat mixture to butter mixture, and crumble them together with fingers until well combined. Spread mixture evenly on a lightly oiled aluminum baking sheet. Bake in a 300° oven for 15 minutes, until crispy and golden.

Fruit:

1 pint fresh or frozen blueberries
2 tablespoons raw honey
1 tablespoon freshly squeezed lemon juice
½ teaspoon vanilla extract

Carefully mix blueberries with remaining ingredients in an 8-inch-square serving dish. Sprinkle baked topping evenly over fruit, and serve. Serves 6.

PEACH AND PISTACHIO CREPES

Per crepe:
184 calories
7 g protein
7 g fat
22 g carb.

1 cup part-skim ricotta cheese
⅓ cup pistachios, blanched, peeled, and ground
¼ cup raw honey
½ teaspoon vanilla extract
¼ teaspoon almond extract
8 Whole Wheat Dessert Crepes (page 208)
4 large ripe peaches, peeled, pitted, and sliced

Blend ricotta, pistachios, honey, and vanilla and almond extract in a small bowl. Lay each crepe flat on a serving plate and arrange ⅛ of the peach slices lengthwise across the center. Add on a tablespoon of the ricotta filling, then fold both sides of the crepe over to enclose it.

Repeat this procedure until peaches and ricotta filling are gone. Serve warm, topped with a little reserved ricotta filling and sprinkled with cinnamon or additional ground pistachios if desired. Makes 8 dessert crepes.

WHOLE WHEAT DESSERT CREPES

Per crepe:
53 calories
2 g protein
2 g fat
7 g carb.

2 eggs
1 cup water
½ cup whole wheat pastry flour
1 tablespoon raw honey
Safflower oil

In a medium bowl whisk eggs until light yellow. Combine water, flour, and honey, add to eggs, and continue to whisk until smooth. Rub a 7-inch nonstick omelet or sauté pan with a paper towel dabbed in safflower oil. Heat pan over a medium heat. With a measuring cup, pour approximately ¼ cup of the crepe mixture (per crepe) into the pan.

Cook it on 1 side for 30–45 seconds or until it starts to bubble on top. Turn it over carefully with a metal pancake turner, and cook it for 10–15 seconds more on the other side. It should be slightly golden on both sides. When done, slide it onto an ovenproof plate, and keep warm until ready to fill.

Rub the pan with the oiled paper towel before making each crepe. Repeat this procedure until crepe mixture is gone. Makes about 8 large crepes.

Fat Buster: For the skinniest whipped topping yet, whip ¼ cup of powdered nonfat milk with ¼ cup ice water for 3 minutes at a high speed. Add 1 tablespoon freshly squeezed lemon juice and 1 packet of NutraSweet, and whip for 3 more minutes. Entire topping contains 64 fat-free calories.

Tidbit: For the ultimate dessert snack, split open dried figs and fill them with a mixture of part-skim ricotta cheese, grated orange rind, and a little raw orange blossom honey to taste. You may also fill them with any of these soufflés or chiffon mixtures. Use a pastry tube to make the filling more decorative. Serve chilled.

LOW-CAL CUSTARDS AND CHIFFONS

These luscious whipped desserts you are about to discover are the stuff that dreams are made of. Especially when you're dreaming of a trim new you. Updated to be lighter and healthier, they're made without calorie-laden flour, cream, or refined sugar. Just nonfattening, essential ingredients whipped up to exquisite perfection. Experience the wonderfully versatile custard or the delicate soufflé, and start enjoying the classics again without a calorie worry.

BEST BASIC CUSTARD

This is a dessert esential—and terribly healthy. You may add your favorite liqueurs, extract flavorings, or dried fruits to the custard before baking. Serve it warm or chilled topped with fresh fruit.

Per serving:
121 calories
7 g protein
5 g fat
14 g carb.

3 eggs
3 tablespoons raw honey
2 cups low-fat milk (nonfat milk may be substituted)
¾ teaspoon vanilla
Dash of cinnamon and nutmeg

Note: If you bake the custard in individual cups, reduce the cooking time to ½ hour.

In a medium bowl, beat eggs until thick and light colored. Stir in honey, milk, and vanilla until well blended. Pour into a 1-quart ovenproof baking dish, and place it in a larger baking pan with water halfway up the sides of the custard dish. Sprinkle the top with cinnamon and nutmeg, and bake in a preheated 325° oven for 1 hour or until set. Makes 6 servings.

KIWI LIME CHIFFON

Put a little culture in your soufflé with this interesting combination of kefir, kiwis, and lime. Without the egg yolks, it's even lighter than a mousse.

Per serving:
143 calories
4 g protein
0 g fat
33 g carb.

1 packet unflavored gelatin, plus ¼ cup water
6 ripe kiwi fruit, peeled
1 cup plain kefir milk
⅓ cup freshly squeezed lime juice
¾ cup raw honey
Grated peel of 1 lime
4 egg whites, warmed to room temperature

In a small saucepan soften gelatin in water for 5 minutes, then stir over a low heat until dissolved. Let it cool. Cut 3 of the kiwi fruit into chunks and drop into a blender. Add kefir and lime juice, and blend while slowly adding honey. Mix into gelatin, along with lime peel, and chill to the consistency of raw egg whites. Then beat again to increase volume slightly.

Meanwhile beat warmed egg whites until stiff peaks form. Gently fold into lime gelatin mixture. Turn into a 1½-quart decorative mold, and chill until set. To unmold, place the bottom in a sink or pan of warm water for about 1 minute, then turn upside down on to a wet serving platter. Slice remaining 3 kiwi fruit, and arrange around the top of the mold. Serves 8.

HONEY LEMON MOUSSE

Per serving:
193 calories
9 g protein
3 g fat
34 g carb.

3 eggs, separated, whites warmed to room temperature
⅓ cup freshly squeezed lemon juice
⅔ cup raw orange blossom honey
1 packet unflavored gelatin, plus ¼ cup cold water
Rind of 1 small lemon, grated
1 teaspoon vanilla extract
¾ cup low-fat cottage cheese
⅓ cup nonfat milk

Mix the egg yolks with lemon juice and half of the honey in a double boiler over simmering water. Stir until hot. Soften gelatin in cold water, then stir into hot egg mixture until dissolved. Mix in lemon rind and vanilla, then remove from heat.

In a large bowl beat egg whites until thick and foamy. Slowly pour in the remaining honey in a fine stream. Continue to beat egg whites until peaks form, then add cooled lemon mixture.

Blend cottage cheese and milk together in a blender or food processor until smooth and creamy. Carefully fold into lemon-egg mixture. Turn into a 1-quart soufflé dish, and chill until set. Makes 6 servings.

PUMPKIN YOGURT CHIFFON PIE

Per slice:
230 calories
6 g protein
10 g fat
34 g carb.

1 cup steamed and mashed pumpkin (canned pumpkin may be substituted)
3 eggs, separated, whites warmed to room temperature
½ cup raw honey
¼ cup pure maple syrup
1 teaspoon cinnamon
½ teaspoon ground ginger
¼ teaspoon each freshly ground nutmeg and allspice
½ teaspoon sea salt (optional)
¼ teaspoon each lemon and orange rind, grated
½ cup low-fat milk (nonfat milk may be substituted)
1 cup plain low-fat yogurt (nonfat yogurt may be substituted)
1 recipe piecrust, unbaked (see Tropical Fruit Pie with Yogurt Piecrust, page 204)

In a large bowl mix pumpkin, egg yolks, honey, maple syrup, spices, salt, and citrus rind together. Blend in milk and yogurt.

In a separate bowl beat egg whites until fluffy, then fold into pumpkin mixture. Pour into prepared crust, and bake in a preheated 325° oven for 45 minutes or until a knife tip inserted in the center comes out clean. Makes 10 slices.

CAROB SOUFFLÉ WITH RASPBERRIES

Here's the pièce de résistance of desserts. Keep it snooty (and healthy) with this carob soufflé garnished with fresh raspberries and a splash of cassis liqueur.

Soufflé:

Per serving:
170 calories
5 g protein
7 g fat
25 g carb.

Note: If you prefer to omit cassis from the soufflé, also omit 3 of the egg yolks.

2 tablespoons butter
1 cup nonfat milk
⅓ cup carob powder, sifted
¼ cup granulated fructose
6 egg yolks
2 tablespoons cassis
1 teaspoon vanilla extract
3 egg whites, warmed to room temperature

Melt butter in a double boiler over simmering water and stir in milk, carob, and fructose until blended. Remove from heat. Beat egg yolks until light yellow. Add a little of the carob sauce to the yolks and continue to beat. Then pour entire mixture into the double boiler and stir over a very low heat until it thickens slightly.

Stir in liqueur and vanilla and let it cool. In a medium bowl, beat egg whites until stiff but not dry. Carefully fold them into cooled carob mixture.

Lightly butter and sprinkle with fructose a 9-inch soufflé dish, and place it in a pan of hot water about 1 inch below the rim of the dish. Pour soufflé mixture into the dish and bake in a preheated 350° oven for 25 minutes or until firm. Serve at once.

Garnish:

1 pint fresh raspberries
¼ cup cassis

Gently toss raspberries with liqueur and garnish servings of soufflé. Soufflé makes 8 servings.

CELEBRATED MEALS

A TOUCH OF CLASS

Mushroom and Oyster Bisque
Crown Roast of Lamb
with Saffron Rice
Tomato Pudding
String Beans Dijonnaise
Carob Soufflé with Raspberries
Rosé wine

FAT-FREE FROSTIES

Are you guilty of having ice cream fantasies? Have you been romancing the cone and flirting with calories? Do you dream of eating rich and getting thin? If the answer is yes, yes, yes, then you're ready to try these fat-free frosties. They're not fussy to make, so you can do them faster than you can get to the ice cream parlor and back. And think of all the calories you'll save. Nutra-Sweet is featured here, and you can substitute it for honey without making any adjustments in the recipes. Go ahead and try these guilt-free frozen desserts, and find that now you can feed your fantasies instead of just having them.

COCONUT CARROT ICE MILK

Per serving:
78 calories
2 g protein
2 g fat
15 g carb.

1 cup nonfat milk
1½ cups unsweetened pineapple/coconut juice
1½ cups carrot juice
1½ tablespoons raw honey
½ teaspoon vanilla extract

Pour milk and juices into the can of an ice cream maker. Add honey and vanilla, and stir until dissolved. Process until thick and creamy. Spoon into a 1-quart plastic container, cover, and freeze until ready to eat. Makes about 1 quart or 8 servings.

STRAWBERRY FROZEN YOGURT

This smooth, low-calorie frozen yogurt is light and quick to make. You may replace the strawberries with fresh raspberries, boysenberries, blackberries, blueberries, or any other of your favorite seasonal berries.

Per serving:
59 calories
2 g protein
1 g fat
10 g carb.

1 pint fresh strawberries, hulled and frozen
1 cup plain nonfat yogurt
2 packets NutraSweet, or to taste

Process strawberries in a food processor or blender. Add yogurt and Nutra-Sweet, a little at a time, while blending. Process as quickly as possible so that the yogurt has the consistency of soft-serve ice cream. Serve immediately. Makes about 2½ cups or 4 servings.

GINGERED PEACH FROZEN YOGURT

For those of you who don't have a food processor or ice-cream-making paraphernalia, try this swift handmade frozen yogurt.

Per serving:
116 calories
4 g protein
1 g fat
23 g carb.

1 packet unflavored gelatin, plus ¼ cup water
2 cups plain nonfat yogurt
1 cup fresh peaches, mashed
⅓ cup raw honey
¼ teaspoon ground ginger
⅛ teaspoon almond extract

Soften gelatin in water in a small saucepan. Stir over low heat for several minutes until dissolved. In a medium bowl, mix remaining ingredients until smooth and creamy. Stir in gelatin and continue to mix until well blended.

Pour into two ice cube trays with the sections removed, cover, and freeze for several hours. Remove from freezer 15 minutes before serving. Makes about 3 cups, enough for 6 servings.

BLUEBERRY CUSTARD ICE CREAM

This is the best real ice cream made without cream. It's surprisingly rich.

Per serving:
135 calories
7 g protein
4 g fat
18 g carb.

4 eggs, separated, whites warmed to room temperature
⅓ cup raw honey
4 cups low-fat milk
1 teaspoon arrowroot
½ teaspoon vanilla
1 cup fresh blueberries, pureed

Lightly beat egg yolks in a medium bowl. Slowly stir in honey. In a large saucepan, heat milk, and dissolve arrowroot. Add egg mixture, and stir over a medium heat until thick. Remove from heat, cool, and chill.

In a medium bowl, beat egg whites until soft peaks form. Stir vanilla into chilled milk-egg mixture, and combine with egg whites. Pour into the can of an ice cream maker, and process until thick and creamy. Stir in blueberries, and spoon into a 1½-quart plastic container. Cover, and place in the freezer to harden. Makes about 5 cups, enough for 10 servings.

LOW-CAL BLENDER GELATO

Here is a dietetic takeoff on Gianduia, a popular Italian ice cream, or gelato.

Per serving:
110 calories
7 g protein
8 g fat
5 g carb.

1 cup water
1 tablespoon carob powder, sifted
6 egg whites
¼ cup blanched and peeled hazelnuts, finely ground
¼ teaspoon each almond and vanilla extract
4 packets NutraSweet (or to taste)
Crushed ice
Cinnamon

Blend water and carob until smooth, and place in a medium saucepan along with egg whites. Bring to a boil and whisk as it cooks until egg whites are foamy. Pour into a blender container. Add hazelnuts, almond and vanilla extracts, and NutraSweet, and process once until blended.

Add crushed ice, a little at a time while blending, until mixture is thick and cold. Pour into 4 small ice cream dishes, and place in the freezer for 15 minutes until nearly frozen, but not hardened. Serve sprinkled with cinnamon. Makes 4 servings.

PINK PEPPERMINT SORBET

Per serving:
148 calories
2 g protein
0 g fat
36 g carb.

⅓ cup raw honey (or to taste)
⅔ cup water
4 sprigs peppermint, chopped
Juice of two pink grapefruit, strained
1 egg white, warmed to room temperature

In a small saucepan heat honey, water, and mint, and stir until blended. Strain out the peppermint, and let the mixture cool. Then stir in the grapefruit juice and freeze until semifrozen.

Beat the egg white in a small bowl until stiff, then fold into the grapefruit juice. Freeze again until it becomes a firm mush, approximately 45–50 minutes. Spoon into 4 individual dessert glasses, and serve immediately. Garnish with extra peppermint sprigs if desired.

LATE HARVEST FROST

This is probably the most precious dessert you'll ever eat, but it's so good . . . if you dare!

Per serving:
109 calories
1 g protein
1 g fat
23 g carb.

1 pound ripe juicy pears
8 tablespoons chilled late harvest Riesling wine (4 tablespoons orange blossom or
other delicately fragrant honey may be substituted)

Core, peel, and dice pears. Place them in a single layer on foil in the freezer until firm. When pears are frozen, process them in a food processor or blender, adding the Riesling a little at a time until it has the consistency of a thick slush. Serve at once. Makes 4 servings.

12
BEVERAGES

HIGH-POWERED PROTEIN DRINKS

Protein drinks are a wonderful way to start the day, a great substitute for a skipped meal, and a nutritious snack any time. With today's on-the-go fitness life-styles, we often need something fast, fuel-efficient, tasty, and readily made with staples on hand. So without further convincing, let these super-quick, super-powered drinks go to work for you.

SUPER HIGH-PRO MALTED

Per glass:
443 calories
39 g protein
14 g fat
41 g carb.

Note: For a chocolaty taste, add 1 tablespoon carob powder with an additional ¼ cup nonfat milk.

8 ounces nonfat milk
2 eggs
3 tablespoons protein powder
1 tablespoon raw honey
1 teaspoon malt
Dash of vanilla extract
2 or 3 ice cubes

Process ingredients in a blender until thick and frosty, then serve. Makes 1 large drink.

Tidbits: For what ails you, substitute or add these in some proportion to your drink: cranberry juice as a diuretic, fresh papaya to aid digestion, fresh pineapple or grapefruit to help to metabolize fat, raw bran, dried figs or prunes for better elimination, banana for potassium, powdered nonfat milk for extra calcium, nutritional yeast for a B vitamin boost, cold-pressed wheat germ oil for the power of vitamin E, orange or lemon rind for bioflavinoids, and fresh berries for additional fiber and flavor.

APRICOT HONEY ICED MILK

Per glass:
352 calories
28 g protein
7 g fat
47 g carb.

8 ounces nonfat milk
1 egg
2 tablespoons protein powder
1 tablespoon raw honey
3 fresh apricots, pitted and quartered
3 or 4 ice cubes
Dash of cinnamon

Process ingredients in a blender until thick and frosty, then serve. Makes 1 large drink.

STRAWBERRY SLAM

Per glass:
409 calories
26 g protein
6 g fat
64 g carb.

1 cup fresh strawberries, hulled
4 tablespoons pineapple juice frozen concentrate
3 tablespoons protein powder
1 cup plain nonfat yogurt
3 or 4 ice cubes

Process ingredients in a blender until thick and frosty, then serve. Makes 1 large drink.

LEMON BUTTERMILK ZEST

Per glass:
455 calories
22 g protein
12 g fat
66 g carb.

1 cup buttermilk (or kefir milk)
2 eggs
1 tablespoon freshly squeezed lemon juice
1 teaspoon each lemon and orange rind, grated
3 tablespoons raw honey
1/4 teaspoon vanilla extract
2 or 3 ice cubes

Process ingredients in a blender until thick and frosty, then serve. Makes 1 large drink.

BANANA EGGNOG

Per glass:
479 calories
34 g protein
13 g fat
59 g carb.

1 cup nonfat milk
2 eggs
2 tablespoons protein powder
1 tablespoon raw honey
½ teaspoon vanilla extract
1 banana, peeled, sliced, and frozen
Dash of cinnamon and nutmeg

Process ingredients in a blender until thick and frosty, then serve. Makes 1 large drink.

ALMOND NECTAR FRAPPE

Per glass:
376 calories
27 g protein
9 g fat
54 g carb.

1 cup freshly squeezed orange juice
1 egg
3 tablespoons protein powder
1 large ripe peach, peeled, pitted, and chopped
1 cup diced melon, honeydew, casaba, or cantaloupe
¼ teaspoon almond extract
3 or 4 ice cubes

Process ingredients in a blender until thick and frosty, then serve. Makes 1 large drink.

SUNFLOWER DATE SHAKE

Per glass:
481 calories
33 g protein
17 g fat
56 g carb.

1 cup fresh pineapple chunks
1 cup soy milk
2 tablespoons soy protein powder
¼ cup raw sunflower seeds
¼ cup dates, chopped
2 or 3 ice cubes

Process ingredients in a blender until thick and frosty, then serve. Makes 1 large drink.

TROPICAL COOLERS

Adventuresome note:
To obtain
approximately ⅓
cup of fresh coconut
milk, take 1 whole
husked coconut,
pierce the eyes with
a sharp pick, and
drain out the liquid.
Reserve. Crack the
shell open with a
hammer, and grate
the meat from a
chunk of coconut
into a bowl to make
¼ cup. Save the
remainder of the
coconut for snacks.

    If a whole
coconut is not
available, use
unsweetened
shredded coconut to
make Coconut Milk
(page 102) and to
replace grated fresh
coconut.

Anyone who has been to Hawaii knows the magic that it weaves. The bright sunny days on sparkling blue seas that give way to balmy nights and waving palms, the scent of plumerias carried by the gentle trade winds, and the lilting sound of doves cooing to another morning in paradise, all cast a spell that is hard to forget. If you would like to capture the flavor of that special place, then you're ready to treat yourself to one of these glorious tropical coolers, made with a blend of exotic and domestic fresh fruits that is perfect for Hawaiian time, any time. Simply whip the ingredients up in a blender, then relax and let your senses carry you away while you enjoy a luscious, frosty drink that may be the next best thing to a Mai Tai in Hawaii.

When whipping up these tropical coolers in a food processor or blender, don't overblend, as the ice will melt very fast. If you like your drink extra thick, you may freeze the fruit before adding it to the blender. Another nifty trick is to freeze the amount of milk or juice you are using in an ice cube tray first.

Try these recipes as they are, or mix and match the fruits you like—anything is delicious. Since the sweetness of the fruits depends on ripeness, time of season, and variety, raw unfiltered honey may be added to suit individual tastes. Drizzle it in last while the drink is blending. Remember, though, honey is an extra 65 calories and 17 carbohydrates per tablespoon.

You may also toss in any combination of egg whites, wheat germ, bran, powdered nonfat milk, protein powder, or yogurt. Each of these adds extra body, protein, fiber, and essential nutrients for under 30 calories per tablespoon.

VOLCANO SUNRISE

Per serving:
274 calories
6 g protein
12 g fat
40 g carb.

¾ *cup freshly squeezed carrot juice, chilled*
⅓ *cup fresh coconut milk, chilled (see below)*
¾ *cup fresh pineapple chunks*
¼ *cup fresh coconut, grated*
1 heaping tablespoon powdered nonfat milk
3 or 4 ice cubes
Honey to taste

Process ingredients in a blender until thick and creamy, then serve. Makes one large drink.

MANGO MINT FRAPPE

Per serving:
291 calories
10 g protein
2 g fat
64 g carb.

¾ cup fresh-squeezed orange juice, chilled
1 medium mango, peeled, pitted, and chunked
1 medium nectarine, peeled, pitted, and sliced
1 packet unflavored gelatin, softened in ¼ cup warm water
2 or 3 fresh mint leaves
3 or 4 ice cubes
Honey to taste

Process ingredients in a blender until thick and creamy, then serve. Makes 1 large drink.

ALMOND MILK

Per cup:
198 calories
11 g protein
8 g fat
19 g carb.

½ cup raw almonds, ground semifine
1¼ cups nonfat milk

Place well-ground almonds in a bowl. Scald milk, and pour over the almonds. Cover, and let it set for 2 hours. Strain the almond-flavored milk through a piece of muslin or cheesecloth until all the liquid is extracted. Discard the used almonds. If you prefer a more flavorful Almond Milk, add a few drops of almond extract. Makes about 1 cup.

PINK WAHINE

Per serving (including Almond Milk):
315 calories
17 g protein
10 g fat
44 g carb.

3 guavas
⅔ cup fresh strawberries, sliced
1 cup Almond Milk (above), chilled
1 egg white
2 or 3 ice cubes
Honey to taste

Scoop out the pulp and seeds of the guava and preblend them and the strawberries in the Almond Milk. Strain the mixture through a fine sieve to remove seeds. Then process all ingredients in a blender until thick and creamy and serve. Makes 1 large drink.

HIBISCUS FLOAT

Per serving:
241 calories
5 g protein
1 g fat
50 g carb.

¾ cup unsweetened pineapple juice
½ medium papaya, peeled, seeded, and chunked
½ persimmon, peeled and sliced
2 ounces plain nonfat yogurt
1 tablespoon freshly squeezed lime juice
2 or 3 ice cubes
Honey to taste
4 ounces mineral water

Process all ingredients except mineral water in a blender until thick and creamy. Then add mineral water and serve. Makes 1 large drink.

FROSTY ORCHID FOAM

Per serving:
243 calories
7 g protein
10 g fat
35 g carb.

1 cup fresh coconut milk (see Volcano Sunrise, page 220)
⅓ cup fresh boysenberries
1 medium pear, quartered and peeled
1 egg white
¼ teaspoon vanilla extract
2 or 3 ice cubes
Honey to taste

If you wish, preblend fresh coconut milk and boysenberries, and strain through a sieve to remove the seeds before preparing drink. Then process all ingredients in a blender until thick and creamy, and serve. Makes 1 large drink.

PASSION COOLER

Per serving:
285 calories
6 g protein
1 g fat
63 g carb.

2 passion fruits
⅔ cup freshly squeezed orange juice
½ medium papaya, peeled, seeded, and chunked
½ cup fresh cherries (pitted)
1 heaping tablespoon powdered nonfat milk
3 or 4 ice cubes
Honey to taste

Halve the passion fruits, scoop out the flesh, and place it in a large sieve over the blender. Press the pulp through, using the orange juice as a liquefier to help. Discard the seeds, then process the remaining ingredients in a blender until thick and creamy. Save a few cherries and freeze them to float in the drink. Makes 1 large drink.

KONA COFFEE BREAKFAST WHIP

To start your day off right, here's a drink with everything in it that's good for you, plus your morning dose of freshly brewed Kona coffee. Take it with you for a *wikiwiki* ("very fast") breakfast on the run.

Per serving:
291 calories
27 g protein
1 g fat
44 g carb.

> *1 cup nonfat milk*
> *¾ cup brewed Kona coffee*
> *½ banana, sliced*
> *1 egg white*
> *1 heaping tablespoon raw wheat germ*
> *2 tablespoons protein powder*
> *2 or 3 ice cubes*
> *Honey or pure maple syrup to taste*

Process all ingredients in a blender until thick and creamy, then serve. Makes 1 large drink.

Note: Kona is the famous coffee grown on the Kona Coast of Hawaii (the big island). If it is not available in your supermarket, try a gourmet food store. Or substitute regular coffee.

TROPICAL BANANA NUT
Kids will love this one!

Per serving:
438 calories
20 g protein
13 g fat
66 g carb.

> *1¼ cups nonfat milk*
> *1 medium banana, sliced*
> *2 tablespoons raw unsalted cashew butter (see note)*
> *1 tablespoon carob powder*
> *Pinch each of cinnamon and nutmeg*
> *1 tablespoon pure maple syrup*
> *2 or 3 ice cubes*

Process all ingredients in a blender until thick and creamy, then serve. Makes 1 large drink.

Note: Cashew butter is available in health food or gourmet and specialty stores, or you can make your own with cashews and a food processor —that's all. If cashew butter is unavailable, almond or peanut butter (natural style) is good too. Carob powder (Saint John's bread) is also found in health food stores.

THIRST QUENCHERS AND REFRESHERS

Whet your appetite with a fancy fruit punch or a vegetable juice perk-me-up. These beverages provide just the relaxation, refreshment, and kick you need to keep you going, wherever you're going. You'll find them brisk and inviting —the perfect cure for the common cola.

Tidbit: Make a low-calorie summer cooler by freezing pitted cherries, grapes, or berries and dropping them into a big frosted glass of sparkling mineral water. They'll float like ice cubes.

GINGER SPICE TEA

Per cup:
23 calories
0 g protein
0 g fat
6 g carb.

2 cups boiling water
2 teaspoons camomile blossoms
1 tablespoon blackstrap molasses
2 teaspoons freshly squeezed lemon juice
Pinch each ground ginger and allspice

Combine all ingredients in a teapot. Let it steep for 5 minutes and serve. Makes 2 cups.

ORANGE SPEARMINT TEA

Per cup:
9 calories
0 g protein
0 g fat
2 g carb.

2 cups boiling water
2 teaspoons dried spearmint leaves
2 orange slices
2 whole cloves
2 twists of orange rind

Combine water, spearmint, orange slices, and cloves in a teapot, and let them steep for 5 minutes. Serve with a twist of orange. Makes 2 cups.

MOCHA AU LAIT

Per serving:
179 calories
9 g protein
0 g fat
39 g carb.

1 cup nonfat milk
1½ tablespoons carob powder
1 tablespoon raw honey
1 cup freshly brewed hot coffee
Dash of cinnamon

Heat milk in a small saucepan. Stir in carob and honey until dissolved. Pour hot coffee and milk mixture together into a large mug. Sprinkle top with cinnamon. Makes 1 large serving.

BOYSENBERRY WINE JULEP

Per glass:
220 calories
0 g protein
0 g fat
35 g carb.

1 quart unsweetened boysenberry/apple juice
2 cups semidry white wine
4 mint sprigs

Freeze boysenberry/apple juice in ice cube trays. Pour wine into a blender container and chill. When ready, begin blending wine with several of the juice ice cubes at a time until it becomes a slush. Fill 4 tall glasses. Garnish with mint sprigs.

SPARKLING HAWAIIAN PUNCH

This is an ice fantasy of frozen pineapple juice and fruit floating with flowers in a punch bowl of tropical fruit juices.

Per cup:
110 calories
1 g protein
0 g fat
29 g carb.

2 cups unsweetened pineapple juice
1 cup fresh raspberries or sliced strawberries
4 cups water
1 cup freshly squeezed lime juice
½ cup raw honey
½ teaspoon almond extract
2 cups guava juice, chilled
2 cups papaya juice, chilled
1 bottle (20 ounces) sparkling mineral water
Mint sprigs and flowers for garnish

Freeze pineapple juice and fruit in a 1-quart decorative mold ring (or ice cube trays). In a medium saucepan, bring water, lime juice, and honey to a boil. Stir until dissolved. Let it cool and pour into a punch bowl.

Add almond extract, guava and papaya juice, and mineral water. Unmold frozen pineapple juice ring, fruit side up, into punch bowl. Float mint sprigs and flowers or petals on the top. Serve at once. Makes about 14 cups.

CELEBRATED MEALS

A SMALL FRY AFFAIR

Wheat Germ Chicken
Mandarin Kiwi Coleslaw
Chunky Peanut Butter and Banana Muffins
Strawberry Frozen Yogurt
Buttered Popcorn
Sparkling Hawaiian Punch

VEGETABLE HERB COCKTAIL

There are many "good" commercial vegetable juices available on the market. But they have just one problem: They're pasteurized—and hence, from the bodybuilding standpoint, less healthful than homemade vegetable juice. Following are some vegetables that complement each other, to make a delightful, healthful raw vegetable juice cocktail. For this you will need an electric juicer with a filter. It's a little more difficult than opening a can, but it's so good for you. Add, in any combination and amount, the vegetables you prefer: tomatoes, spinach, sprouts, cucumbers, celery, carrots, bell peppers, scallions, parsley, fresh basil and dill, paprika. One cup of juice will have only about 30 to 40 calories.

If you're on a diet, drink a "dieter's cocktail" before dining. Mix equal parts of warm broth or stock and Vegetable Herb Cocktail together. The mixture of warm protein, fats, and acids increases a natural appetite suppressant in the intestinal tract.

For the party animal, freeze 1 jigger of vodka or vermouth along with water in an ice cube tray. (Yes, a jigger of alcohol to a trayful of water *will* freeze.) Blend the desired number of ice cubes with the Vegetable Herb Cocktail in a blender until slushy. Complete with a dash of Worcestershire or Tabasco sauce. Then make a healthy comeback with a blend of Vegetable Herb Cocktail and kefir or buttermilk.

THE ESSENTIAL LIQUID DIET

Fasting, by all standards, is not considered a sensible diet. And as you know by now, crazy crash diets are out. But everyone still wants to know the secret of "How do you lose weight *quickly*?"

The answer is tricky: "Without losing muscle." Crash diets only deplete the body of water and muscle before they burn up fat. The result is a body that is mostly a smaller version of the fat body.

Manufacturers of commercial liquid diets claim they have the solution to proper rapid weight loss. Their month-long plan is based on a formula that ranks close to the recommended dietary ratio of 60 percent carbohydrate, 25 percent protein, 15 percent fat, and supplies 100 percent of the U.S. RDA of vitamins and minerals on 300 to 400 calories per day.

With all due respect, their theory has credibility but also several problems. The ratio of carbohydrate, protein, and fats is correct, but there isn't enough of them to sustain a healthy body, particularly for larger people. Anything less than 600 calories a day is starvation. Equally important however is the problem of food value. These liquid diets are not raw but completely processed. They contain no fresh food, no living enzymes to nourish and regenerate a living body. The body will then go into its muscle tissue for nourishment as well as fuel. Existing on such a diet for any length of time is unhealthy and self-defeating.

Here is a liquid diet, based on a well-meaning premise, that meets the Muscular Gourmet standards of health as well. Two servings daily total approximately 600 calories and provide 45 grams of protein which is 100 percent of a woman's daily need (not 75 percent like the commercial liquid diets), 90 grams of carbohydrates and 14 grams of fat. The drink sticks closely to the 60 percent carbohydrate, 25 percent protein, 15 percent fat balance, but leans a little more toward the protein. Men should increase the ingredients proportionally by ⅓, totaling 900 calories per day.

The Essential Liquid Diet is actually a complete meal, because it contains eggs, milk, fruits, and grains and is naturally high in vitamins, minerals, fiber, and essential amino acids necessary for the synthesis of protein. It's difficult to get 100 percent of your U.S. RDA of all nutrients naturally for 600 or 900 calories of food a day, so you would be wise to take a multiple vitamin and mineral supplement and extra vitamins E, C, and calcium, preferably before you go to bed.

Twice a day whip in blender until thick and frosty:

½ cup freshly squeezed orange juice
1 raw egg
½ banana
3 tablespoons powdered nonfat milk
1 packet unflavored gelatin
1 tablespoon raw wheat germ
1 tablespoon raw bran
3–4 ice cubes

For variation you may use any freshly squeezed juice, but not canned or frozen. For convenience you can squeeze enough for a few days and keep it tightly closed in the refrigerator. You may use any fresh or frozen (without sugar) fruit that equals 40 calories per serving, but the banana is best because it is always in season and makes the drink thick and sweet. You may use spices like cinnamon and nutmeg and flavoring extracts such as vanilla and almond.

No liquor please. Drinking alcohol is not on the diet, but you may have black coffee, tea, or mineral water with a twist of lime or orange peel. Drink as much water as you like, preferably four 8-ounce glasses per day.

A last word about the raw egg. To make it more digestible, run it under hot tap water for a minute before cracking it and putting it into the blender. You can have the egg under the tap while you're preparing everything else, then add the egg in last. This recipe will make about one 16-ounce drink twice a day. It's delicious and satisfying, and you won't feel like you're on a diet at all.

If you are an average person with an average dietary intake, you will be cutting back about 1,700 to 1,800 calories a day, which equals a loss of about one-half pound. Because the diet supplies about 100 percent of a person's daily protein requirement, the weight you lose will stay off, which indicates a loss of mainly fat, not muscle. If you're a large or extremely active person—who burns 3,000 calories a day, for instance—you would only have to cut your consumption to about 1,250 calories to achieve a loss of about one-half pound a day. For this you would simply double the recipe.

If you're a person in good health, you can safely stay on the diet for 2 to 4 weeks, but check with your doctor before you do so. The duration of the diet should be determined by how you feel, the extent of your physical activity, and by when you have finally reached your goal. This diet should not be used to lose more than 10 to 15 pounds at a time.

When you begin eating normally again, do not go over the minimum recommended calories for a person of your sex, age, and height—*not once*—for at least the length of time you were on the Liquid Diet. You have just given your metabolism a jolt, and your body is more than ready to hoard calories as soon as you go over your limit. Let your metabolism stabilize itself. This is a good time to begin your Muscular Gourmet life-style diet for a steady plan of achieving and maintaining successful weight control.

INDEX